OH,
FUDGE!

OH, FUDGE!

Lee Edwards Benning

A CELEBRATION OF AMERICA'S FAVORITE CANDY

HENRY HOLT AND COMPANY

NEW YORK

Published by Henry Holt and Company, Inc.,
115 West 18th Street, New York, New York 10011.
Published in Canada by Fitzhenry & Whiteside Limited,
195 Allstate Parkway, Markham, Ontario L3R 4T8.

Library of Congress Cataloging-in-Publication Data
Benning, Lee Edwards, 1934–
Oh, fudge! : a celebration of America's favorite candy / by Lee
Edwards Benning. — 1st ed.
p.   cm.
ISBN 0-8050-1196-X
1. Fudge.   I. Title.
TX791.B42   1990
641.8'53—dc20   89-27487
                                                              CIP

Designed by Marysarah Quinn
Printed in the United States of America

BOMC offers recordings and compact discs, cassettes
and records. For information and catalog write to
BOMR, Camp Hill, PA 17012.

CONTENTS

PREFACE

To be honest, I never intended to write a cookbook, much less one on fudge. I am, unfortunately, one of those people who can gain five pounds just reading a recipe.

It all started innocently enough one December evening in 1988. My husband, Arthur, upon awaking from his postprandial nap, announced at 11:00 p.m. that he was going to make a batch of fudge.

Now, for Arthur to cook is not unusual. He makes the best macaroni salad, mustard dip, and marinated cucumbers I've ever eaten. But he's a throw-it-together man, an if-it-doesn't-fit-wedge-it man. So I had my doubts about his candy-making abilities. Especially when I discovered this was not just any fudge, but a recipe clipped from a newspaper, and you know how accurate some of those are.

One look at it, and I knew why this particular recipe had reached out and grabbed him. It was for buttermilk fudge, and my husband, who doesn't eat chocolate, simply dotes on anything buttermilk. So, there we were like Dr. Kildare and his chief surgical nurse: Arthur calling out the ingredients and I fetching and slapping measuring spoons in his hand.

In the midst of all this, our son called home from college. His reaction to our making fudge at that hour was typical of the classic younger generation's belief that parents, left unsupervised, will sooner or later take leave of their senses.

Once the whole concoction was assembled, Arthur noted that it had to simmer for forty-five minutes and would I call him when it was done. He was going to watch "The Tonight Show." There I was, a home economist, with this pot bubbling away on my range, and I had not the slightest idea why it had to cook so long. When Arthur returned to check on the progress of the fudge, it was to discover me surrounded by cookbooks, checking fudge recipes. But, despite my hundreds of cookbooks, I found very little information on fudge. The next thing you know, Arthur was suggesting I write a cookbook on it. I demurred, fast! I was up to my neck in a historical novel. The last thing I needed was to get involved in a cookbook. Cookbooks, as far as I was concerned, were for reading and some even for using, but not for writing. And although the fudge turned out quite good, I thought that was the end of it.

Two days later Arthur turned to me and said, "Oh, fudge!"

"What's wrong?" I asked with trepidation. Arthur's a mild-mannered man, not in the habit of invoking anything or anybody.

"Nothing; it's the perfect title for the book."

As you can gather, my husband doesn't take no for an answer. One hundred and forty pounds of granulated sugar, fifty pounds of superfine sugar, twenty-four pounds of brown sugar, and, hurray! only five more pounds of me later, I had the makings for a book . . . and I had the answers to my questions. In the process, I have corresponded with fascinating women all over the country, been given access to the rare book room at Winterthur Museum in Delaware, fed dimes into a ravenous copier at the Schlesinger Library in Boston, met an Irish-man who could pass for a leprechaun, sampled some awfully expensive, awful factory fudge, learned some nasty-rasty drinking songs, and taught a home economics class for a week. Oh, yes, I also learned the best way to judge the worth of any cookbook: If it says to cook candy or caramel to one specific temperature or for x number of minutes, it doesn't know what it's talking about. If nothing else, I've just saved you some money.

In retrospect, writing this cookbook was an experience I wouldn't have missed for the world. I just can't wait to see what recipe my husband brings home next. Knowing him, it will be a challenge . . . and I wouldn't be surprised to find myself writing another cookbook.

IOUs

That's what acknowledgments really are. If you, gentle reader, enjoy perusing such lists, as I do, then allow me to introduce you to some of the most helpful people in the world—good guys to know.

If, on the other hand, you are one of those named herein, let me assure you no mere mention in a book will suffice to discharge completely what I owe you. However, 'tis better than nothing, and the best I can do until you call in your IOU.

In semichronological order, then, my thanks go to:

Marilyn Marter, columnist for *The Philadelphia Inquirer*, who published a recipe, source unknown, in her "Between Neighbors" column that started me on my quest to solve the mystery of fudge.

Fred Carbone, who gave up one of his infrequent days off to photograph fudge.

Jane Jordan Browne, who believed and encouraged and, thank goodness, sold the project to the right house.

Elizabeth Crossman, who took a chance on an unseasoned cookbook writer, with hopes I haven't let her down.

Bruno A. Quinson, president of Henry Holt and Company, Inc., whose letter made a big difference, one he may never know.

Elaine Tait, *The Philadelphia Inquirer* food editor, who answers her own phone and gave generously of her time, her advice, and her encouragement to a total stranger.

Dr. Sarah Short, Ph.D., Ed.D., professor of nutrition, Syracuse University, who did her best to explain the inexplicable: sugar chemistry.

Robert Lawinger, manager of Jim Garrahy's Fudge Kitchens, Inc., Dutch Wonderland, Lancaster, Pennsylvania, who demonstrated all there was to know about making fudge, only I didn't know it . . . then!

James "Seamus" Garrahy, who not only agreed to answer every question and do so truthfully but was a man of his word. With thanks for the laughs, the information, the tour, and the record album!

Joseph Schwartz, Ph.D., principal of Springfield High School in a suburb of Philadelphia, who took me seriously when I suggested turning one of his classrooms into a test kitchen.

Joan Zeller, home economics teacher, Springfield High School, who not only lent me her class but taught me a lot, too.

Mrs. Zeller's seventh-period coed cooking class—my test kitchen for thermometer calibrating, recipe testing, ingredient substituting, quantity cooking: Robbin Barbee, Dennis Lingg, C. D. Smith, Joe Beckham, Jeanne LoRusso, Dawn Hildebrand, Jennifer Pisarcik, Jennifer Messina—and to all the rest of you who forgot to sign your papers.

The ladies who work at Arthur's employer, Gray & Rogers: Cynthia Hillsley, who provided recipes, oldies and goodies; Kathy McLaughlin, who lent a designing hand right from the very beginning; Megan McMillen-Damiano, who has the most discerning tastebuds and an enormous amount of tact to go with them.

Fante's Philadelphia and King of Prussia, who retinned copper pots, suggested equipment, and, most important, helped underwrite this project with the aid they give starving cookbook writers. Is there an oxymoron there?

John Mariani, author of *The Dictionary of American Food & Drink* (Ticknor & Fields, 1983).

Susan Spaech of Spaech Candy Store, Syracuse, New York, who's carrying on her husband's family tradition . . . deliciously. And who proved it is possible to make a white vanilla.

Donna DeShain, of nationally famous Ronsvalle's Old-Fashioned Homemade Chocolates in Syracuse, New York, candy dipper and friend *extraordinaire* to the owner, Mrs. Donna Ronsvalle, bless her.

Anna Marie Coccia, manager of the test kitchens, Knox Gelatin (Division of Lipton), who proved corporations could be helpful and, more important, knowledgeable.

Jay Silverman of Braun Espanola S.A., who managed to get me the chopper attachment that made so many of these chocolate fudge recipes possible.

Alicia and John ("Houdi") Goodolf of Chester Valley Old Books, outside Philadelphia, who are doing wonderfully in their new location, though I wish they hadn't moved: thanks for collecting all those once-loved books, as well as an antique cocoa can.

I threw him a curve and he caught it: John Nice in quality control, Rosenberger's Dairies in Hatfield, Pennsylvania.

That threesome of learned ladies at Vassar who helped unravel the history of fudge: Elizabeth Daniels, Vassar historian; Beth Schnei-der, alumnae office; and Nancy Mackechnie, curator of rare books and manuscripts, Vassar College.

Another of my unofficial researchers, Wilma R. Slaight, archivist, Margaret Clapp Library, Wellesley College, who went duty far and beyond the need to respond to an unknown writer.

Maida Goodwin, archives specialist, Smith College, who first in-troduced me to the Maria Parloa connection and gave me a vital clue.

Carolyn Rittenhouse, archivist at Bryn Mawr, who looked and looked but "Muggle" was the best she could do—and that was perfect.

Julia Timberlake and Nancy Burleson, at the Wardlaw-Hartridge School, in Plainfield, New Jersey, who brought Emelyn Hartridge to life for me.

Stephanie Williams and, especially, Mark O'Brien, communica-tions associates, General Foods, USA, who tracked down and copied the key documents in the mystery of the Seven Sister fudges.

Francis O'Neill of the Maryland Historical Society, who verified vital information.

Eleanor McD. Thompson, librarian in charge, the Henry Francis du Pont Winterthur Museum in Delaware, who worked on this project as if it were her own.

Jonathan Segal, an old friend and new editor at Alfred A. Knopf—congratulations to both—who used his influence on my behalf.

Craig Claiborne, who went out of his way to answer a way-out request.

Margaret Engel, author of *Food Finds* (Harper & Row, 1984), who didn't call collect but gave of herself and her knowledge freely.

Dean and Jerry Scheerens, Marshall's Mackinac Trail Fudge, for the samples that demonstrated why people rightly think of Mackinac Island, Michigan, as the fudge capital of the world.

Carol Jackson of Jackson-Mitchell Pharmaceuticals in Montecido, California, for introducing me to goat's milk . . . and goat's milk fudge!

All the talented and cooperative men and women on the staffs of our local public libraries outside Philadelphia, and in particular, Trudie Buri and Connie Hall of Wissahickon Valley Library and Larry Forry and Patricia Kelly of the Montgomery County Norristown Library.

John Riley in the curator's office at Mount Vernon who researched Martha Washington Bon-Bons and found none.

Kim Hohl, Bert Barnett, and particularly John Tarbet of the National Park Service, Eisenhower National Historic Site, Gettysburg, who tracked down the original recipe for Mamie's fudge.

Joan Cashen and Don Durkee of Durkee-Mower, Inc., manufacturers of Marshmallow Fluff—with many thanks for both the history and the information on the recipe.

Michael Desmond of the John F. Kennedy Library, Boston, for his research into the food likes of the President.

Carol A. Freese of Ingredients & Equipment in Conshohocken, Pennsylvania, who introduced me to professional cooking equipment, beginning with candy thermometers.

Barbara Jo Metzler of the Candy Americana Museum and Wilbur Chocolate's Factory Candy Outlet in Lititz, Pennsylvania, who gave me a tour, a box of samples, and the desire to master Opera Fudge.

Miko Sakata, product manager for Karo, a division of Best Foods, and Dr. Phil Wells of Best Foods, CPC International, in Englewood Cliffs, New Jersey, who explained the facts of glucose and dextrose and maltose and fructose to me.

William Dunn of Dunn Health Foods in Warminster, Pennsylvania, who helped me in my search for a substitute for maple sugar . . . at a reasonable price!

Nicholas Verderamo, sales service manager of David Michael & Company in Philadelphia, who explained the facts of flavors (and extracts) and lots more.

Elizabeth Jackson, who not only told me of a very special recipe but tracked it down.

Mary Jane Peters, who parted with a family treasure in memory of her late sister, Ruth Cake, who is sorely missed.

Jack Williams, a great source of fun and games and jokes.

Last, but certainly not least, the marvelous staff of Jim Garrahy's Fudge Kitchens: vice-presidents Gregory Riggeal and Timothy Wrynn; treasurer Joyce Maitland, who tracked down a copy of Mamie's letter for me; and ex-officio, Mark Nesbit. They made my visit to a Fudge Palace not just informative but fun.

And finally, I must acknowledge the freedom given me by those corporations and associations who never bothered to answer my letters.

ONE

The History and Lore of Fudge

Oh, fudge! or should I say, "Ah, fudge"? The very word "fudge" conjures up images of thick, rich, sumptuously smooth squares of sweet temptation. Can't you taste it now? That first dainty bite meeting just the slightest resistance. Then, as you penetrate the sugary crust, immediate surrender; the fudge literally melts in your mouth. No wonder it takes willpower to nibble, not gnaw; a true aficionado to savor, not devour.

Ask a professional fudge-maker, and he'll tell you that is bad fudge, that the crust comes from the corn syrup setting up on a too-warm slab. But that, too, is the beauty of fudge: sugary, chewy, fluffy, creamy, caramely—whatever its shape or form, each has its devotees.

Just as fudge is more than a sweet, it is more than merely chocolate. Today it's butterscotch and coconut and peanut butter and almost any flavor you can imagine, including apple, brandy, candied cherry, Chambord, cinnamon, coffee, ginger, hazelnut, lemon, lime, maple, melon, mocha, molasses, orange, pineapple, pistachio, raisin, raspberry, rum, strawberry, and on and on.

Herein you'll find all those flavors and more—over 240 taste treats in all—in a book that finally gives fudge its proper recognition as a major ingredient in the world of candy. And the favorite of millions of Americans, including our First Families. You'll find recipes for fudges of every shape and color, as well as those first cousins, fondants and divinities and nougats and brittles and caramels and taffies.

As you peruse them, try to imagine a world without fudge in any form. Unbelievable, isn't it? Yet fudge is a comparative newcomer to the candy scene—a purely American contribution a little more than a hundred years old.

It is foreign to the Chinese despite the fact that their knowledge of sugar dates back to the seventh century, when they sent ambassadors to India to discover the secret of sugar refining. It is from the Sanskrit word for sugarcane, *sarkara*, that we get the word "sugar." The Sanskrit for solidified sugar, *khanda*, gives us "candy," as in the verb "to sugar or grain or crystallize or solidify." In other words, to become fudge. Only recently has "candy" become a synonym for a "sweet." Indeed, cookbooks written by classicists and purists list all caramels, fondants, fudges, and so on in the index under "confections," not "candies."

The Spanish never came close to discovering fudge, yet they were the ones to introduce sugarcane seedlings to the New World on Columbus's second voyage in 1493 . . . and the first to see chocolate in 1502 when Columbus returned to Spain with strange orange-and-red cucumber-shaped pods filled with almond-shaped white or purplish seeds. How smug those courtiers felt, confirmed in their superiority to ignorant natives, when told that the beans were revered as a gift from paradise, offering universal wisdom to those who ate of them. And how they laughed when they discovered that the beans, not gold, served as money for the natives. Four would buy a pumpkin, ten a rabbit, eight or ten the services of a prostitute, and one hundred a live slave.

Nor did the courtiers think much better of the other spice Columbus brought back, a long, skinny bean of a dark-brown color. When told it was considered an aphrodisiac, they mockingly named it *vainilla*, the diminutive of the Spanish word for vagina.

They soon changed their minds. Perhaps it was the tale Hernando Cortés told that *xoco-latl* ("choco-lat") enhanced sexual potency; Montezuma, with his vast harem, drank fifty gobletsful a day. Cortés had originally been more interested in the golden goblet in which the Aztec emperor's "bitter water" was served. Upon learning of the drink's "medicinal" qualities, Cortés, an opportunist if there ever was one, promptly usurped both goblet and drink, adding sugar to the latter. Once the Spanish discovered the delights of chocolate, they were soon as pro-chocolate as the Aztecs. Although there is no record of anyone having drunk himself to death on hot chocolate, chocoholics soon came into being in Spain. (One has to wonder if this might not have been Montezuma's real revenge.)

So important did the Spanish consider chocolate that in the early sixteenth century they entrusted the secrets of it to the monasteries, which retained absolute control over it for more than a century until it went north as part of the marriage portion of Spanish princess Maria Theresa of Austria to the king of France.

The mighty French were no more able to resist the influence of *xoco-latl* than the Spanish. Once it was introduced to the court at

Versailles in 1659, the Sun King, Louis XIV, promptly created the position of Royal Chocolate Maker to the King.

Yet fudge was not discovered in France, the birthplace of confectionery, the land of spun-sugar architectural fantasies so vast and heavy they required several stout shoulders to carry in to the feast. Despite their knowledge of marzipan and marshmallows, nougats and pastilles, fondant and caramel (the latter two, father and mother to fudge, respectively), the French learned of that most popular of all confections from America during this century. Some say fudge was brought back to the Old World in packages mothers sent to their Yankee doughboy sons, but no one will swear to it.

We do know that an entry in *Harmsworth's Household Encyclopedia* (London, 1920) officially confirms the presence of fudge in Great Britain. It is defined as "A sweetmeat that hails from America, but is now popular in other countries also. [It is] made from white or brown sugar, milk, cream, or condensed milk, butter and flavored with chocolate, coffee and vanilla essence. Margarine can be used instead of butter, but the toffee does not set so well nor is the taste quite so rich or good."

While some cookbook writers accepted the methodology and approved of the ingredients, other Britons refused to use the word "fudge" and instead called the confections "tablets." Why tablets? Did attaching a pharmaceutical term ameliorate against the sinful richness and goodness of the sweet? We'll never know. And that is typical of fudge, the mystery sweet.

We don't even know for sure exactly who first made it, although every source agrees fudge was the result of an accident, a botched batch of some other confection. (Imagine making such a goof, denying it, and losing your rightful place in history as the discoverer of fudge.) We are not even sure exactly which batch of what got botched. Although a few non-Americans insist that it was toffee, everyone else agrees fudge came from a candied or grained caramel.

Hundreds of experiments have proved to my satisfaction that fudge could not result from candying a high-cooked confection—it had to be the end-product of taking the ingredients for caramel and handling them as if making a fondant . . . maybe even deliberately, who knows?

If we can't agree on exactly what or how fudge happened, you can imagine how even more elusive the dating of it is.

One thing we do know is that it wasn't in existence in 1849 when J. M. Sanderson assembled the second edition of his *Cook and*

Confectioner; The Complete Cook. Printed in Philadelphia and currently in the library at the Henry Francis du Pont Winterthur Museum, the book was meant for professionals and included between its red covers 196 pages on cooking and 154 pages on confectionery. In those pages, Sanderson described everything anyone would ever want to know about making sweets—from the clarification of raw sugar, which took the white of an egg and half a teacupful of bullock's blood, to the making of Spanish baskets of cooked sugar from do-it-yourself plaster-of-Paris molds.

In fact, many of the techniques he describes are used today. Fortunately for us, we don't have to cope with some of the more elaborate ones. For example, we don't have to crush our sugar, clarify it with egg whites and blood, skim it and strain it and filter it and add a little lime to neutralize the acid found in raw sugar. The sugar we buy is unbelievably pure and rarely needs skimming.

The nine essential points or degrees in boiling sugar that he lists have remained much the same although with today's thermometers, we can more accurately gauge when sugar will pass through the various stages.

Sanderson is the one who explained that "candy" meant the graining of a cooked sugar and proclaimed that the prevention of candying was "the chief desideratum" of the confectioner. This theme is sounded to this day in cookbooks for professionals and for amateur candy-makers.

Sanderson gives exhaustive lists, recipe after recipe, for syrups and bonbons (fondant-creams) and coltsfoot (horehound) candy and prawlings and rocks and hardbakes and stomachics and caramels and nougats . . . but nowhere does he mention or even assemble the ingredients for the sugar-and-cream confection we know as fudge. His book is just too complete to have omitted fudge . . . unless it didn't exist back then.

Then again, there is always the possibility that he fudged this aspect of candy-making, perhaps considering it beneath him or too amateurish for inclusion in a book for professionals.

One of the most complete compilations of recipes for everything from making bread to removing stains was Marion Cabell Tyree's *Housekeeping in Old Virginia, Containing Contributions from Two Hundred and Fifty of Virginia's Noted Housewives, Distinguished for Their Skill in the Culinary Art and Other Branches of Domestic Economy* (1879). Reprinted in 1965 by Original Favorite Recipes Press, Inc., it contains recipes for what is now called fondant and a type of divinity and taffy, in addition to macaroons and caramels. But nothing in this book remotely resembles fudge.

In 1885 the public was treated to *Dr. Austin's Indispensable Handbook and General Educator. Useful and Practical Information pertaining to The Household, the Trades and the Professions* . . . by George L. Austin, M.D. Turn to page 368 and his "Confectionery Department," and you'll find taffy and butterscotch and chocolate caramels and chocolate cream drops and bonbons and horehound candy and cough candy (two kinds) . . . and so on, and so on. Dozens and dozens of recipes. But not a one for any fudgelike candy, and this is 1885.

So, when did fudge begin?

Stories abound. In one treasured Michigan family chronicle, two youngsters ruined a batch of Dad's caramel, but Granny came arunnin' to the rescue. The story ends there, but presumably resulted in fudge. Fruitless trips to the Library of Congress turned up nothing, while research in the British archives resulted in a saga of pre–Civil War escapades at a northern Michigan boarding school for girls.

So, just when did fudge as fudge the candy begin?

For that, we need to consult a slim file folder in the archives of Vassar College in Poughkeepsie, New York. In it sits a letter written on December 11, 1921, by Emelyn B. Hartridge (class of 1892) to a beloved history professor, trying to coax the latter into coming to visit when the two "could make caramels." Here it is, the first verifiable story of the origin of fudge.

Writes Miss Hartridge, "Fudge, as I first knew it, was first made in Baltimore by a cousin of a schoolmate of mine. It was sold in 1886 in a grocery store [at 279 Williams Street] for 40 cents a pound. . . . From my schoolmate, Nannie Hagner . . . I secured the recipe and in my first year at Vassar, I made it there—and in 1888 I made 30 pounds for the Senior Auction, its real introduction to the college, I think."

Emelyn Hartridge went on to found the Hartridge Boarding School for Girls in Plainfield, New Jersey (now the coed Wardlaw-Hartridge Day School). She is remembered as such a dreaded tyrant that staff and alumnae have difficulty believing this was the same woman who knelt on the floor for hours on end and stirred cream and sugar and chocolate together over a spirit lamp to produce thirty pounds of fudge for the Senior Auction held June 2, 1888. Thirty-three years later, with a personal staff that included a cook, head laundress, janitress, and two maids, she was still personally making fudge to raise money for the Vassar Book and Gift Shop. In the pre–World War I years, Vassar girls made fudge in dormitory kitchenettes, which remained in operation until 1940.

Hurrah for Miss Hartridge, I say, dreaded tyrant though she may have been. Within months of her introduction of the sweet to Vassar, "fudge" had spread to other schools—Smith and Wellesley, in particular. Bryn Mawr girls opted for an easier way of ingesting sugar and milk and chocolate: a beverage called Muggle.

But why name it "fudge"?

When fudge was accidentally made, did someone exclaim, "Oh, fudge!" in the manner of Mr. Burchell in Oliver Goldsmith's *Vicar of Wakefield* . . . and did the others exclaim, "Eureka, that's it!"? Or did someone draw the obvious comparison between people splurging on fudge and the Fudge family of English tourists gorging themselves on French gourmet foods in the satire of the Irish poet Thomas Moore? "The Fudge Family in Paris," written in 1818, was a best-seller and remained enormously popular decades later for the pointedness of its wit:

> *Yet, who can help loving the land that has taught us*
> *Six hundred and eighty-five ways to dress eggs?*

What a literate, romantic possibility. Unfortunately, a more mundane solution is likely. Dictionaries dating back as early as 1811 (*Dictionary of the Vulgar Tongue*) list "fudge" as "nonsense." By the early 1900s, the term had become more codified, as in:

a noun: A nonsensical story; humbug; rubbish; frequently used as an interjection indicating contempt . . . as, for example, when John Russell Lowell in *A Fable for Critics* (1848) compared Edgar Allan Poe to a Dickens character who was a murderer and halfwit, "There comes Poe, with his raven, like Barnaby Rudge,/ Three-fifths of him genius, and two-fifths sheer fudge."
a verb: Intransitive. (1) to accomplish, fabricate, or contrive in a careless or blundering manner; bungle. . . . Sailor's slang: to fake an observation; to work out an alleged position at sea by mathematics, not by observation.

Since all agree that fudge was the result of a happy accident, it is logical to assume that the name referred to the "arranging confusedly" or "bungling" of a batch. Certainly that is the only explanation for early cookbooks referring to a single recipe as "fudges," as in "he fudges, she fudges"—a present-tense verb. Of course, when considering the alternatives, especially the 1980-style synonyms for ruining something, we can only be grateful that fudge came about in a quieter, gentler time, a time when "Oh, fudge!" and "Golly Ned!" were considered powerful expletives.

However the name came to be, do not assume it to have been immediately and universally accepted. Quite the contrary. At first it seemed to apply only to the chocolate version. The earliest recipe I've found calling for fudgelike ingredients and methodology is in the *American Domestic Cyclopedia, A Volume of Universal Ready Reference for American Women in American Homes* by M. Lupton (New York, 1890). It is not called fudge but "Vanilla Candy" and advises the cook to "stir until hard and eat when you please."

Ten years later, when Frank A. De Puy's *New Century Home Book* was published in New York, fudge was there and warranted its own section, with a selection of six recipes, only two of which were chocolate. And with this book, a trend in fudge-recipe writing was begun: the giving of a basic recipe followed by variations. (Who am I to argue with a ninety-year-old tradition? I'll be doing the same—only with a vastly larger number of both master recipes and variations.)

Already professional cooks and fudge-recipe writers were aware of the fallibility, or should I say, *failability* of any fudge recipe. As Mr. De Puy noted in his basic recipe, "The success of fudge depends upon its being removed from the fire at the right moment."

In the meantime, the girls at Vassar were setting the recipe for fudge to music (to the tune of "Smiles") and glorifying the fudge pan in verse:

> *We love the sight of the fudge-pan bright,*
> *We love the sight of the spoon,*
> *And better by far than the light of the star*
> *Is the gas, now outshining the moon.*
> *Then gather around with whispers profound*
> *For the bell has rung ten at night,*
> *With the transom shut, at our very last cut*
> *We'll sing to the fudge-pan bright . . .*
> (*Vassar Miscellany* 24, no. 8 [May 1895])

At Wellesley the candy evolved in less than four years from a simple, rather haphazardly put together concoction to a fixed recipe. (What was "fudge" to the girls at Vassar was "penuci"—Mexican-Spanish for coarse sugar—at Wellesley.)

Betty Scott, in the 1898 Wellesley College Yearbook, *Legenda*, recalls fudge-making in her freshman days.

the lamp . . . was placed conveniently in the center of the floor. Into a large tin box was rattled a score or so of sugar lumps, bedewed with a thin mixture of condensed milk and water and a scant sprinkling of Huyler's cocoa; thus ensconced comfortably, though with some necessary display of talent in balancing, upon the lamp chimney . . . the result of these experiments, the fudge of this period, was typically New England—stern, hard and cold . . . molded unalterably to one form, stamped indelibly with the pattern of its environment, usually three fluted teacup saucers, from which, deftly loosened by the insertion of a knife blade, it rolled off, round, ribbed and rocky.

That was in 1894, when fudge was "composed of such ingredients as circumstances offered." By 1898 she notes that not only had its mobility of character ended but its ingredients had become "fixed and known quantities: cream, fresh butter, granulated sugar, Baker's Chocolate" but also the tin box balanced atop a lamp chimney had been replaced by what had become the traditional gift from senior to freshman: the chafing dish!

Further evolution of fudge occurred that same year when, for what may well have been the first time ever, fudge was used as a frosting for a cake. Served at the Wellesley Tea Room from 1898 on, it was featured as recently as 1982 in full-page ads for Baker's Chocolate in women's magazines. However, the recipes given were not the originals.

Fudge as frosting or candy was proving to be a fickle confection. As anyone who has ever made fudge knows, it can try one's soul. For example, back in 1903, a Smith student, Myrtis Benedict, wrote to her sister Miriam about her experiences making fudge.

It cooked awfully slow and wasn't done when the lights were out [lights out, literally, was at 10:00 P.M.]. So we lit a candle and still watched it try to cook. At last we beat it and set it outside the window to cool. It just wouldn't get hard so we took it in as it was, then went and called in all the rest of the third floor girls, pulling them out of their warm beds, and we sat around on the floor with the chocolate stuff and a bag of crackers in the middle, and ate chocolate sandwiches, spreading the fudge on the crackers you see.

It's the first, but not the last, mention of fixing a fudge failure in the literature of fudge. You'll find a whole chapter on it at the end of this book.

Somewhere around the turn of the century, fudge made its way out to the Midwest and to what, eventually, would become known as the fudge capital of the United States—Mackinac Island, off the coast of northern Michigan in Lake Huron. Philip Murdick opened a candy shop there in 1887, and by 1900 he was augmenting his offerings of penny candies with pans of slab-made fudge.

Within the next five years, fudge made it to the big time, in the cookbook sense, appearing in one book after another. But the name was still creating problems. In the *Consolidated Library of Modern Cooking & Household Recipes* by Christine Terhune Herrick (editor-in-chief) and Marion Harland *et al.* (New York, 1904), we find vanilla fudge is called "Cream Caramels" and chocolate brown sugar fudge called "Fudges," which is a single recipe using brown and white sugar, milk, butter, and chocolate. The same recipe without chocolate is named "Ponouchi." And, finally, there was "Comanche," which directs one to pour the brown fudge into a buttered pan and pour the white fudge over it.

Almost one hundred years later there is still disagreement as to how one spells (in chronological order) penuci-ponouchi-panocha-penuche. (Modern dictionaries are no help other than cross-referencing the latter two.)

Two years earlier *Woman's Favorite Cookbook* by Annie R. Gregory "assisted by 1000 housekeepers" contained another recipe for "fudges," contributed by Stanley Miller. Among other recipes, including a Butter Scotch for Colds made from lard, were four nonfudge contributions by the Julia Child of the nineteenth century, Maria Parloa. In such high esteem was she held that her recipes were identified as by "Miss Maria Parloa."

In 1908 a booklet entitled "Choice Recipes by Miss Maria Parloa and other Noted Teachers" was issued by Walter Baker & Company. On page 31, in a section headlined in bold, capital letters "RECIPES

FOR MAKING FUDGE," recipes for Vassar Fudge, Smith College Fudge, Wellesley Marshmallow Fudge, and three others appeared for the first time.

Although only the Vassar fudge has any basis in historical fact ingredientwise, Miss Parloa was a genius! Those three fudges are the basis for as many as 90 percent of all fudge recipes in existence today. And, modernized, they are three of the master recipes you'll find in this book. Furthermore, with these recipes as well as with Double Fudge, Chocolate Fudge with Fruit, and Fudgettes, Miss Parloa was the first to attempt to solve the how-will-I-know-it's-done-without-testing problem. She specified the exact number of minutes to boil.

Upon Miss Parloa's death in 1909, a co-author was hired—a woman who specialized in doing company-sponsored cookbooks. The booklet was revised, pralines and Turkish paste added, and the whole renamed "Chocolate and Cocoa Recipes by Miss Parloa, and Home Made Candy Recipes by Mrs. Janet McKenzie Hill." By the way, this pamphlet is the one usually cited in candy and/or chocolate chronicles as the first time a fudge recipe appeared in print.

The pamphlet was reissued periodically to meet demand during the next fourteen years, and somewhere along the line—copies of all editions do not exist—all three recipes were revamped. Thus by 1926 when the booklet was reissued under the title "Chocolate and Cocoa Recipes by Noted Cooks, and Home Made Candy Recipes by Mrs. Janet McKenzie Hill," the Smith and Wellesley fudges, which had not been historically accurate to begin with, had been rendered even less so, and the Vassar Fudge had had its chocolate content doubled, which certainly can't have displeased Walter Baker & Company.

From Nannie Hagner to Emelyn Hartridge to Vassar to Smith to Wellesley to Mackinac Island to Maria Parloa . . . from there, everywhere. Eventually, fudge even reached the most famous kitchen in America, that of the White House.

It seems that First Families, like normal people, have sweet tooths. Although recipes for Martha Washington Creams (a.k.a. Dolley Madison Creams) and Mount Vernon Fudge are apocryphal, according to the curator at Mount Vernon, we know that since the middle of the last century at least, candies were no strangers to the White House. Evidently Herbert Hoover was so fond of sweets that, according to *The President's Cookbook* by Poppy Cannon and Patricia Brooks (1969), White House menus during his administration often began with home-made candies.

When you think of fudge and First Families, there is but one recipe that comes to mind. One version or another of it has appeared in dozens and dozens of spiral-bound "Personal Collection" cookbooks under many different but somewhat similar names. It may be the most famous candy recipe in the United States.

You may know it as Double Chocolate Fudge or Dorchester Fudge, but more frequently it is called Mamie's Fudge or Mrs. Eisenhower's Fudge or Mamie's Million Dollar Fudge or Million Dollar Fudge. Supposedly, President Eisenhower named it thusly for the money it raised for the war effort and for charity during World War II.

The recipe takes almost as many forms as it has names—and some of the permutations are unbelievable. You'll find the original in chapter 13. It came from the Eisenhower farm in Gettysburg. A variation of it has graced Durkee-Mower Marshmallow Fluff containers since World War II and is one of the two most reprinted and requested brand-name fudge recipes of the past fifty years; the other appeared on a can of cocoa. Both are included in this book.

When Mrs. Eisenhower left the White House, fudge evidently went with her. Jacqueline Kennedy (Onassis), despite being a Vassar girl, left the cooking to her French chef, and the closest the Kennedys came to a simple American dessert was strawberries and vanilla ice cream; crème brulee, chocolate mousse, and baked Alaska were the more common desserts served.

Lady Bird Johnson prefers a quick chocolate peanut candy, dropped by the teaspoonful like divinity.

You would guess that Rosalynn Carter, with a peanut warehouse in the family, enjoys peanut brittle. But hers is a truly different brittle, using raw peanuts.

Nancy Reagan is fond of that masterpiece of baked fudge, the brownie. She makes hers extra-special by combining it with jelly and topping it with meringue.

Barbara Bush, who admits to a liking for fudge, has an apple crisp recipe that is easily adapted and changed into fudge. The result, as taste-tested by children of all ages, is an all-American winner.

But judge all these for yourself; the First Lady recipes appear in chapter 13.

What confection will reign supreme at the White House in years to come, no one knows. But we do know this: More than a new confection was brought to life in that dorm room in preparation for the Vassar Senior Auction; a lasting tradition was started.

Admit it now, your earliest memory of your mother's cooking was licking the spoon . . . and the very best spoons for licking were those that had just scraped from the pan the remnants of a glorious batch of fudge.

If you were like me, your first attempt at cooking might well have been your very own batch of fudge. I remember it well, as does my mother, although she wasn't home. I cluttered up the kitchen, dirtied every pot and pan in sight, burned my fingers, and produced a rock-solid mess that wasn't dented by a kitchen mallet.

Challenged, I eventually not only learned to make a really good fudge, but also discovered that the promise of fudge drew teenage boys like honey to a bee . . . as it had to my mother and her mother before her. And that strong young man's arm was certainly appreciated when it came time to beat fudge the old-fashioned way.

If you don't remember taffy-pulling parties, ice cream socials, maple sugaring get-togethers, candy club cook-offs, and Girl Scout badge-earning candy sessions, then you are either under thirty or under-privileged. In either case, it's not too late. They say what goes around comes around. And taffy pulls, penoche parties, and fudge-making shindigs are back with a sweet vengeance.

Irma Rombauer, of the famous *Joy of Cooking* cookbook, felt so strongly about fudge-making that she begged her readers, "The fudge pot remains the young cook's initial baptism by fire, so please, in spite of its drawbacks, give your children free rein." James Beard had fond memories of making fudge. "A dark day was always a time to make candy, and on such occasions one went to a friend's house after school and messed up the kitchen magnificently making a penoche."

For a while there, health consciousness in America seemed to sound the death knell for fudge. However, results of a ten-year study by the U.S. Food and Drug Administration suggest that the calories in fudge not only are not empty but can even be good for you. (Your teeth are another story—but a quick-dissolving candy like fudge is not as destructive as, for example, those chewy dried fruit skins they sell in health-food stores.)

Sugar not bad for you? Seems hard to believe, doesn't it? Although sugar did not become a major constituent of our diets until the nineteenth century, during the twentieth, few substances have received worse press. It has been cited as a cause of heart disease and diabetes and has been implicated in hyperactivity and even criminal behavior. However, the FDA has declared sugar not guilty. In fact, sugar is now recognized as playing an important part in a well-balanced diet. Besides providing quick energy, it improves the palatability of other foods, as well as serving as a preservative.

For an energy lift, little else can compare to fudge as a source of the essential carbohydrates the brain requires to function. Human adults require about 100 grams of carbohydrate per day. That branch of sports medicine known as human-performance research has found that an athlete's performance can be increased not only by carbo-loading beforehand but also by consuming glucose-loaded carbohydrates during exercise. By nibbling slowly on that piece of fudge instead of gulping it down you will increase your energy availability by 20 percent.

The latest research shows that having a piece of fudge with a glass of milk can actually help prevent osteoporosis. For some reason, the glucose in the fudge enhances calcium absorption by as much as 20 percent, according to one study—an important factor for older Americans.

But what of the fat in fudge? Fat per se is not all bad. It has satiety value, which tells your body it should be content to stop eating—one reason we feel so good after eating this sugar-butter-milk confection. Cholesterol—bad cholesterol—is what should be avoided, the cholesterol found in palm oil. Homemade fudge has none of that and, relatively speaking, little of the other cholesterol. Commercial fudge is another story. Some of the most famous in the country contains not just sugar, evaporated milk, chocolate, and butter; the fifth largest component is "hydrogenated vegetable oil (palm kernel, cocoanut [sic] and palm)" . . . and it is these oils that have turned out to be the real cholesterol culprits. But what of chocolate? you ask. There's a lot of chocolate in fudge, and it's high in cholesterol. True, but chocolate is high in the right kind of cholesterol, the beneficial one. Maybe the Aztecs knew what they were talking about when they considered chocolate a health food. Of course, the kinds of heart attacks they suffered came atop a pyramid and at the end of a knife.

Speaking of chocolate, it is made from the cacao, fruit of the evergreen genus *Theobroma* (Greek for "food for the gods"), which is not to be confused with the South American coca shrub (*Erythroxylon coca*), the leaves of which contain cocaine. Cacao is a concentrated food containing about 40.3 percent carbohydrates, 22 percent fat, 18.1 percent protein, and 6.3 percent ash with small amounts of water and fiber. It has only a mild stimulating affect caused by theobromine

(2.2 percent) and caffeine (0.1 percent). But that is enough to make a great many people feel good after eating it.

Moreover, the combination of sugar and chocolate yields concentrated energy plus stimulation, which has made candy a mandatory ration for soldiers since the time of Napoleon. In fact, when the English blockade prevented sugar from arriving in France, Napoleon offered a reward of 100,000 francs to anyone who could figure out how to manufacture sweeteners from starch.

During the War between the States, there was renewed interest in the conversion of starch to sugar in America. Finally, in 1866, sugar was made from corn in a factory in Buffalo, New York. The troops got their sweetening, America a new industry, and candy-makers got a greater chance of success, for corn syrup acts as a stabilizer, a "candying" inhibitor that prevents graininess during candy-making. It also increases the hygroscopic aspect of fudge (its tendency to absorb water from the atmosphere).

When fudge-makers added corn syrup to their recipes, they created a damned-if-you-do, damned-if-you-don't situation that haunts us to this day. Too much corn syrup and "candying" was prevented and voilà, you have what I call fudge soup. Too little corn syrup or none at all, and the fudge candies easily but can become unpleasantly sugary. Get the right amount and your work still may be undone if you attempt to cook fudge on a wet or humid day. Finding the perfect balance has meant testing hundreds of recipes . . . many of which—the ones that work—you'll find within these pages.

Just remember, if there are foods to die for and foods to diet for, fudge is both.

TWO

The Selling of Fudge

Almost as old as man's love of sweets is his desire that someone else cook them. For example, thousands of years ago, the ancient Egyptians were careful not only to lay in an ample supply of sweets for the afterworld via tomb paintings and magical formulas but also to ensure cooks were there to prepare them in the form of servant replicas, the *shawabtis*, or miniature wooden figurines.

Six hundred years before the birth of Christ, the making of sweets had become a business venture. The sweetmeat shops in Rome also proved to be great tourist attractions although only the very wealthy could afford to patronize them. (A condition that would continue for centuries, due to the high cost of wild honey. Nor did it improve much after the discovery of sugarcane, for until the last century, sugar sold for as much as $270 a pound in 1990 dollars.)

For two thousand years, sweets did not change much, but the selling of them did. For example, in the fifteenth century, German gingerbread bakers were making sticky, sugary concoctions from dried fruit, nuts, sesame or poppy seeds, and spices. Still bound with honey, cut into pieces, and rolled in flour, chopped nuts, and seeds to keep them from sticking together, they would have seemed familiar to a Roman from Nero's time. (The recipe for Date-Nut Roll you'll find in chapter 6 is a direct descendant of those early sweets.) And, still, they were reserved for the nobility; the general public could look, but not touch . . . and certainly not taste.

Then the monasteries and apothecaries became involved. But these newcomers to the "sweets" game were early believers in research and development, and they came up with confections closer to what we know as candy, using the newly introduced vanilla, sugar, and cocoa, though they had not yet found a way to make chocolate. More important, they found a way to reduce costs enough to sell to the public. For the monasteries, this was only a sideline, as it remains today. But the apothecaries were doing big business—marshmallows, for example, were one of their early and most wanted medications.

The bakers were soon forced out and replaced by "grocers" who received royal patents not only to bake cakes and gingerbread but to compete against the apothecaries in producing sweets for sale to the public. Soon, faced with a growing demand for sweets, some grocers abandoned bread- and cake-making to specialize in producing sweets.

It took twenty-one hundred years, but eventually we had come full circle: The sweet shop was back in business.

Across the Atlantic, history would once again repeat itself. In the beginning, the Dutch bakers of the colony of New Amsterdam, later called New York, made sweets for celebrations in the seventeenth century. For Christmas and New Year's Eve parties, they offered sugar wafers, marshpanes, macaroons, pasteys, roundels, and sugar plums, many decorated with gold leaf. Theirs was a virtual monopoly until up jumped the apothecaries. In 1712 an apothecary in Boston advertised the sale of fruits, spices, sugars, sweetmeats, chocolate, almonds, and sugar candy. (Some consider this to be the first actual candy shop in America.) Soon pharmacists were opening their own shops and offering sugar candy in New York and Philadelphia and all the major cities along the Atlantic coast. And soon, as in Europe, grocers were cashing in on the action.

By the end of the 1800s a flourishing business was done in "penny candies." But now the pharmacies and grocery stores were replaced by a rash of penny candy stores—all with children as steady customers. And they were ready when, in 1911, another candy wave hit the nation—the manufactured candy bar, an individually wrapped concoction of chocolate, caramel, nuts, and nougats. After the introduction of the candy bar, many of the popular candies were packaged in five- and ten-cent sizes.

Today there are two thousand varieties of confections, most of which have hundreds of different variations, including as many as five hundred different formulas for nougats and probably double that for marshmallow. But one thing hasn't changed in the last twenty-six centuries: our fascination with candy-making . . . and candy-making as a tourist attraction.

For example, in August 1901, Excelsior Publishing Company of New York issued no. 64 in its line of "Popular Hand-Books," *The Candy Maker, a Practical Guide to the Manufacture of the Various Kinds of Plain and Fancy Candy*. It listed fewer than 150 recipes for candies including ices (sherbets), punches, and syrups, but included valuable advice for would-be candy-shop entrepreneurs. "The workman in full view," the editors noted, "has proved the most certain means of attracting the public eye; and we have in remembrance at least two instances of firms having risen from the slender capital of a few dollars to a large wholesale trade by the use of this device. The public is curious about most mechanical operations, and people will stop to see almost anything done in the street or in full view of the passer-by, especially if the performance requires some particular knowledge."

Almost ninety years later, across the country, wherever there are tourists, there are candy shops. And the most successful of them all, the ones attracting the most attention, have large plate-glass windows, with three-inch-thick $750 marble slabs in front of those windows. Walking around and around the slabs, right there in full view of the passerby, are serious, obviously expert, candy-makers, changing lakes of chocolate into thick, rich loaves of fudge.

A VISIT TO A FUDGE PALACE

He made his fortune in fudge.

James Garrahy didn't intend it that way . . . it just happened, in that mid-sixties era that spawned both dropouts and entrepreneurs.

Today, if you go into any of his Fudge Kitchens coast to coast, look around for Seamus, as he prefers to be called; it's Gaelic for James. You might recognize him from his outdoorsy look, or the twinkle in his eye. And when he speaks, there's a hint of a brogue that instantly gives away his ancestry. By his own description, he's 117.4 percent Irish; the overage is probably good Irish whiskey. And all things being equal, he'd rather be sailing the high seas than overseeing a growing empire of fudge palaces.

It all started one Saturday afternoon in 1963 over a glass of beer or two, when a fellow classmate at the University of Detroit, Gary McClellan, was recounting tales of his year on Mackinac Island and just happened to mention that he had the recipe for Jack Murdick's famous fudge.

"Right then and there, we decided to forgo the pleasure of another beer, and soon found ourselves building fudge trays out of plywood," Garrahy recounts.

"I'm a measure once and cut twice kind of carpenter," he says, "but we got the job done. So now we had some trays and a recipe . . . but no store."

Off they went, first to Canada and then to a few other spots they knew in the Great Lakes region, looking for the perfect location with lots of tourist foot traffic.

They found it up in Northern Michigan at Sault Sainte Marie, where in the old days people had to park to take the ferry across to Canada or down through the locks. There was but one problem. "We found this wall near a sidewalk, a good location but just a big, blank stone wall, back of a candy warehouse. So back we went to Detroit and applied for a small business loan. We were all of twenty-three years old. And the SBA said, 'Well, gentlemen. First thing you have to do is get two letters from banks stating they will not lend you money.' Seems the SBA can't compete with regular banks.

"And, boy, was that easy! No problem there. So we got the two letters, went back to the SBA and in thirty days we had five thousand dollars. This was 1964 and that was a lot of bucks.

"We took the money and took out the brick wall and put in a plate-glass window and floors and ceilings and bought equipment: marble slabs, copper kettles, little stoves, and all that stuff. Neat, beautiful fudge shop. But we didn't know how to make fudge. We had a good recipe, but that was the extent of it. And all the folks in the town—there were like seventeen thousand people—were saying, 'Well, when's the fudge coming, guys?' This was going to be their first fudge shop in what is a real big fudge area. And we said, 'Well, the shop's not quite ready yet.'

"We decided we'd better start learning to make fudge. So, we waited until night, coated the window with Glass Wax, and, under subdued candlelight, tried to make fudge. You could either drink it with a straw or build your house with it. We couldn't get it right. So we'd pack it up in boxes, carry it out into the woods, and pitch it because we didn't want anybody to know we didn't know how to make fudge. And all our furry friends would clap their paws together. 'Hot damn, they blew another batch. Hey, Max, Seamus—over here, man!' Good chow for them. Finally, one night, the maple pecan happened. The right temperature, right mixing, right creaming, everything. It finally came out, and we had fudge.

"The next day we sold that batch of maple and we kept making fudge. We did $19,600 that year. We were in the fudge business.

"The second year we went to Niagara Falls, Ontario, and found a location. And I can remember, the rent in Niagara was five thousand dollars for the season."

Garrahy sold the Niagara shop in 1967 and, for personal reasons, dropped out of the fudge business. But within four years, he was back in it, this time in Gettysburg, Pennsylvania. That's when and where he met Roy Smith, who owned about half the tourist places in town. Roy was willing to sell Seamus a spot for a fudge shop, and thanks to his advice, Garrahy soon opened a second shop in Intercourse, Pennsylvania. It made $75,000 the first year and to this day remains a strong operation, appealing to tourists who visit the Amish country as well as doing a major mail-order business. Roy Smith became friend, business adviser, and mentor.

Lancaster and the Pocono Mountains resort area were next. In the past twenty-five years Garrahy has built a chain of shops crossing the United States and opened six in England. Today he's still growing, still expanding, his most recent shop opening in Jackson, Wyoming. But you will not find any Garrahy fudge stores at the New Jersey shore. He tried it there and made his only big mistake: He hadn't counted on the toughness of the competition.

During his years in business, his shops have sold so much fudge that they measure it in tons. Ask him how many, and he picks up the phone. "At the moment, right now [June 1989], the last call: 3,168 tons. We do 230 to 240 tons a year, twenty-five pounds at a time by hand." Which works out to approximately 19,000 batches per year, handmade.

When he started in business back in 1964, the fudge sold for $1.20 a pound. Now it's up to $7.50, but he confides his nets were higher at $1.20. Like many fudge shops, Seamus offers a buy-three-slice deal and get a fourth free, which brings the price down to $5.25 to $5.35 per pound. Although people complain about the price, it really doesn't stop them from indulging their love of fudge. An experimental month-long lowering of prices at shops in California at Solvang and Universal City made no appreciable difference in volume or gross. The following month, when the price went back up, volume did not fall off.

With one exception, all of Garrahy's fudge shops in the United States sell the same seven flavors: chocolate pecan, plain chocolate, chocolate peanut butter, rocky road (chocolate with marshmallows and pecans), vanilla pecan, maple pecan, and peanut butter. The exception is the Gettysburg shop, which still makes Mamie Eisenhower's favorite, plain vanilla. Carefully kept out of daylight to preserve the fading ink at Fudge Kitchen headquarters in Gettysburg is one of Seamus's proudest possessions, a handwritten letter from Mamie Doud Eisenhower dated July 18, 1978, thanking him for a box of Vanilla Fudge candy, her favorite.

Back to the seven flavors. Why just seven? "In season to make seven is tough. You go from vanilla to chocolate, then if you have to make another vanilla, you have to clean the kettle and scrub the table. So, it's really hard to make enough every day to keep up with the demand.

"Takes an act of God and Congress for us to go to a new flavor. But the Brits did that. They said, 'Ooh, marshmallow is awful.' They don't want peanut butter either. So we make rum raisin, chocolate, maple walnut, caramel, toffee, chocolate walnut, and chocolate orange in England." The story around the Garrahy kitchens is that the Chocolate-Orange Fudge is not only sinfully delicious, it also has aphrodisiac qualities.

Garrahy says nothing makes him more proud than his employees. Many of them start at age fifteen or sixteen and go up through the ranks. In 1988 there were 428 employees on the payroll in the United States and another fifty or sixty in England. And most of them know how to make fudge!

Employee training is strictly "hands-on." The first year most just make the mix and clean and scrub. The next season they learn to make fudge.

"Some folks learn in two batches . . . some never learn," Garrahy says. "I'd say it takes a full season of making it to get down all the little tricks of the trade—you know, temperature, barometric pressure, humidity, slab temperature, different ingredients; they all enter into it."

And you thought fudge-making was simple. Well, take it from this millionaire fudge-maker, it's not! (Not his way; however, mine is much simpler and a perfect in-home method.)

Jim Garrahy's Fudge Kitchens make fudge by one method only— by creaming it on a marble slab. It is cooked in large copper kettles over gas fires and stirred with wooden paddles. The fudge is then poured onto a 750-pound Vermont marble slab with stainless bars to keep it from running off the slab and then worked into a large loaf and sliced. Part of the Garrahy magic is keeping the marble slab and the creaming operation very visible. People are naturally curious to see what's going on—and the more they watch, the more likely they are to purchase some fudge.

Temperature is perhaps the most serious matter the fudge-maker must contend with—not only the cooking temperature, but also the room temperature and the slab temperature. The first batch is cooked to a higher temperature because the slab will be cold. As the marble warms, the fudge comes off the fire at a lower temperature. Along about the sixth or seventh consecutive batch, the marble gets too hot, and the cooking temperature has to go up again.

That's on a normal day. But when the weather outside doesn't cooperate, the slabs may have to be cooled or warmed by other means. In winter, electric blankets have been used. On especially hot days, blocks of ice are sometimes used to cool the slab and keep production humming along.

Gregory Riggeal, right-hand man and vice-president of James Garrahy's Fudge Kitchens, points out, "You can always tell the manager of a fudge shop. That's the one who doesn't make the first batch. A cold slab can cause the twenty-five-pound batch to take as much as two hours to cream. That takes a lot of scraping and folding . . . and really gets to your arms and shoulders."

Of course, not all of us have marble slabs. Seamus says he has made fudge at home on Formica countertops; of course, by the third batch, the glue underneath the counter had melted. The glass-topped kitchen table didn't last even that long. The glass shattered at first pour.

(My first suggestion is to use a jelly-roll pan if you want to try the slab method. My second is that you don't even try it—use the simpler in-home method described in chapter 3 and leave slab fudge to the professionals.)

Besides correcting for the temperature of the slab and the weather outside, altitude makes a big difference. For example, at the new shop in Jackson Hole, they expect their fudge to come in around 222°F (105.5°C) instead of 238°F (114.5°C) because water boils at that altitude at around 180°F (82°C) instead of 212°F (100°C).

So next time you're in one of Jim Garrahy's Fudge Kitchen shops, watching employees work the fudge back and forth or square it or loaf it or curl and shape it, be respectful: genius at work.

That genius might even be Seamus Garrahy himself. He keeps his hand in . . . says it's like riding a bicycle, you never forget how. If you are lucky enough to see him, you're in for a treat—other than his fudge, I mean. He may break into a rasty drinking song, of which he and some friends proudly have recorded an album, or tell you a tale of how he came to install a firepole from his third-level office to the ground floor. He might even describe how he served as second mate on *The Bounty*, the last of the wooden-hulled sailing ships, the one built for Marlon Brando's *Mutiny on the Bounty*, when Ted Turner wanted it moved to its present southern location in 1986.

Alas, Jim "Seamus" Garrahy will, one of these days, answer the call of the sea. He says he will never give up his ownership of the fudge empire, but the wind in the sails and the green hills of Ireland will keep him from his now-frequent visits to his shops. He hopes to charter boats out of an Irish seaport, perhaps even start a "boat and breakfast" there.

There exists one other hotbed of fudge-making activity worthy of mention here, for its history as well as its still-famous fudge delights. That is Mackinac Island, Michigan, the source of the original Garrahy recipe. If you have ever stepped off the ferry (in season) or walked over the bridge, you know the air is redolent with the unmistakable fragrance of fudge.

Although the first candy shop opened there in 1887, it wasn't until the 1900s that fudge was available, and today there are at least eleven fudge shops fighting for your dollar. Murdick's Fudge Kitchen and May's Candy are the oldest, but coming on strong are JoAnn's Fudge (twenty years old), Ryba's Fudge Shop (fifteen), and Kilwin's (ten years). Although all proclaim they have the original recipe or are the original store (one through the simple expedient of buying the ground the first shop stood on), most old-timers disagree. The general consensus among those who know is that only two shops in the area use the original recipe (and that by virtue of inheritance), and neither is on the island. The two are Marshall's main store and branch, located at either end of the bridge over the Straits of Mackinac, in Mackinaw City and St. Ignace. (Supposedly a third shop, owned by a Murdick descendant in Charlevoix, Michigan, also uses the recipe.)

The original shop, opened in 1952 by Jim Marshall and his wife, Oradelle, was called Marshall's Driftwood Fudge. At that time there were four fudge shops on the island and four flavors of fudge. Today under management of the Marshalls' son, Dean, and his wife, Jeannie, they've added a second shop, changed their name to Marshall's Mackinac Trail Fudge, and now have as many as twenty-five different flavors of slab fudge. In season you can sample such unique flavors as chocolate peanut butter, strawberry, butter pecan, chocolate cashew, chocolate chip, piña colada, chocolate mint, triple chip, cherry, chocolate caramel, and chocolate orange. Not only do they have fudge and more fudge, but they make a magnificent nougat-centered pecan roll as well as caramels, brittles, and chocolate barks. See page 284 for their toll-free number for mail order.

According to Seamus Garrahy, the original fudge recipe can be found in any library. The employees at Marshall's say not even they know the exact mix. The fudge palace recipe (see page 277) I have developed for you is as close as anyone can come to approximating Garrahy/Mackinac Island Fudge in a regular kitchen.

THREE

Ten Steps to Making No-Fail Fudge at Home

The truth is you don't have to read this chapter to make my fudge recipes. Each of them is self-sufficient. Why, then, do I bother to include this chapter? For one thing, it has nice-to-know hints and shortcuts. For another, it's for all those people out there who want to know why certain recipes work and others don't . . . who want to take out a little insurance that no surprises are lurking in the fudge pot . . . who want to use recipes from other cookbooks and be guaranteed they'll work.

This is also written to set the record straight because, for too long, certain myths about fudge-making have gone unquestioned and thus have become self-perpetuating. Read some or all of this chapter and discover how to stave off disaster, how to go creative, how to never, ever, have to beat a batch of fudge again . . . and more.

TEN EASY STEPS

"Ten steps to making fudge," you say. "That many? Why, there aren't that many steps in making a cake! Sounds too complicated for me. Where'd you put the microwave fudges?"

To which I reply: "Suppose I said 'How to make fudge in ten little words.' Would that sound so bad? Because that's what it is: Prepare, dissolve, boil, test, shock, seed, stir, watch, add, pour . . . and I'll add one more, the best of all—eat!

You might have noticed that nowhere in that list is the word "beat." With my method, you don't. Doesn't that in itself make it worth hearing me out? I promise you, I'll do my level best, might even throw in a laugh or two, to liven up the reading.

To begin at the beginning. You've undoubtedly heard that making fudge is neither art nor science, but a little of both. And it's true.

31

Even professional fudge-makers don't know for sure why certain things happen. Nor do I. But the method I've developed works. It makes the art more exact while allowing you to be scientific in varying it. Using it, you can develop your own fudge flavors just as they do at Marshall's near Mackinac Island.

Listen to the voice of wisdom, obtained the hard way by botching more batches of fudge than you'd care to know about: Cooking fudge is easy if you know what to look for, listen for, test for, taste for, and feel.

STEP 1: PREPARE

In other words, get your act and equipment together.

Measuring cups, dry and liquid
Measuring spoons
Wooden spoon
Pastry brush for washing down sides of pans
Custard cups, at least two, each holding approximately ½ cup of water, to use for testing sugar syrups in ice-cold water
Tall glass filled with ice cubes
Saucepan: minimum size for fudge is 2-quart; 3-quart is safer; some fudges will take a 4-quart or even larger pan
Optional: Candy thermometer

Depending on how you plan to stir the fudge, you'll need:

A wooden spoon, *or*
An electric mixer (stand-alone with heat-proof bowls or heavy-duty portable), *or*
A food processor (standard size with metal blade)

MYTH 1: YOU HAVE TO USE A CANDY THERMOMETER

To those who insist that a candy thermometer is necessary, I say "Oh, fudge!" More fudges have failed just because their cooks relied on a candy thermometer. You don't need one! And you certainly should never *rely* on one. The people at Taylor Thermometer won't like me for telling you that, but it's true. Many professional confectioners never use one. Do I? Yes. But not to tell me when a fudge is done, because it can't, only testing can. I use it for two other purposes. First, because when I make fudge, I use its cooking time to do something else, too, such as making out shopping lists. Thus, from across the room, a glance at the thermometer will advise me as to what stage the syrup's at without my having to come and peer into the pan. Second, I have to use it for recipes I'm testing and/or developing. How else could I provide those of you who are believers in the thermometer with temperature guides for each recipe? Even in that case, its use is after the fact—to tell me at what temperature the fudge came in each time.

A word to the wise: If you see a recipe in another cookbook that says cook to a single, specified number of degrees, such as 234°F (112°C), watch out. You're courting disaster. No cookbook author, including me, can predict at what temperature a fudge will come in in *your* kitchen. I can't even do it reliably in my own. I've had the same recipe come in at a different temperature each time I made it. Once my kitchen was very cool; another time, the air conditioner was off; the third, the dishwasher had changed the humidity. Frequently, outside, out-of-your-control weather conditions will be an influence. (You'll find, for example, that on cold days fudge will ball at least two degrees lower than the same fudge on a hot day. It has to do with the humidity and evaporation of water.)

So, if you don't need a thermometer, why do so many cookbooks tell you to use one? For one thing, it's a security blanket of sorts— for both of you; and for another, it makes the writer seem authoritative.

Certainly, fudge-shop operators use thermometers. But even though they make essentially the same recipe over and over, they know before they start that each batch will come in at a different temperature. They spend months, sometimes years, learning how to predict temperatures, depending, for example, on whether this is the first or fifth batch done. So great is their reliance on the thermometer that let it go off a degree or two, and these fudge-makers are sunk and making gunk.

Unless you have some way to suspend your thermometer so that it hangs in the middle of the pan, what you will be registering is the temperature around the edge, not the middle, and the syrup will be hotter there than inside. See for yourself. Move the thermometer about, see differences of not just a degree or two but sometimes five or ten.

The most accurate home measure is the saccharometer, perfected by Antoine Baume (1728–1804), which is an instrument to determine the density of liquids and used primarily in home wine-making. It will tell you exactly how much liquid has evaporated off. I have such an instrument, but I'll bet you don't, so let's forget that one.

MYTH 2: "SOFT BALL" IS AN EXACT STAGE

One of the craziest things I came across when researching this book was a major discrepancy among ordinary cookbooks, professional manuals, and confectionery textbooks. All say to cook fudge to the "soft ball." But they don't mean the same thing, nor do they even agree on the same temperatures.

For example, according to one of the most comprehensive confectionery cookbooks for the public, *Candy* (1981), in the Time-Life The Good Cook series:

> *soft ball*: "A rapidly flattening lump . . . [that when gathered into a ball and removed from water] immediately loses shape and flattens" at 234°F to 240°F (112°C to 115.5°C)

According to a college food science textbook (based on the *Handbook of Food Preparation*, prepared by the American Home Economics Association, revised edition, Washington, D.C., 1964):

> *soft ball*: "Dropped into very cold water, syrup forms a soft ball which *does not flatten* when removed from water—234°F to 240°F (112°C to 115.5°C).

And according to *The Modern Pastry Chef* by Wm. J. Sultan (Sultan AVI Publishing, 1977), a professional candy/confectionery manual:

> *soft ball*: "droplet when placed in cold water will tend to form a soft ball when rolled between the fingers" at 242°F to 245°F (116.5°C to 118.5°C)

So when pros and experienced amateurs don't agree, what's a poor girl to do? I quote a textbook for students of confectionery: "Most experienced sugar boilers will use the hand test to assess the degree of cooking; for students the approximate temperatures are given." Of course, if you don't know what the test should do, that isn't very helpful either.

From my experience, rarely does a fudge come to the ball at as low a temperature as other cookbook recipes say it does, at 234°F (112°C). *The average ball temperature for most of my recipes was 238°F (114.5°C).* And the ball should not flatten after removal from cold water unless you apply pressure or wait for it to soften from the heat of your hands . . . and, if you taste it, it should be slightly chewy.

ABOUT THERMOMETERS

If you already own a thermometer, you can skip this and go directly to Step 1a: Prewarm. If you aren't planning to use one, skip this and Prewarm and go to Step 1c: Measure. If you opt to use a thermometer and need to buy one, read on; it will save you time and money.

First, check the gauge. You want one that measures in individual degrees, not ranges labeled (or rather abbreviated) *sb* (soft ball) and so on.

Second, make sure the mercury column is visible.

Third, if it is a round dial thermometer, be sure it is properly calibrated. With some, most of the space on the dial is given over to low- and high-temperature readings, and everything else is compressed into a small arc in the middle. That one will drive you nuts.

Fourth, check the location of the sensor. You want it to come as close to the bottom of your fudge pan as possible without touching it. There is a half-inch difference between the bottom of the stem and the bulb on my two professional thermometers. The sixty-dollar one that goes from 80°F to 400°F in two-degree increments has a sensor-bulb so far up the stem that it can only be used for large, large batches. A third one, sold at restaurant supply stores, is an "instant" read and has a dimple sensor almost three inches up on the stem. This will only measure the temperature of any froth unless you double or triple recipes, which I doubt you're going to do. My guess is you're just going to make a pound at a time, not go into business.

Fifth, note how it fastens to the pan. Whatever mechanism used should be not only adjustable up and down to take into account the different size pans you will use, but also flexible in the sense that there is allowance made for turned lips or edges on pans. In the best of all possible worlds, that mechanism would also allow the thermometer to protrude into the center of the pan. But we can't have everything.

Finally, it would be nice if it were accurate. However, there is no way to check that at the store although some thermometers do carry a guarantee. I must own close to twenty thermometers, ranging in price from a couple of dollars for an off-the-wall blister-pack no-name to more than sixty dollars for a copper commercial candy-maker's instrument. If there's one thing those twenty thermometers have in common, it's inaccuracy. Some have been known to be okay one day, gone the next. When Joan Zeller's class of high school home economics students in Springfield Township, Pennsylvania, tested twelve thermometers, only three were accurate. And those three could easily have been rendered inaccurate by subjecting them to sudden hots and colds.

I do get a lot of use out of the small "instant" thermometer or probe usually used for checking microwaved foods—I'll explain why later.

If you are planning to use a regular thermometer, heed my words:

Step 1A: Prewarm Thermometer

Prewarming the thermometer is real simple. Just place it in a saucepan of cold water, bring the water to a boil, and let it simmer away while you're making the fudge in another pan.

This serves several purposes. To begin with, you can check the thermometer's accuracy. After the water has boiled for five minutes, the thermometer should register 212°F (100°C) if you are at sea level. (Don't know whether you're at sea level or not? Call your library; this is one of the facts most of them keep handy.)

At high altitudes, different stages of candy-making will register six to twelve degrees lower. For example, your thermometer, if accurate, should register the boil at two degrees less for every one thousand feet above sea level:

TEMPERATURE AT WHICH WATER BOILS

at sea level	212°F	100°C
at 500 feet	211°F	99.8°C
at 1,000 feet	210°F	99°C
at 2,000 feet	208°F	98°C
at 3,000 feet	206°F	96.9°C
at 4,000 feet	204°F	95.9°C

What do you do if your thermometer's off a few degrees? Don't sweat it. You're not going to rely on just the thermometer anyway. And you can add or subtract from temperature ranges given in any recipe to allow for the inaccuracy. (Example: According to your thermometer, water boils at 215°F [101.5°C], so your fudge will probably come in at 241°F [116°C], or three degrees higher than my usual 238°F [114.5°C]. If the water boiled at 210°F [99°C], you'd expect your fudge to be ready at 236°F [113.5°C]).

The other reasons for prewarming the thermometer? The pan of hot water will come in handy for washing down crystals, parking your wooden spoon, melting chocolate in a bowl over (or warming premelted chocolate), and cooling the thermometer down and soaking it clean later. Besides, saying "prewarm your thermometer in another pan of water" is so much more couth than "get yourself a slop pot."

Step 1B: Select Saucepan

Selecting the proper saucepan is of far greater importance than you might think, especially if you are using a thermometer. The trick here is to make sure the pot is deep enough so that the bulb of the thermometer is covered by the syrup, not just froth. Also that the saucepan lip is compatible with your thermometer clip—many aren't. Best check to make sure.

MYTH 3: FUDGE POTS SHOULD BE TALL AND HEAVY

Although most cookbooks will tell you to use a tall saucepan, a wide one is better. The larger the surface area, the quicker evaporation can take place. Also, a tall pot requires more vigorous stirring to bring the sugar into solution.

The heavier the better is not necessarily true, either. I find, for example, that Calphalon takes longer than others to get up to temperature. Equally bad, it retains so much heat that the fudge continues to cook long after it is taken from the heat.

I have made fudge in enameled pans, in antique copper pans, in old, banged-up Revere pans, in iron pans, in a cheap, nonelectric wok (it works super)—in just about any pan you can name with the exception of glass. (I don't care if the advertising says it can go from freezer to oven and vice versa; I'm just too cowardly to stick a pan heated to 238°F [114.5°C] in a sink filled with cold water. If you do it and it works, let me know.)

Whatever pan you choose should heat evenly without having hot spots on the bottom; that usually means having a heavy base. It should also be smooth inside with no exposed rivets on the interior to make cleaning clinging crystals a problem. To make nondairy-based candies, it should have a tight-fitting lid.

My preference is a double-walled stainless-steel pan that heats evenly, which eliminates a lot of stirring with milk-based fudges, and cools quickly when placed on cool or wet surfaces.

My second choice is an antique heavy copper saucepan; however, since I cook on an electric range and copper is such a super conductor, I must use a diffuser under the pot. Also, although copper is the pot of choice of professional candy-makers, it is less forgiving than others—and cools the fudge down too rapidly. (If you decide to use one, be sure to use hot water in your sink.) Besides, such pans are neither easily found nor paid for. And the idea of spending tens upon tens of dollars for a fudge pot boggles my mind.

If you use heavy, nonsuperconductive pans, you'll need to cook over higher temperatures. If you use supersensitive ones, cook over low heat to prevent scorching or burning.

The most important thing is not what kind of saucepan you use, but what size. Although I'll specify sizes as we go along, for other recipes it might be wise to have a rule of thumb. Allow 1 quart for each cup of sugar, another quart if the recipe calls for milk or cream, and still a third one if baking soda is used.

Step 1C: Measure Ingredients

Unlike baking, measuring need not be so exact for fudge. The actual boiling of the sugar syrup will self-correct the sugar/liquid proportions through evaporation. So there's no need to level off the sugar measure or jam-pack the brown sugar or use exactly half a can, to the half-ounce, of evaporated milk or scrape out every last drop of corn syrup. If you wet measuring cups or spoons before measuring corn syrup or honey, it pours out more easily. I have been known to dip my spoons in the thermometer hot-water bath—hot water seems to work even better. In the case of flavorings, I'll recommend amounts, but I expect you to be the judge, adjusting up or down to suit your taste. However, when it comes to baking soda or cream of tartar, do use amounts specified.

Unless otherwise stated, all recipes have been devised to yield about one pound of fudge.

MYTH 4: NEVER SUBSTITUTE INGREDIENTS

If you're been told never to substitute ingredients, that's just plain silly. How do you think those hundreds of fudge recipes were developed over lo! these many years? Where you might come to harm substituting, I'll try to warn you—otherwise, go to it. Half the cookbooks written vary their fudge recipes by the simple expedient of substituting ingredients: brown sugar for white, light cream for heavy, and so on. So of course you can substitute. (If you believe in following recipes religiously, you can skip this section and go to Step 1D: Dump Ingredients.)

If you're feeling creative and want to substitute, you have my blessing, but you should know what you are doing. For example, most of my recipes call for butter, which has a higher melting point than margarine. If you wish to substitute margarine, realize it will melt long before the sugar does. Nor will it be as effective as butter for "seeding" purposes (we'll get to that a little later on). Nor do I personally think fudge made with margarine is as creamy as that made with butter. On the other hand, who's going to complain? By the way, although you can use unsalted butter if you wish, salted butter is an asset in fudge-making because it helps regulate the boil. And that's why so many recipes specify salt. But, yes, you can leave it out.

When it comes to substituting other dairy products, just remember, you can't make a real white fudge if you use evaporated or condensed milk; caramelizing has already started with those. Furthermore, you'll need to adjust the butterfat content of recipes when you start using different milk products.

> *To use light cream instead of heavy cream*, add 3 tablespoons butter for every cup substituted.
>
> *To use half-and-half instead of heavy cream*, add 4 tablespoons (½ stick) butter; instead of light cream, add 2 tablespoons more butter for every cup substituted.
>
> *To use undiluted evaporated milk instead of heavy cream*, increase butter by 5 tablespoons (⅝ stick); instead of light cream, add 2 tablespoons more butter for every cup substituted; instead of half-and-half, use the same amount, ounce for ounce.
>
> *To use whole milk instead of heavy cream* (which I don't really recommend), for every cup substituted, add 6 tablespoons (¾ stick) butter; instead of light cream, add 2½ tablespoons butter; instead of half-and-half, add 1½ teaspoons (½ tablespoon) butter; instead of evaporated milk, double the quantity of milk used, which is going to take forever to boil down.
>
> *To use buttermilk or sour cream instead of the same amount of milk or cream*, add baking soda to compensate for the acidity. The rule of thumb is 1 teaspoon baking soda per cup of buttermilk or sour cream.
>
> *To use whole milk instead of buttermilk*, use the same amount but add 1 tablespoon lemon juice or vinegar per cup plus the baking soda.
>
> *To use chocolate milk in place of any other dairy product* is a waste of money. You'll have to add so much butter and extra chocolate anyway . . . don't bother.

Speaking of chocolate—and to some people fudge isn't fudge unless it's chocolate—you can make substitutions here, too, if you adjust the recipe. You'll find that most of my recipes call for plain, old, unsweetened chocolate, which is cheaper, in the long run, than chips, for example. However, some people resent having to melt or grate the chocolate first. Although I have a hand blender with a chopper attachment that grates the chocolate beautifully, I usually simply smash it. Stick the chocolate in a plastic bag and whack away at it with a mallet or tack hammer or even a saucepan—whatever's handy. Otherwise I zap it, unwrapped and unwhacked, in the microwave in a micro-proof cup or bowl on HIGH for 1½ to 2 minutes, stirring after 60 and 90 seconds. I have also been known to put the smashed chocolate in a bowl and put it to melt over the thermometer bath.

However, if you find other forms of chocolate more convenient or don't have unsweetened chocolate on hand, you can substitute if you adjust the recipe to allow for the differences in the cocoa butter content. For every ounce (square) of unsweetened chocolate, use:

3 tablespoons cocoa plus 1 tablespoon butter, or
½ cup (3 ounces) semisweet chips; cut butter back by 1 tablespoon,
   and reduce sugar by ¼ cup, or
1 packet unsweetened premelted baking chocolate

There are some substitution no-nos that you ought to be aware of:
Beware of substituting milk chocolate chips for semisweet; the milk chocolate ones take much longer to melt.

Since gelatin and butterfat are incompatible, be wary of substituting in recipes that call for gelatin and/or marshmallow creme.

Don't use granulated sugar for confectioners' sugar in uncooked recipes, the results will be grainy. In emergencies, you can make a close approximation of confectioners' sugar by putting granulated in your blender and pulverizing it.

What about omitting ingredients? I think that's rather chancy and don't recommend it. If I were to make one exception, it would be salt—that you can manage without. I would particularly caution you against omitting the corn syrup—it's the fudge-maker's best friend, although many of us have a love-hate relationship with it. However, if it's a rainy day (What are you doing, making fudge on a rainy day? You know humidity is a fudge's worse enemy!) and you're out of corn syrup and you can't get to the store, you can substitute honey, lemon juice, or even vinegar (ounce for ounce, providing the recipe doesn't call for more than ¼ cup). You can even skip those and add a little acid, such as ¼ teaspoon cream of tartar. All of these chemically change the nature of sugar and make it smoother, thus preventing it from getting grainy. Personally, if it's rainy, I suggest you either turn on the air conditioner full blast or forget the fudge.

ABOUT SPECIFIC INGREDIENTS

Evaporated milk: A concentrated form of milk that can be recon-stituted by adding an equal amount of water. Usually used in caramel recipes when there is a need to force the amount of milk solids in the recipe without diluting it.

Condensed milk, sweetened: Another concentrated form of milk; much of the water has been removed and corn syrup added, which makes it perfect for uncooked fudges. It sometimes dark-ens in color during storage.

Half-and-half: Contains not less than 12 percent milkfat.

Light (table) cream: Contains not less than 18 percent milkfat.

Heavy (whipping) cream: Contains not less than 36 percent milkfat. It is the dairy product of choice for most fudges, except micro-wave fudges.

Buttermilk: Product remaining when fat is removed from milk or cream and contains not less than 8.5 percent milk solids, *not fat.* Most of today's buttermilk is homogenized and blander than it used to be; still, it will need to be neutralized by the addition of baking soda.

Brown sugar: Light brown unless the recipe calls for dark or brown-ulated. You can substitute white granulated and add ¼ cup unsulfured molasses for every 2 cups called for.

Corn syrup: Use light unless dark is specified. The dark (or blue label), which is the original kind, dates back to 1902 and is still made from refiners' syrup plus caramel syrup with salt added. Eight years later, light (red label) came on the market. Sup-posedly the different labels were needed so that illiterate stock boys could tell the difference between cans identical in every way except for their contents.

Golden syrup a.k.a. refiners' syrup: Use light corn syrup instead, ounce for ounce and vice versa.

Maple syrup: Be sure to use pure and add a pinch of baking soda per cup. Some maple syrup is extremely acidic and will need more baking soda. If it doesn't foam up alarmingly, add baking soda in ⅛ teaspoon increments until it does.

Maple sugar: Unless you are fortunate enough to live in New En-gland, this can be impossible to find. However, you can sub-stitute pure maple syrup by the following formula: use ¾ cup syrup for every cup of maple sugar specified, then reduce liquid in recipe by ¼ cup also.

Confectioners' sugar (also known as 10X or powdered sugar): Has 3 percent cornstarch added to prevent lumping. More expensive than granulated. A waste of money for most cooked candies, essential for *uncooked*.

Loaf or cube or lump sugar: Frequently specified in old cookbooks because it was made from the first refined syrup crystallized and was the purest. These days it is pressed into molds that are lightly lubricated with edible oil. And those oil traces will form a scum. So, if you're using an old recipe that calls for sugar cubes, substitute superfine. In England, preserving or mineral-water sugar is now advised for sugar boiling.

Superfine, bar sugar, ultrafine, or Castor sugar: All basically the same fast-dissolving sugar that is especially good when a white fudge is desired.

Flavorings: Try to use pure ones whenever you have a choice. The one exception is artificial vanilla (vanillin), which is colorless and a necessity if you want a pure white fudge. For other fudges, stick with the pure. I make my own vanilla by soaking vanilla beans in rum (two 3-inch-long beans to ½ cup light rum). It takes about two weeks, but the result is glorious. As you use up your homemade vanilla, just add more rum. Speaking of which, remember that when recipes call for liqueurs and liquors, if they are added when the fudge is hot, all the alcohol is boiled off and only the flavoring remains. So if a recipe calls for rum, use the real thing. By the way, extracts and flavorings, by law, are not the same (the former are usually stronger although double, triple, and even twentyfold strength flavorings are available— one company makes eleven thousand different ones). If you choose to use flavoring oils, a rule of thumb is ⅔ teaspoon flavoring oil for every teaspoon of supermarket extract. But follow your own taste buds.

Step 1D: Dump Ingredients

. . . into your saucepan and let the sugar soak and begin to dissolve while you're finishing up your preparations—it'll speed up the cooking time. Generally speaking, all of the ingredients go in at one time except optional ingredients or the flavoring and butter that are added after the fudge is cooked.

Step 1E: Butter Saucepan

For all fudges made with dairy products, butter the sides of your saucepan from about one inch above the ingredients to the top. It will help prevent crystals from clinging to the sides, although some fudges increase so much in volume that they self-clean their crystals. And it helps prevent the fudge from boiling over (although nothing will stop it if your saucepan's too small to begin with). Always butter sides of dishes used for microwaving fudge to prevent boiling over.

Step 1F: Grease Fudge Pan

Personally, I spray my fudge pan, using one of those nonflavored vegetable sprays. I also use 5 × 10-inch (actually 4¾ × 10 × ¾-inch) disposable toaster oven pans (and then defeat my purpose in using them by sticking them in the dishwasher to clean and reuse). These will hold one pound of fudge very nicely. For larger batches, I use an 8 × 8-inch square pan, but in a pinch, a bread pan will do fine.

If you are not using a disposable pan and especially if you are using a nonstick pan that you don't want to take a chance on cutting, make yourself a wax-paper liner. After spraying or greasing the pan, cut a piece of wax paper the same width of the bottom and let it extend up two sides or the ends, then grease or spray that, too. It's very convenient for lifting the fudge out of the pan.

Three more things and we can begin making fudge. You'll find all my recipes for fudge call for adding something—flavoring, butter, chocolate—immediately after you take the fudge off the heat. This addition is used to "seed" the fudge.

Step 1G: Freeze "Seed" Butter

In the case of a butter seed, you'll get best results if you put the butter in the freezer while the fudge is cooking. While at the freezer, be superefficient and . . .

Step 1H: Fill Glass with Ice Cubes

Take the glass with the ice cubes to the sink and fill it with water for testing the candy later on. Why use a glass? Making fudge can be thirsty work.

While at the sink, one last step:

Step 1I: Fill Sink with Half an Inch of Water

Why put water in the sink? You're going to use it to cool down the fudge in an approximation of how the professionals do it. More on that later. Trust me.

Except with gelatin-based fudges, it doesn't really matter whether you use hot or cold water in the sink. One will cool down and the other will warm up while the fudge is cooking. Just make sure you put in enough to come up half an inch on the sides of your saucepan. Too little and you won't protect the sink. Too much and the fudge will cool down too fast, especially about the sides.

Step 2: DISSOLVE

In this step you're about to do a little sugar chemistry known as creating a supersaturated solution. Although sugar will always dissolve in water, as it does in your morning coffee, you know it takes a bit of nudging or stirring. However, if you loaded your coffee up with teaspoon after teaspoon of sugar, at a certain point it would refuse to accept more.

But, if you reheated your coffee, it would not only accept that extra teaspoon, but more still. And, when the coffee cools down again, you'd find that if the boiling was carried out correctly, all that extra sugar would remain dissolved. That is a supersaturated solution (it is also sickeningly sweet coffee!).

So, using a wooden spoon, start nudging that sugar mixture into solution over low heat. You'll need to stir constantly, but not vigorously—in a figure-eight pattern, please, which covers the bottom of the pan more thoroughly—to keep the sugar from scorching. Why a wooden spoon? For one thing, metal can get hot. Second, later on you'll be using that spoon for testing at a critical point where a metal spoon could cause premature graining.

At approximately 224°F (107°C), the sugar will have dissolved. If butter is used as part of the recipe and not as a seeding medium, it will have melted. Gritty sounds will cease, and the spoon will glide over the bottom of the pan. In those fudges containing gelatin, you may continue to see undissolved granules on the spoon. If gelatin, no problem, they'll dissolve later. (Test by drawing a finger through the spoon—watch out, it may be very hot—and feeling to see if granules are soft or sugary.) If they're sugar granules, delay bringing fudge to a boil until they go into solution. With a nondairy-based fudge or candy, the opacity disappears, and it will become clear.

Step 3: BOIL

Increase the heat and bring to a full, rolling boil.

Now's the time to prevent premature graining. If you forgot to butter the sides of the pan—or if you're making a nondairy-based candy—cover the pan with a square of wax paper and a tight-fitting lid. Steam 1 to 2 minutes to dissolve sugar crystals. (Listen carefully. If the mixture sounds angry enough to boil over, take that lid off, and fast!) When you remove the lid, check to see if crystals still cling to the side. If so, repeat the steaming.

The other and safer method is to wash those crystals down with a pastry brush dipped into the hot water from the thermometer bath, using as little water as possible. Yes, I know other books say to use cold water, but I don't know why. Cold water is self-defeating because it lowers the temperature you're trying to raise. Why is using as little water as possible important? Because you're about to start boiling off the water, so why use more?

Once the mixture reaches a boil, lower the heat while maintaining the boil. That's so you don't have to stir any more than necessary. Stirring retards evaporation, which is what you're trying to achieve. You'll also find that it can make some mixtures bubble up alarmingly, especially those containing baking soda, which already have a tendency to expand.

It rarely happens, but you may find a scum appearing on the top of the mixture. Skim it off, and vow never to buy that brand of sugar again.

Finally, if you've decided to use a thermometer, now is the time to introduce it into the fudge. You haven't done this before because it would have gotten in the way of your stirring and would have required washing down to get rid of sugar crystals. But now it's time for its big entrance. Just make sure you attach it so that its tip doesn't touch the bottom of the pan.

Boil until the froth made up of large bubbles subsides and individual bubbles become pronounced and noisy. In most cases, you'll see implosions scattered here and there, and you can hear them pop individually. These reverse bubbles look like minivolcanoes or craters, especially in chocolate fudges. In all cases, the mixture will thicken and become syrupy when poured from the spoon. Depending on your ingredients, it may thicken considerably and change color significantly. With chocolates particularly, it will become very shiny.

If you're using a thermometer, this will happen around 238°F (114.5°C) at sea level, but it could be higher or lower. To read the thermometer, be sure to scrunch down if necessary so that it's at your eye level. If things are obviously happening to the fudge, but the temperature reading hasn't budged, something may be interfering with the sensor. Remove the thermometer and give it a little shake with a snap of the wrist as you would an oral thermometer, then return to the fudge. This happens most frequently with thick or frothy fudges.

Step 4: TEST

Here it is, the moment of truth! Time to test.

Testing hasn't changed much over the last 150 years . . . and is covered in more detail in the appendix on testing and temperatures. Confectioners of the classical or continental school advocate the "dip-stick method" of testing using a wooden stick, a clay pipe-stem, or, for the brave, a finger first dipped in cold water, then in the syrup, and then back into cold water. It's fast, it's clean, it's easy—it can burn! Julia Child uses this method; coward that I am, I do not recommend it.

The method I use is very simple, very basic:

1. *Use about ½ cup clean, ice-cold water.* Use ice water so your water will be the same temperature as mine. To keep it ice-cold, don't pour it into the custard cup until just before you test. Don't let ice get into the cup.

2. *Using a wooden spoon, pour half a spoonful of syrup into the ice water in the custard cup.* The wooden spoon is to keep from cooling off the syrup or causing premature graining of the syrup. You can tell a lot from what happens to the syrup. If it dissipates immediately, it is not ready to test. If it forms a round, flat mass on the bottom of the cup, it is probably not ready but you can proceed to step 3 if you want to be sure. If the end of the pour remains elevated, get a move on, it should be ready. If the whole thing looks like a stalagmite, sticking up in the air, get that pan off the heat fast—you're at least at the soft-ball stage.

3. *Gather syrup into a ball.* The easiest way, especially on your fingers, is to let the syrup cool a second or two, then pour out the water into the sink as you gather up or roll the syrup into a ball. If it won't gather or, once out of water, the ball falls apart and is runny and gooey, like a thick gelatin, stop. The syrup is not ready yet.

4. *Look, feel, and taste the ball.* If the ball is fairly round and holds its shape, hold it out before you on your fingers. After a moment or two, the heat from your hand should begin to flatten it. Try giving it a gentle pinch. Does it yield without collapsing? Taste it. As with spaghetti, here is one place melt-in-your-mouth is undesirable. If it immediately dissolves, it's not ready! If it offers some resistance or is a bit chewy—what's known as al dente—your fudge is ready.

If you should have to retest, use a clean custard cup and fresh ice water. Don't reuse water from the previous test. The hot syrup will have raised its temperature and that can distort the results.

MYTH 5: YOU MUST REMOVE PAN FROM HEAT WHILE TESTING

Removing the pan from the heat while testing the syrup made sense during the days of roaring, uncontrollable fire in the old coal- or wood-burning kitchen stove, but no longer. Unless you're cooking on high, don't bother. In the first place, you're just cooling the fudge down and, if it's not ready, you will have to heat it longer to bring it back up to temperature. In the second place, the syrup doesn't boil off quickly until it reaches the caramel stage. If you use a thermometer, you'll discover that the temperature creeps, slowly, laboriously up that scale until it's in the vicinity of 245°F (118.5°C) when it takes off like gangbusters. So, unless you're going to take forever to do the test, chances are you'll come back to find the fudge and the temperature unchanged. And in the third place . . .

MYTH 6: BEWARE OF OVERCOOKING FUDGE

I say, it is better to overcook than to undercook fudge. Even if you were to cook it to as high a temperature as caramel, you can still force it to "candy"—remember, that's how fudge started in the first place—but there's not much you can do with undercooked fudge "soup," although I list some options later on. From what people have told me, I think nine out of ten fudge failures occur not because of premature candying or graining but because it hasn't cooked long enough. Human nature being what it is, we have a tendency to rush things—a fatal mistake with fudge. I speak from experience—I used to be the "undercook kid."

Step 5: SHOCK

The secret of good fudge is controlling the "candying," or graining, which you do through a combination of methods. The most effective is to shock it out of equilibrium by a change of temperature, comparable to pouring the fudge onto a marble slab. That's accomplished by placing the saucepan in a sink that is partially filled with water for ten minutes or so to cool down.

MYTH 7: SHAKING THE PAN
WILL BRING ON DISASTER

Very few fudges are so fragile that you must handle them very carefully. And in fact, if you're planning to finish the fudge in your electric mixer or food processor, you can not only shake the fudge but actually pour it into the mixer's metal, heatproof bowl or the food processor's plastic bowl with steel blade inserted.

In any case, the fudge should then be placed in the sink to cool down. (With the plastic processor container, you'll need to add enough cool water in the sink to come up at least one inch on the sides. Leaving the blade in place keeps the water from seeping up through the tube in the middle.)

MYTH 8: YOU CAN PUT FUDGE ON ICE
TO COOL IT DOWN

Actually, this is both half myth, half truth. You *can* put your fudge on ice in case of emergency or when time is at a premium. But you must begin stirring immediately to prevent congealing, and that results in a sugary fudge. And never, ever do it with gelatin-based fudges unless you plan to use a food processor to candy them; otherwise, they get lumpy. I find this method very treacherous and don't recommend it. If you do it anyway, and the fudge congeals, you can rescue it by using your food processor. See chapter 11.

STEP 6: SEED WITH FLAVORING OR BUTTER

Okay, you've changed the fudge's temperature externally, now do so internally through a chemical action/reaction. Just add an alcohol-based flavoring, that tablespoon of butter you put in the freezer, or nuts or chocolate morsels or whatever. The act of the alcohol burning off or butter melting (which it does at a high temperature and thus more effectively than margarine) releases heat and begins to bring the fudge out of solution.

Once "seeded," let the fudge sit without stirring until it cools to lukewarm. A hand held above the fudge should not feel much heat. And most important of all, a "skin" should form on top of the fudge. If you touch it with a spoon, it should indent. Double-check by stirring to see if the fudge on the bottom is beginning to set up and get thick— the spoon will meet some resistance. If it does, proceed to step 7. If not, continue to let cool. Any fudge with a lot of corn syrup in it (¼ cup or more) is safer to stir at a high temperature than other fudges, because corn syrup inhibits grain formation.

If you're using a thermometer and have left it in place, the fudge is ready to stir when the thermometer registers approximately 110°F (43.5°C) right, square in the middle of the pan. If you are not using a candy thermometer, you can use an instant microwave probe to check the temperature in the center of the pot. The most important thing with such a thermometer is to make sure it doesn't touch the bottom of the pan.

STEP 7: STIR

The purpose of not stirring until cool is to keep the fudge from becoming sugary. The lower the temperature at which it is agitated, our third method of crystallization, the smaller the crystals formed and the creamier the fudge.

In fact, if you stir at a high temperature, you can get a coarse grain, and later, say in a day or two (should you happen to have any fudge left), it may develop spots. The spots are harmless but unattractive.

If you haven't done so before, return the thermometer to its hot-water bath to soak itself clean. Now, choose your weapons. You can stir by hand with a wooden spoon or with an electric mixer, either stand-alone or portable, or with a food processor equipped with a steel blade. But the key word is "stir."

MYTH 9: YOU MUST BEAT VIGOROUSLY

The myth that you must beat vigorously is another holdover from the days of yore before fudge-making became semiscientific through the use of shocking and seeding. Or perhaps it was simply the macho thing to do, like hand-churning ice cream. Today, knowing what we do, to beat is a waste of time and energy—yours! After you've gone to all this trouble to make the fudge crystallize properly, let chemistry and physics do the work for you. So, whichever method you choose, stir rather than beat.

STIRRING BY HAND

Once you've learned the knack of stirring fudge by hand with a wooden spoon, you may find it's less trouble than getting out the food processor or electric mixer. It does, however, take more time.

How does one stir? To begin with, do it while the pan remains in the sink. Then, lazily. Stir around the sides so that the interior portion comes into contact with the colder metal. Then through the center. Pause now and again. Walk away and take a sip of ice water. Come back and give it another lick or two. Listen for it to "snap" with each stroke, which proves it's turning. In the case of summer fudges, gelatin may start setting up on the bottom so you will need to use a scraping motion to free it.

ELECTRIC MIXING

You can use either a portable (if it is powerful and the batch is not too large) or your regular electric mixer with a flat whip, if it has one. You want to use low speed and stop frequently to check the gloss of the fudge and to allow the fudge to react. Watch for distinct mixer waves that show the fudge is beginning to candy. At this point, it will begin offering resistance to the beater. Then increase the speed to medium, giving it short bursts, but pausing often.

FOOD PROCESSING

If you've had a change of heart and decided not to stir or use the mixer, you can still use the food processor. Simply pour—yes, you can scrape the pan—the cooled fudge (it must be 110°F [43.5°C] or less) into a food processor bowl equipped with a steel blade. Remove the pusher from the feed tube so you can peer inside. You want to use short pulses and long pauses between them. It will take anywhere from one to three minutes. If it takes longer than that or if the container gets quite warm, the fudge was probably too warm to begin with. So, speed things up by wrapping a cold, wet dish towel around the processor bowl while it's working.

STEP 8: WATCH

No matter which method you use, fudge will "candy." Look for it to:

get thicker
lose its sheen
become lighter in color or streaked with lighter shades
give off some heat
suddenly stiffen

If you stir it by hand, once you hear the "snap," watch for fudge to thicken, light streaks to appear, and the fudge to get dull. Sometimes, with lighter fudges, the change in color is not terribly obvious. But if you walk away from the fudge, often when you come back, you'll notice the difference.

When you use an electric mixer, you have to watch the mixer waves closely. They must become very distinct. Watch for light streaks and a change in gloss. The most common problem that occurs with the electric mixer is not pausing long and often enough to compensate for the speed with which the fudge is being beaten.

With the food processor, I have visions of a nation of fudge-makers peering down that feed tube. It is absolutely imperative that you pause frequently because the fudge can candy so unbelievably quickly. Watch for light streaks, for the mixture to flow back sluggishly toward the center, for it to lose its sheen. Keep the saucepan nearby so you can compare the gloss with whatever fudge is left in the pan. Pour as soon as it dulls. It sets up quickly and usually will finish setting up the moment it hits the metal pan.

STEP 9: ADD

Before the mixture candies completely is the time to add any optional ingredients. But do it fast. Adding a large quantity of any ingredient, particularly hot or melted chocolate, will finish candying the fudge. If you've waited too long, you can put nuts in the bottom of the greased pan and pour the fudge over them. This is the technique to use for a half-and-half fudge: one half plain or with nuts, the other half with mini-marshmallows or chips.

STEP 10: POUR, SCORE, AND STORE

For a nice even fudge, pour and spread quickly. Or you can pour it in waves down the middle of the pan and get an irregular but freehand approximation of the mounding fudge shops get with their slab-made fudge.

To get rid of air pockets in thinner fudge, drop the pan on the countertop from a height of about three inches, banging it smartly.

Let the fudge cool and completely harden by placing the pan in a cool place. When the fudge firms up, score it with a knife to make cutting it easier later. A word to the wise: *Never* wet a knife before cutting fudge. The fudge shops use a straight rather than a tapered blade to cut portions, and little plastic knives for individual squares. You'll probably use a kitchen knife. Opt for a narrow- or medium-width blade (the wider the blade, the more the fudge may stick to it). Fudge is also a lot easier to cut if you remove it from the pan so that you can press down on both ends of the knife rather than saw. Here the wax paper you used to line the pan will come in handy, both in taking the fudge out of and in putting any back into the pan.

Store fudge in airtight containers (resealable plastic bags do fine—one 8×8-inch pan or two 5×10-inch pans fit into a 1-gallon size). Most fudge will keep a week or so at room temperature. Others are better off stored in the refrigerator, still in their airtight coverings. I'll let you know which is which. The reason for keeping them airtight is fudge's attraction for and to humidity. If left uncovered, or even simply foil-wrapped, fudge will soak humidity out of the air at room temperature, and today's frost-free refrigerators dehydrate fudge if it is simply placed loosely covered or uncovered inside.

With very few exceptions—for example, that containing marshmallow creme—fudge freezes beautifully. If well wrapped, it will keep three to six months. After that it may start to get sugary. You can always remelt it and use it as sauce.

MYTH 10: YOU MUST NEVER DOUBLE OR TRIPLE A RECIPE

Yes, you heard me right, it's a myth that fudge recipes cannot be doubled or tripled. I know other cookbooks will tell you that's a no-no! But recipes that can be doubled outnumber those that can't by about ten to one. In fact, many of the recipes in this book began as professional recipes for twenty-five to one hundred pounds.

Seamus Garrahy goes one step further; he says the bigger the batch, the better. When he took his recipe for a twenty-five-pound batch and quartered it for at-home fudge parties, the fudge wasn't as good as that made from the full recipe.

To double most recipes, all it takes is a *big* saucepan or a stockpot. Also, you'll need to cream the fudge by hand in most cases, although you can divide the fudge into portions and do them one at a time with a mixer or food processor.

And that's it! How to make fudge in ten little steps: prepare, dissolve, boil, test, shock, seed, stir, watch, add, pour. And those ten steps apply to any fudge recipe, guaranteed 99.99 percent of the time.

Now, have I forgotten anything? Ah, yes. If, when you pour your fudge, it doesn't get hard immediately, chill it in the refrigerator for several hours.

I promised you a joke or two. Would you settle for a truism? With apologies to Ogden Nash, allow me to remind you that candy is dandy; true, liquor is quicker. But not only won't sex rot your teeth, but neither will chocolate according to the latest dental research.

ADDITIONAL THINGS YOU MAY WANT TO KNOW ABOUT FUDGE AND OTHER CANDIES

1. Always have everything in readiness before beginning a batch.

2. Use the best-quality granulated sugar for boiling and the best-quality confectioners' for kneading.

3. Fudge requires a well-balanced formula that contains sugar, corn syrup, and milk solids, as well as optional fondant and marshmallow creme. The proportion of sugar in a fudge formula has less effect on grain size than the manner in which a batch is handled during candy-making. Most frequently, excessive heat is responsible for the development of a coarse-grained fudge. Agitating a batch of fudge at a low temperature results in the formation of fine sugar crystals.

4. Never stir syrup after the sugar is dissolved—the only object in stirring is to prevent the sugar from settling and burning when it is first put on the heat. (An exception is when milk is involved. Then continue to stir enough to prevent the milk from burning.)

5. Never allow the crystals to remain on the side of the pan; wipe them off with a pastry brush dipped in hot water.

6. Fudge containing large amounts of milk should be cooked quickly; otherwise the fudge develops a dark color. Slow cooling also darkens the milk in a batch of fudge. Dark specks appear in a fudge whose milk has been burned during cooking—convert it to chocolate immediately if they're really evident. Or you can pour the fudge into a clean pan (preheat it by pouring the hot water from your thermometer pan into it) without scraping the bottom of the original pan, and then continue cooking.

7. Beware of cooking with sweetened condensed milk. Although it cooks up faster, it is more apt to scorch. If scorching is minor, simply stir it in; condensed milk gives a caramel flavor to begin with. Better yet, replace the sweetened condensed milk in a recipe with cream or evaporated milk, compensating for the difference in solids content by adding butter. Sweetened condensed milk is best used in uncooked fudges.

8. When using chocolate, cook over low heat to avoid burning it.

9. Add evaporated milk slowly to prevent fudge from getting a rough texture.

10. Most fruits and fudge do not mix—the enzymes in fruit "melt" the fudge. Dried fruits are the exception unless reconstituted.

11. Certain recipes call for the use of fondant. The addition of ⅔ cup fondant to 1 pound fudge when fudge has cooled to about 180°F (82°C) will shortcut the setting up of seed crystals of a finer size in the fudge. Fondant is the ultimate and best seed (also the most work to use). It forces the cooked sugar to come out of solution but with an ultrafine crystal. Commercial fudges are usually made with fondant. Agitating a fudge also gives it a fine grain. However, fondant-induced grain is finer than grain produced solely by agitating.

12. Avoid cutting the fudge when it is too firm or not firm enough. If it is too firm, portions are likely to crumble; if it is too soft, the set of the fudge will break. (This is why we score the fudge when it is still warm—so it can be cut easily later.)

TO RECAP THE BASIC
TEN-STEP RECIPE

STEP 1: PREPARE: Prewarm thermometer; select the right size saucepan; measure all ingredients except those used to seed or optionals, and dump into saucepan; butter upper sides of saucepan. Grease and, if necessary, line a 5 × 10-inch pan. If seeding with butter, freeze 1 tablespoon. Fill glass with ice cubes and water and sink half-inch full of water.

STEP 2: DISSOLVE sugar, stirring constantly with wooden spoon over low heat until butter melts, gritty sounds cease, spoon glides smoothly over bottom of pan. Increase heat to medium and bring to boil.

STEP 3: BOIL after washing down any crystals that may have formed with pastry brush dipped in hot water from thermometer bath, using as little water as possible. Introduce prewarmed thermometer. Reduce heat while retaining boil. Stir no more than necessary.

STEP 4: TEST in ice-cold water when mixture thickens and bubbles become noisy. Ball, formed in ice water, should hold its shape until heat from your hand begins to flatten it and should be al dente— slightly chewy. Approximately 234°F to 240°F (112°C to 115.5°C).

STEP 5: SHOCK by placing saucepan in sink.

STEP 6: SEED by adding, without stirring, flavoring, chocolate, and/or frozen butter. Then allow to cool.

STEP 7: STIR when lukewarm and "skin" forms on top (110°F [43.5°C]). Return thermometer to its hot-water bath to soak clean. Stir fudge thoroughly but not vigorously by hand, with electric mixer, or with food processor. Pause frequently to allow fudge to react.

STEP 8: WATCH for fudge to thicken, lose its sheen, become lighter in color or streaked with lighter shades, give off some heat, suddenly stiffen. If mixing by hand, fudge will "snap" with each stroke; by mixer, mixer waves will become very distinct; by food processor, fudge will flow sluggishly back to center when processor is stopped.

STEP 9: ADD any optional ingredients before fudge totally candies.

STEP 10: POUR, SCORE, AND STORE when cool in airtight container in refrigerator or at room temperature.

EAT

FOUR

Basic Fudge Recipes

SUGAR & CREAM FUDGE

CHOCOLATE PEPPERMINT SUGAR & CREAM FUDGE
PEANUT BUTTER SUGAR & CREAM FUDGE
CHOCOLATE–PEANUT BUTTER SUGAR & CREAM FUDGE
PLAIN VANILLA SUGAR & CREAM FUDGE
BUTTERSCOTCH SUGAR & CREAM FUDGE
COCONUT SUGAR & CREAM FUDGE
PISTACHIO SUGAR & CREAM FUDGE
MALTED MILK SUGAR & CREAM FUDGE
CHOCOLATE-BANANA SUGAR & CREAM FUDGE
BANANA SUGAR & CREAM FUDGE
COFFEE SUGAR & CREAM FUDGE
VANILLA-ALMOND SUGAR & (SOUR) CREAM FUDGE
CHOCOLATE-ALMOND SUGAR & (SOUR) CREAM FUDGE
PEANUT BUTTER CHIP SUGAR & (SOUR) CREAM FUDGE
STRAWBERRY-WALNUT SUGAR & (SOUR) CREAM FUDGE
CHERRY-ALMOND SUGAR & (SOUR) CREAM FUDGE

BROWN SUGAR FUDGE

HONEY BROWN SUGAR FUDGE
CHOCOLATE HONEY BROWN SUGAR FUDGE
ORANGE BROWN SUGAR FUDGE
COFFEE BROWN SUGAR FUDGE
PEANUT BUTTER BROWN SUGAR FUDGE
SESAME SEED BROWN SUGAR FUDGE
GINGERBREAD BROWN SUGAR FUDGE
COLA CANDY BROWN SUGAR FUDGE
PRALINE BROWN SUGAR FUDGE

MARSHMALLOW CREME FUDGE

ALTERNATE MARSHMALLOW CREME FUDGE
MARBLEIZED MARSHMALLOW CREME FUDGE
MARBLEIZED PEPPERMINT MARSHMALLOW CREME FUDGE
PEANUT BUTTER MARSHMALLOW CREME FUDGE

ULTIMATE FUDGE

COCONUT ULTIMATE FUDGE
PIÑA COLADA ULTIMATE FUDGE
BLACK VELVET ULTIMATE FUDGE
CHESTNUT ULTIMATE FUDGE
CHOCOLATE-CHESTNUT ULTIMATE FUDGE
CHOCOLATE CASHEW ULTIMATE FUDGE
PISTACHIO ULTIMATE FUDGE

MAPLE ULTIMATE FUDGE
MAPLE NUT ULTIMATE FUDGE

SEASHORE FUDGE

CHOCOLATE SEASHORE FUDGE
CHOCOLATE-WALNUT SEASHORE FUDGE
PISTACHIO SEASHORE FUDGE
PEANUT BUTTER SEASHORE FUDGE
MARBLEIZED CHOCOLATE-VANILLA SEASHORE FUDGE
HONEY-VANILLA SEASHORE FUDGE
DRUNKEN SEASHORE FUDGES
BRANDY ALEXANDER SEASHORE FUDGE
CHOCOLATE BRANDY ALEXANDER SEASHORE FUDGE
DRAMBUIE OR SCOTCH SEASHORE FUDGE
KAHLÚA SEASHORE FUDGE
KAHLÚA-MOCHA SEASHORE FUDGE
GRASSHOPPER SEASHORE FUDGE

SUMMER FUDGE

BLACK CHERRY SUMMER FUDGE
GRAND MARNIER SOUFFLÉ SUMMER FUDGE
KEY LIME SUMMER FUDGE
LEMONADE SUMMER FUDGE
LEMON-LICORICE SUMMER FUDGE
ORANGE SHERBET SUMMER FUDGE
RICH RASPBERRY SUMMER FUDGE
PEACHES 'N' CREAM SUMMER FUDGE

To me, a collection of recipes should resemble a closet full of clothes, with no two exactly the same. But in every closet hangs that little black dress or navy-blue suit—the garment of choice whenever in doubt as to what to wear. *Oh, Fudge!* has one, too, only I call it Bread & Butter Fudge. You can serve it plain, you can dress it up, you can combine it with chips and goobers and pretzels. If you can think of a flavor, you can make it with this the most basic of basic recipes.

Then there are the three fudges that made history: Vassar, the typical Sugar & Cream Fudge; Smith's tangier version, thanks to molasses, Brown Sugar Fudge; and for those of us who like never to fail, Wellesley's Marshmallow Creme Fudge to the rescue.

If you're one of those strong-willed creatures who indulges only rarely in fudge, but then demands it be the richest, most voluptuous fudge in town, extra-rich Ultimate Fudge is for you.

Then, again, you may be convinced the best fudge made is found on the Boardwalk at Atlantic City or Ocean City. In which case, make your own Seashore Fudge, but since the classic recipe comes in only four or five basic flavors (the shops double this by throwing in some nuts), I give you a whole slew of Drunken Seashore Fudge suggestions to relieve the monotony.

Finally, there is the way-out, adventurous, versatile, just-crying-for-some-creativity-on-your-part fudge, Summer Fudge. Made with the flavored gelatin of your choice, it opens up a whole world of fruit-flavored, delicate fudges.

So, welcome to the wonderful world of basic fudges. It should be pointed out that any basic flavor—chocolate, coconut, peanut butter, and so on—can be made with any one of these basic fudges . . . and that almost any kind of nut, not to mention mini-marshmallows, can be added, as well. Use quantities given in any basic recipe to adapt any of the other recipes.

Bread & Butter Fudge

They don't come any simpler, any more versatile, and not much better than this. A simple five-ingredient fudge, utilizing heavy cream, that can be made into almost any flavor you can imagine: milk chocolate, dark chocolate, butterscotch, peanut butter, chocolate mint, coconut, strawberry, pistachio, butter rum, even Christmasy with diced red and green candied cherries, and so on.

> *2 cups granulated white sugar*
>
> *1 cup heavy (whipping) cream*
>
> *¼ pound (1 stick) butter*
>
> *1 tablespoon light corn syrup*
>
> *1 teaspoon vanilla extract or choice of flavoring*
>
> Optional: *1 cup coarsely chopped nuts, mini-marshmallows, coconut, chopped pretzels, M&M's—whatever you can dream up*

STEP 1: PREPARE: Prewarm thermometer; use a 3-quart saucepan; butter upper sides of saucepan; measure all ingredients but vanilla and optionals and dump into saucepan. Grease and, if necessary, line a 5 × 10-inch pan. Fill glass with ice cubes and water and sink half-inch full of water.

STEP 2: DISSOLVE sugar, stirring constantly with wooden spoon over low heat until butter melts, gritty sounds cease, spoon glides smoothly over bottom of pan. Increase heat to medium and bring to a boil.

STEP 3: BOIL after washing down any crystals that may have formed with pastry brush dipped in hot water from thermometer bath, using as little water as possible. Introduce prewarmed thermometer. Reduce heat while retaining boil. Stir no more than necessary.

STEP 4: TEST in ice-cold water when mixture thickens and bubbles become noisy. Ball, formed in ice water, should hold its shape until heat from your hand begins to flatten it and should be al dente—slightly chewy. Approximately 234°F to 242°F (112°C to 116.5°C).

STEP 5: SHOCK by placing saucepan in sink.

STEP 6: SEED by adding, without stirring, vanilla or other flavoring. Then allow to cool.

STEP 7: STIR when lukewarm and "skin" forms on top (110°F [43.5°C]). Return thermometer to its hot-water bath to soak clean. Stir fudge thoroughly but not vigorously by hand, with electric mixer, or with food processor. Pause frequently to allow fudge to react.

STEP 8: WATCH for fudge to thicken, lose its sheen, become lighter in color or streaked with lighter shades, give off some heat, suddenly stiffen. If mixing by hand, fudge will "snap" with each stroke; by mixer, mixer waves will become very distinct; by food processor, fudge will flow sluggishly back to center when processor is stopped.

STEP 9: ADD any optional ingredients before fudge totally candies.

STEP 10: POUR, SCORE, AND STORE when cool in airtight container in refrigerator or at room temperature.

YIELD: 1 POUND. Recipe is easily doubled and can be frozen.

VARIATIONS

Chocolate Bread & Butter Fudge

In step 1, add to other ingredients in saucepan, 2 squares (2 ounces) unsweetened chocolate, grated or pounded, or ⅓ to ½ cup cocoa, or 1 cup (6 ounces) semisweet chocolate chips, or 2 packets premelted chocolate.

Frosted Bread & Butter Fudge

Prepare fudge as usual; in step 10, when cool, melt ½ cup (3 ounces) any kind of chips over hot water or in microwave and spread on top of fudge. Note milk chocolate chips take longest to melt.

Peanut Butter Bread & Butter Fudge

Add ⅓ cup (2 ounces) peanut butter chips with other ingredients in step 1, *or* add ¼ cup peanut butter in step 6 when you seed, but don't stir it in until fudge is lukewarm.

Peanut Butter Chocolate Chip Bread & Butter Fudge

Add ⅓ cup (2 ounces) peanut butter chips in step 1 and ½ cup (3 ounces) semisweet chocolate chips in step 9, *or* add mixture of ⅓ cup peanut butter and ⅓ cup (2 ounces) milk chocolate chips in step 9.

Mocha Chip Bread & Butter Fudge

Add 2 to 3 tablespoons instant coffee in step 1, add ½ cup (3 ounces) milk chocolate chips in step 9.

Candied Bread & Butter Fudge

In step 9, use 1 cup of any one of these or any combination of the following: candied pineapples, candied cherries, orange and lemon peels, plus ½ cup sliced or chopped nuts.

Date & Nut Bread & Butter Fudge

In step 9, use ½ cup chopped pitted dates and ½ cup coarsely chopped walnuts. Figs can be substituted for dates.

Rum-Butterscotch Bread & Butter Fudge

In step 6, replace vanilla extract with ½ ounce rum. Add 1 cup (6 ounces) butterscotch chips either in step 1 or in step 9.

Cinnamon Bread & Butter Fudge

In step 6, in addition to vanilla, add ⅔ teaspoon cinnamon oil flavoring. After pouring fudge in step 10, sprinkle top with 2 teaspoons ground cinnamon mixed with 2 teaspoons confectioners' sugar. If fudge has cooled too much, lightly butter it so sugar-cinnamon mixture will adhere.

Bread & Butter(Milk) Fudge

This is your basic fudge, stepping out in style. It rivals the best the fudge stores can produce, and is smooth, creamy, butterscotchy with a hint of tang. Like its predecessor, Bread & Butter Fudge, it lends itself to many variations—and these, because of the buttermilk, will have just a little more kick to them.

> *2 cups granulated white sugar*
> *1 cup buttermilk*
> *¼ pound (1 stick) butter*
> *1 tablespoon light corn syrup*
> *1 teaspoon baking soda*
> *1 teaspoon vanilla extract*
> Optional: *1 cup coarsely chopped walnuts*

Follow directions for Bread & Butter Fudge but use 6-quart saucepan. In step 1, put everything but vanilla and nuts, if desired, in pan. Stir constantly with wooden spoon over low heat until sugar is dissolved. Then bring to a boil. Watch it—it will really swell up. Cook until mixture thickens. Because of acid in buttermilk, it will ball at a comparatively high temperature (236°F to 242°F [113.5°C to 116.5°C]). Shock. Seed with vanilla. Stir when cool until it candies. Then add nuts, if desired. Pour. When cool, score.

YIELD: 1 POUND. Recipe can be doubled, if you have a large enough saucepan, and can be frozen.

Rum-Raisin Bread & Butter(Milk) Fudge

In step 6, seed, without stirring, by adding 1 cup golden raisins soaked for 1 hour in ¼ cup light rum and then drained but not squeezed. You want some of that rum flavor (remember, the alcohol burns off). Omit the vanilla.

Slow-Cooked Bread & Butter(Milk) Fudge

A very, very creamy fudge. In step 1, combine sugar, buttermilk, butter, corn syrup, and baking soda in 6-quart saucepan and cook over very low heat for 1 hour. Stir occasionally to make sure it is not sticking to bottom of pan. Then bring to a boil and proceed as usual, using vanilla to seed in step 6.

Sugar & Cream Fudge

a.k.a. Vassar Fudge

This is it, the first, the one, the only, the original fudge—the fudge that the girls at Vassar first cooked over their gas lamps. It seems only fitting that this was also the fudge I used to perfect making fudge in a food processor.

It is also the simplest recipe of them all and makes a very simple, straightforward, delicious fudge—an old-fashioned fudge that may seem a little too sugary for some. To others, this is what fudge is all about! The trick here is to make sure you cook it long enough, or it will remain soup. Once you get it to the right ball, if you shock, seed, and stir, it grains easily, maybe too easily. Thus the use of warm water in the sink to slow the cooling down, the use of a single ingredient to seed it, and the need to wait to stir until the fudge has cooled.

One other thing: Remember that under the best of circumstances, chocolate fudges grain easily—it's the nature of chocolate.

In order to control the graining, you can add 1 tablespoon light corn syrup. Or you can substitute 5 ounces evaporated milk plus 3 ounces regular milk for the cream, but the fudge will not be as rich.

2 cups granulated white sugar

1 cup heavy (whipping) cream

2 squares (2 ounces) unsweetened chocolate, grated or smashed

1 tablespoon butter

Optional: *½ cup chopped nuts*

STEP 1: PREPARE: Prewarm thermometer; use 2-quart saucepan; butter upper sides of saucepan; measure all ingredients except butter and optionals and dump into saucepan. Grease and, if necessary, line a 5 × 10-inch pan. Freeze the tablespoon of butter. Fill glass with ice cubes and water and sink half-inch full of hot water.

STEP 2: DISSOLVE sugar, stirring constantly with wooden spoon over low heat until butter melts, gritty sounds cease, spoon glides smoothly over bottom of pan. Increase heat to medium and bring to a boil.

STEP 3: BOIL after washing down any crystals that may have formed with pastry brush dipped in hot water from thermometer bath, using as little water as possible. Introduce prewarmed thermometer. Reduce heat while retaining boil. Stir no more than necessary.

STEP 4: TEST in ice-cold water when mixture thickens and bubbles become noisy. Ball, formed in ice water, should hold its shape until heat from your hand begins to flatten it and should be al dente—slightly chewy. Approximately 234°F to 240°F (112°C to 115.5°C).

STEP 5: SHOCK by placing saucepan in sink.

STEP 6: SEED by adding, without stirring, frozen butter. Then allow to cool.

STEP 7: STIR when lukewarm and "skin" forms on top (110°F [43.5°C]). Return thermometer to its hot-water bath to soak clean. Stir fudge thoroughly but not vigorously by hand, with electric mixer, or with food processor. Pause frequently to allow fudge to react.

STEP 8: WATCH for fudge to thicken, lose its sheen, become lighter in color or streaked with lighter shades, give off some heat, suddenly stiffen. If mixing by hand, fudge will "snap" with each stroke; by mixer, mixer waves will become very distinct; by food processor, fudge will flow sluggishly back to center when processor is stopped.

STEP 9: ADD optional ingredients before fudge totally candies.

STEP 10: POUR, SCORE, AND STORE when cool in airtight container in refrigerator or at room temperature.

YIELD: 1 POUND. Recipe is easily doubled but not if you are using a food processor. Can be frozen.

FLAVOR VARIATIONS

Chocolate Peppermint Sugar & Cream Fudge

In step 1, replace unsweetened chocolate with ⅓ cup (about 2 ounces) chocolate-peppermint chips.

Peanut Butter Sugar & Cream Fudge

In step 1, replace unsweetened chocolate with ½ cup (3 ounces) peanut butter chips or heaping ¼ cup creamy peanut butter.

Chocolate–Peanut Butter Sugar & Cream Fudge

In step 1, replace unsweetened chocolate with 3 tablespoons peanut butter and ½ cup (3 ounces) chocolate chips.

Plain Vanilla Sugar & Cream Fudge

Eliminate unsweetened chocolate in step 1 and seed with butter and 1 teaspoon vanilla in step 6. Be sure mixture is no warmer than lukewarm when you begin to stir.

Butterscotch Sugar & Cream Fudge

In step 1, replace unsweetened chocolate with ½ cup (3 ounces) butterscotch chips.

Coconut Sugar & Cream Fudge

Eliminate unsweetened chocolate in step 1; add 1 cup coconut in step 9. For more intense flavor, add ⅔ teaspoon coconut flavoring oil then.

Pistachio Sugar & Cream Fudge

In step 1, replace unsweetened chocolate with ½ cup chopped pistachio nuts. In step 6, seed with butter and 1 teaspoon pistachio flavoring.

Malted Milk Sugar & Cream Fudge

In step 1, replace unsweetened chocolate with 2 tablespoons malted milk mix powder. Double that for stronger malted flavor.

Chocolate-Banana Sugar & Cream Fudge

In step 1, add 1 good-size ripe banana mashed (½ cup or more). In step 6, seed with butter and 1 teaspoon banana extract, *or* ⅔ teaspoon banana flavoring oil, *or* 1 tablespoon banana liqueur, *or* 1 teaspoon rum.

Banana Sugar & Cream Fudge

Follow recipe for Chocolate-Banana Sugar & Cream Fudge, but eliminate unsweetened chocolate in step 1.

Coffee Sugar & Cream Fudge

In step 1, replace unsweetened chocolate with 3 tablespoons instant coffee.

Vanilla-Almond Sugar & (Sour) Cream Fudge

There are some people who are convinced this is the creamiest of them all. It certainly is less apt to sugar on you since the sour cream, being acidic, acts as a grain-retardant. This means that the cooling down period need not be so long.

> 2¼ cups (1 pound) granulated white sugar
>
> 1 cup sour cream
>
> 2 tablespoons (¼ stick) butter
>
> ¼ teaspoon salt
>
> 1 teaspoon rum
>
> 1 tablespoon vanilla
>
> 1 cup whole almonds, or ⅓ cup each almonds, walnuts, pecans

Follow basic directions for Sugar & Cream Fudge but use buttered 3-quart saucepan. In step 1, put everything but rum, vanilla, and nuts in pan. When mixture comes to a boil, reduce temperature quickly and watch it carefully—it will really swell up. Cook until mixture thickens—it should cling to spoon. Because of acid in sour cream, like buttermilk fudges it will ball at a comparatively high temperature (236°F to 242°F [113.5°C to 116.5°C]) and "candy" very slowly.

Shock. In step 6, seed with rum and vanilla. Cool, then stir until it candies. When watching for signs that it is candying, the most important is the presence of light streaks. If they're there, even if fudge seems as elastic as caramel, it will candy. Add nuts. Pour. When lukewarm, score.

YIELD: 1 POUND. Recipe does not double easily unless divided into two batches when shocked. It can be frozen.

Chocolate-Almond Sugar & (Sour) Cream Fudge

In step 1, add 2 ounces grated or smashed unsweetened chocolate. In step 6, eliminate rum and all but 1 teaspoon vanilla to use as seed.

Peanut Butter Chip Sugar & (Sour) Cream Fudge

In step 9, add ½ cup (3 ounces) peanut butter chips. Eliminate nuts or replace with peanuts.

Strawberry-Walnut Sugar & (Sour) Cream Fudge

The just barely acidic quality of this fudge lends itself to making fruit-extract-flavored fudges. Make exactly the same as the Vanilla-Almond Sugar & (Sour) Cream Fudge but omit the vanilla and in step 6 add ½ tablespoon strawberry extract *or* 1 small bottle strawberry flavoring oil. Substitute 1 teaspoon Grand Marnier for the rum. Three to 4 drops red food coloring are also optional. In step 9, replace almonds with walnuts.

Cherry-Almond Sugar & (Sour) Cream Fudge

If possible, use cherry extract or ½ small bottle cherry flavoring oil in place of vanilla in step 6. Otherwise, use 1 to 2 teaspoons kirschwasser to seed in place of rum and vanilla. In step 9, add ½ cup chopped candied (*not* maraschino) cherries, as well as ½ cup chopped almonds. To go hog wild, add ½ cup shredded coconut.

Brown Sugar Fudge

a.k.a. Smith College Fudge, Ponouchi, Penuci, Penuche, Panocha, and so on

You'll be surprised at what a difference changing the sugar can make in fudge. The use of brown sugar, which is not as refined as granulated, helps control the graining and gives the fudge a distinctive taste. At one time, sugar came in no less than fifteen grades, ranging in color from white to yellow to brown. It is from the latter that this fudge gets its real name of *panocha*, the Mexican-Spanish word for "raw sugar." We met it first back in 1905 when it was called Ponouchi. You may know it as penuci, penocha, or penuche—no difference, and all are pronounced the same: as puh-NOO-chee. In one of its incarnations, it is known as praline.

Historically this fudge has been known as Smith College Fudge although the Wellesley girls were actually the ones to call their fudge penuci.

1 cup granulated white sugar

1 cup firmly packed light brown sugar

½ cup heavy (whipping) cream

2 to 3 tablespoons molasses (original recipe calls for 4, which is too strong for my taste; you may find even 3 too much. Its presence, however, guarantees that fudge will candy properly.)

2 squares (2 ounces) unsweetened chocolate, grated or smashed

4 tablespoons (½ stick) butter

1½ teaspoons vanilla extract

Optional: *½ cup chopped walnuts, pecans, hazelnuts (filberts)*

STEP 1: PREPARE: Prewarm thermometer; use a 2-quart saucepan; butter upper sides of saucepan; measure all ingredients except vanilla and

74

optionals, and dump into saucepan. Grease and, if necessary, line a 5 × 10-inch pan. Fill glass with ice cubes and water and sink half-inch full of water.

STEP 2: DISSOLVE sugar, stirring constantly with wooden spoon over low heat until butter melts, gritty sounds cease, spoon glides smoothly over bottom of pan. Increase heat to medium and bring to a boil.

STEP 3: BOIL after washing down any crystals that may have formed with pastry brush dipped in hot water from thermometer bath, using as little water as possible. Introduce prewarmed thermometer. Reduce heat while retaining boil. Stir no more than necessary.

STEP 4: TEST in ice-cold water when mixture thickens and bubbles become noisy. Ball, formed in ice water, should hold its shape until heat from your hand begins to flatten it and should be al dente—slightly chewy—between 230°F and 240°F (110°C and 115.5°C). Because of molasses and brown sugar, it can ball at a lower temperature than some other fudges.

STEP 5: SHOCK by placing saucepan in sink.

STEP 6: SEED by adding, without stirring, vanilla. Then allow to cool.

STEP 7: STIR when lukewarm and "skin" forms on top (110°F [43.5°C]). Return thermometer to its hot water bath to soak clean. Stir fudge thoroughly but not vigorously by hand, with electric mixer, or with food processor. Pause frequently to allow fudge to react.

STEP 8: WATCH for fudge to thicken, lose its sheen, become lighter in color or streaked with lighter shades, give off some heat, suddenly stiffen. If mixing by hand, fudge will "snap" with each stroke; by mixer, mixer waves will become very distinct; by food processor, fudge will flow sluggishly back to center when processor is stopped.

STEP 9: ADD optional ingredients before fudge totally candies.

STEP 10: POUR, SCORE, AND STORE when cool in airtight container in refrigerator or at room temperature.

YIELD: 1 POUND. Recipe is easily doubled and can be frozen.

VARIATIONS

Honey Brown Sugar Fudge

In step 1, eliminate unsweetened chocolate and replace molasses with ¼ cup honey. The honey causes fudge to ball at a higher temperature.

Chocolate Honey Brown Sugar Fudge

In step 1, replace heavy cream with light cream or evaporated milk and replace molasses with ¼ cup honey.

Orange Brown Sugar Fudge

In step 1, eliminate molasses and unsweetened chocolate but add 1 tablespoon corn syrup. In step 6, add 1 tablespoon grated orange zest plus, if you can get it, 1 teaspoon pure orange extract. If you'd like to try a little experimenting, add some chopped wedges of orange jellied candy in step 9.

Coffee Brown Sugar Fudge

Photographer Tana Hoban was the inspiration for this. Eliminate molasses and chocolate. In step 1, add 1 tablespoon corn syrup and 2 to 3 teaspoons instant coffee. In step 6, seed with 1 teaspoon lemon extract instead of the vanilla. *Or* if for a more subtle lemon flavor, add a piece of zest with the other ingredients in step 1, seed with 1 teaspoon vanilla in step 6, and remove zest in step 7, just before stirring.

Peanut Butter Brown Sugar Fudge

In step 1, eliminate molasses and chocolate; replace heavy cream with ¾ cup milk and ¼ cup creamy peanut butter. To intensify the peanut butter flavor, add ⅓ cup salted peanuts in step 9.

Sesame Seed Brown Sugar Fudge

In step 1, use all brown sugar and add 1 tablespoon vinegar instead of molasses; eliminate unsweetened chocolate. In step 6, reduce seed to 1 teaspoon vanilla. In step 9, add 1 cup of toasted sesame seeds. (Toast in oven at 250°F for 10 to 15 minutes. Let cool before adding to fudge.)

Gingerbread Brown Sugar Fudge

In step 1, replace heavy cream with ½ cup light (table) cream and eliminate unsweetened chocolate. In step 6, seed with 1½ teaspoons vanilla extract plus

⅓ *teaspoon salt*
½ *teaspoon ground cinnamon*
¼ *teaspoon ground nutmeg*
⅛ *teaspoon ground cloves*

Excellent with ½ cup coarsely chopped walnuts added in step 9.

Cola Candy Brown Sugar Fudge

By all rights, the cola should be Dr Pepper since that's where the idea originated. However, I have made it with other colas, including decaffeinateds, and find it equally piquant although in some cases, the cola will give it a very definite maple sugar taste. In step 1, replace the cream with 1 cup cola soda. For a less definite cola flavor, use dark brown sugar. Eliminate molasses and unsweetened chocolate. Freeze 1 tablespoon of the butter to use as seed. In step 9, just before it grains, add ¼ cup (heaping) marshmallow creme plus 2 cups pecan halves. If you reserve a few pecans and drop fudge by tablespoons onto waxed paper, topping each with a pecan, you have . . .

Praline Brown Sugar Fudge

The American praline was born down South, supposedly in New Orleans, and refers to a candy patty originally made not only to look like a cookie but from pecans and just enough cookie dough to make the pecans stick together. Later, someone decided to keep the shape and the name but make it from a brown sugar fudge to which pecans are added. Dropped like cookie dough into round patties about two to three inches in diameter, it is sold in roadside candy stores the length and breadth of the South and used to be a fixture on every corner in the French Quarter of New Orleans.

In step 1, eliminating molasses is optional—you'll get a more Southern praline with it, a milder one without—or compromise and use only 1 tablespoon. Eliminate unsweetened chocolate. In step 3, when mixture begins to thicken, add 1½ cups pecan halves slowly so as not to break the boil or cool mixture too quickly. If this concerns you or you don't want to stir constantly, you can wait to add the pecans with a reduced seed of 1 teaspoon vanilla in step 6. (If you cook pecans right from the beginning, they float at first, then sink and, unless you stir constantly, have a tendency to burn.) Or put the pecans in mounds on the wax paper and drop spoonfuls of fudge on top of them. And if you want, you don't have to make patties at all, simply add your pecans and pour into a greased pan. It will still taste like a praline.

Marshmallow Creme Fudge

a.k.a. Wellesley Fudge, White House Fudge, No-Fail Fudge, and so on

Variations of this fudge appear on marshmallow creme containers, in cookbooks and magazine articles. They are all touted as fail-safe and/ or no-fail. Unfortunately, that's not true. This fudge has been known to flop—especially if one goes by boiling times rather than testing for the ball—and when it fails, it's a doozie! Almost, but not completely, impossible to resurrect. However, the beauty of working with marshmallow creme is that it can simplify the fudge-maker's life. It incorporates shocking, seeding, and cooling in one step. Because of that same marshmallow, though, the fudge must be stirred by hand. Mixers and food processors break down the creme and the fudge may separate. Devotees of a chocolatey, chewy fudge swear by this recipe. Once you get the hang of it, you will, too. Please note, this is one of the few fudge recipes that does not freeze well. After freezing, these fudges have a much grainier texture.

> 2 cups granulated white sugar
>
> 1 cup light (table) cream
>
> 2 squares (2 ounces) unsweetened chocolate, grated or smashed
>
> 2 tablespoons (¼ stick) butter
>
> One 7-ounce container marshmallow creme
>
> Optional: 1 cup coarsely chopped nuts

STEP 1: PREPARE: Prewarm thermometer; use 3-quart saucepan; butter upper sides of saucepan; measure all ingredients except marshmallow creme, and dump into saucepan. Grease and, if necessary, line an 8 × 8-inch pan. Fill glass with ice cubes and water and sink half-inch full of water.

STEP 2: DISSOLVE sugar, stirring constantly with wooden spoon over low heat until butter melts, gritty sounds cease, spoon glides smoothly over bottom of pan. Increase heat to medium and bring to a boil.

STEP 3: BOIL after washing down any crystals that may have formed with pastry brush dipped in hot water from thermometer bath, using as little water as possible. Introduce prewarmed thermometer. Reduce heat while retaining boil. Stir no more than necessary.

STEP 4: TEST in ice-cold water when mixture thickens and bubbles become noisy. Ball, formed in ice water, should hold its shape until heat from your hand begins to flatten it and should be al dente—slightly chewy. Approximately 234°F to 240°F (112°C to 115.5°C).

STEP 5: SHOCK by placing saucepan in sink.

STEP 6: SEED by adding marshmallow creme.

STEP 7: STIR thoroughly and by hand without waiting for fudge to cool. Pause frequently to allow fudge to react. Return thermometer to hot-water bath to soak clean.

STEP 8: WATCH for fudge to thicken, lose its sheen, become lighter in color or streaked with lighter shades, give off some heat, suddenly stiffen. As it begins to candy, fudge will "snap" with each stroke.

STEP 9: ADD any optional ingredients before fudge totally candies.

STEP 10: POUR, SCORE, AND STORE when cool in airtight container in refrigerator or at room temperature.

YIELD: 1 POUND WITH A RATHER CHEWY TEXTURE. Recipe is not easily doubled. If frozen, the texture will change.

VARIATIONS

Alternate Marshmallow Creme Fudge

If you wish a less chewy texture, in step 6 seed with 2 tablespoons frozen butter. In step 7, stir when lukewarm. Incorporate marshmallow creme in step 8 when just beginning to thicken.

Marbleized Marshmallow Creme Fudge

Follow alternate directions above, waiting to swirl a 7- to 8-ounce container Marshmallow Fluff through fudge until step 9, then pour immediately.

Marbleized Peppermint Marshmallow Creme Fudge

Follow alternate directions above, adding ½ teaspoon peppermint flavoring to marshmallow creme. (You may also wish to add several drops red food coloring.)

Peanut Butter Marshmallow Creme Fudge

In step 1, eliminate unsweetened chocolate and substitute ¼ cup peanut butter *or* ⅓ cup (about 2 ounces) of peanut butter chips. If you are fond of marshmallow peanut butter sandwiches, you may wish to follow the marbleized method of waiting to add creme until step 9 and then swirling it through.

Ultimate Fudge

How rich is rich? Well, if *Forbes* magazine were to put out a list of the richest fudges in America, this would rank number 1 or 2.

> 1 cup heavy (whipping) cream
> 1 cup unsweetened evaporated milk
> 2¼ cups (1 pound) granulated white sugar
> 1 tablespoon plus ½ teaspoon light corn syrup
> 1½ teaspoons vanilla extract

STEP 1: PREPARE: Prewarm thermometer; use 3-quart saucepan; butter upper sides of saucepan; measure all ingredients but vanilla, and dump into saucepan. Grease and, if necessary, line a 5 × 10-inch pan. Fill glass with ice cubes and water and sink half-inch full of water.

STEP 2: DISSOLVE sugar, stirring constantly with wooden spoon over low heat until butter melts, gritty sounds cease, spoon glides smoothly over bottom of pan. Increase heat to medium and bring to a boil.

STEP 3: BOIL after washing down any crystals that may have formed with pastry brush dipped in hot water from thermometer bath, using as little water as possible. Introduce prewarmed thermometer. Reduce heat while retaining boil. Stir no more than necessary.

STEP 4: TEST in ice-cold water when mixture thickens and bubbles become noisy. Ball, formed in ice water, should hold its shape until heat from your hand begins to flatten it and should be al dente—slightly chewy. Approximately 236°F to 244°F (113.5°C to 118°C).

STEP 5: SHOCK by placing saucepan in sink.

STEP 6: SEED by adding, without stirring, vanilla. Then allow to cool.

STEP 7: STIR when lukewarm and "skin" forms on top (110°F [43.5°C]). Return thermometer to its hot-water bath to soak clean. Stir fudge thoroughly but not vigorously by hand, with electric mixer, or with food processor. Pause frequently to allow fudge to react.

STEP 8: WATCH for fudge to thicken, lose its sheen, become lighter in color or streaked with lighter shades, give off some heat, suddenly stiffen. If mixing by hand, fudge will "snap" with each stroke; by mixer, mixer waves will become very distinct; by food processor, fudge will flow sluggishly back to center when processor is stopped.

STEP 9: ADD optional ingredients for variations before fudge totally candies.

STEP 10: POUR, SCORE, AND STORE when cool in airtight container in refrigerator or at room temperature.

YIELD: 1 POUND. Recipe is easily doubled and can be frozen.

VARIATIONS

Coconut Ultimate Fudge

Although many coconut fudges are referred to as "sauerkraut" candy because the coconut was originally shredded on the same cutter used to shred cabbage for sauerkraut, this one even looks like sauerkraut. In step 1, use 3-quart pan, and replace heavy cream with ⅔ cup (half of a well-stirred 15-ounce can) of cream of coconut for piña coladas. In step 2, you will need higher heat to bring to a boil and should stir frequently. In step 6, seed with 1 tablespoon ice-cold butter and ½ teaspoon vanilla. Add 1 cup shredded coconut in step 9.

Piña Colada Ultimate Fudge

In step 9, add ½ cup of diced dried pineapple in place of or in addition to coconut (in which case, reduce coconut to ½ cup).

Black Velvet Ultimate Fudge

Add 2 squares (2 ounces) grated or smashed unsweetened chocolate in step 1. In step 6, seed with 1 tablespoon ice-cold butter and ½ teaspoon vanilla.

Chestnut Ultimate Fudge

Drain 10-ounce jar of chestnuts packed in vanilla syrup and substitute syrup for equal amount of heavy cream in step 1. In step 9, add the chestnuts, coarsely chopped.

Chocolate-Chestnut Ultimate Fudge

Drain 10-ounce jar of chestnuts packed in vanilla syrup and substitute syrup for equal amount of heavy cream in step 1 as well as 2 squares (2 ounces) unsweetened chocolate, grated or smashed. In step 9, add 1 cup (more or less) coarsely chopped chestnuts.

Chocolate Cashew Ultimate Fudge

Add 2 squares (2 ounces), grated unsweetened chocolate in step 1. In step 6, seed with 1 tablespoon ice-cold butter and ½ teaspoon vanilla. In step 9, add 1 cup chopped cashews.

Pistachio Ultimate Fudge

In step 6, seed with 1 tablespoon ice-cold butter and replace vanilla extract with 1 teaspoon pistachio flavoring, plus several drops of green food coloring. (Add more, if necessary, in step 7, when you begin to stir.) In step 9, just before fudge completely candies, add ½ to 1 cup chopped pistachio nuts.

Maple Ultimate Fudge

This is a slow cooker, but you don't have to stir—in fact, you shouldn't—while it's boiling. It balls at a fairly low temperature and smells heavenly while cooking. Use a 5-quart saucepan because, when it comes to a boil, it threatens to boil over. For a plain maple flavor eliminate vanilla. In step 1, add 1 cup pure grade A Vermont maple syrup. Measure out 1 teaspoon baking soda, but add only a pinch (⅛ teaspoon) to begin with. If maple syrup is not pure and mixture doesn't foam up high when it comes to a boil in step 3, add rest of teaspoonful. In step 6, seed with 1 tablespoon ice-cold butter and vanilla, if desired.

Maple Nut Ultimate Fudge

Follow directions for Maple Ultimate Fudge. In step 9, add 1 cup walnuts or pecans *or* ½ cup of both. Pour into an 8 × 8-inch pan.

Seashore Fudge

This is it, the fudge people remember from trips to Atlantic City and Ocean City in New Jersey. (Personally, I think the salt air may have something to do with their fondness for it.) In any event, this fudge can be as good as or better than any you've tasted down there . . . and you have the advantage of a wider choice of flavors. In fact, this makes such a good-sized batch, you could divide it in half and make up two different flavors from one.

THE PLAIN BASE

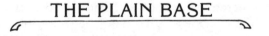

4 *cups granulated white sugar*

⅓ *cup light corn syrup*

2 *level tablespoons honey*

1 *cup unsweetened evaporated milk*

6 *tablespoons (¾ stick) margarine or butter*

½ *teaspoon salt*

Choice of flavorings, see pages 87–88.

STEP 1: PREPARE: Prewarm thermometer; use 5-quart saucepan; butter upper sides of saucepan; measure all ingredients except optionals and your choice of flavorings, and dump into saucepan. Grease and, if necessary, line several small loaf pans or one 8 × 12-inch pan. Fill glass with ice cubes and water and sink half-inch full of water.

STEP 2: DISSOLVE sugar, stirring constantly with wooden spoon over low heat until butter melts, gritty sounds cease, spoon glides smoothly over bottom of pan. Increase heat to medium and bring to boil.

STEP 3: BOIL after washing down any crystals that may have formed with pastry brush dipped in hot water from thermometer bath, using as little water as possible. Introduce prewarmed thermometer. Reduce heat while retaining boil. Stir no more than necessary.

STEP 4: TEST in ice-cold water when mixture thickens and bubbles become noisy. Ball, formed in ice water, should hold its shape until heat from your hand begins to flatten it and should be al dente—slightly chewy. Approximately 236°F to 242°F (113.5°C to 116.5°C).

STEP 5: SHOCK by placing saucepan in sink. To make two different flavored fudges from same batch, divide now into two batches by pouring other half into heat-proof bowl. Work the bowl first.

STEP 6: SEED by adding, without stirring, flavorings or chocolate. Then allow to cool.

STEP 7: STIR when lukewarm and "skin" forms on top (110°F [43.5°C]). Return thermometer to its hot-water bath to soak clean. Stir fudge thoroughly but not vigorously by hand, with electric mixer, or (in two batches) in food processor. Pause frequently to allow fudge to react.

STEP 8: WATCH for fudge to thicken, lose its sheen, become lighter in color or streaked with lighter shades, give off some heat, suddenly stiffen. If mixing by hand, fudge will "snap" with each stroke; by mixer, mixer waves will become very distinct; by food processor, fudge will flow sluggishly back to center when processor is stopped.

STEP 9: ADD any optional ingredients for variations before fudge totally candies.

STEP 10: POUR, SCORE, AND STORE when cool in airtight container in refrigerator or at room temperature.

YIELD: 2 POUNDS. Recipe is easily doubled if you have a powerful mixer and a large enough stockpot, and it can be frozen.

THE FLAVORS

Chocolate Seashore Fudge

In step 6, seed with 2 teaspoons vanilla extract. When ready to stir in step 7, add 3 squares (3 ounces) unsweetened chocolate, partially melted, *or* 1½ cups (9 ounces) semisweet chocolate chips, melted and cooled.

Chocolate-Walnut Seashore Fudge

Follow directions for Chocolate Seashore Fudge but add 1½ cups coarsely chopped or broken walnuts in step 9.

Pistachio Seashore Fudge

In step 6, seed with 2 teaspoons pistachio extract and a few drops of green food coloring. Can also add ½ cup or more chopped pistachio nuts in step 9.

Peanut Butter Seashore Fudge

In step 6, seed with 1 teaspoon vanilla. Just before stirring (step 7) add approximately ½ cup creamy peanut butter *or* 1½ cups (9 ounces) peanut butter chips (do not need to melt). Just before fudge completely candies, you can also add ½ cup chopped roasted peanuts, but cut the peanut butter back to ⅓ cup.

Marbleized Chocolate-Vanilla Seashore Fudge

In step 6, seed with 2 teaspoons vanilla. After fudge has almost completely candied in step 9, add 2 squares (2 ounces) melted unsweetened chocolate *or* 2 packets premelted baking chocolate (warmed by immersing in thermometer bath) and barely swirl through. Pouring it out will finish mixing it.

Honey-Vanilla Seashore Fudge

In step 1, increase honey to ⅓ cup. In step 6, seed with 2 teaspoons vanilla extract (add more if you really like vanilla).

Drunken Seashore Fudges

Actually this is a misnomer, because when the alcohol-based additions hit the hot fudge, the alcohol goes bye-bye, just as it does when you add plain old vanilla extract. However, this particular fudge lends itself to the flavors of "strong drink" . . . and you could eat hundreds of pounds without getting drunk. Fat? Now, that's another story. Use the same base and follow the same directions as for Seashore Fudge, but for flavorings use one or more of the following:

Brandy Alexander Seashore Fudge

To seed in step 6, add 1 ounce brandy, 1 ounce creme de cacao—and stand back, the fumes of the alcohol burning off are powerful.

Chocolate Brandy Alexander Seashore Fudge

Besides the brandy and creme de cacao from the last variation, add 2 squares (2 ounces) melted unsweetened chocolate *or* 2 packets premelted baking chocolate in step 7.

Drambuie or Scotch Seashore Fudge

You really have to be a scotch lover to go for this, but scotch lovers I know like it. Add 1 ounce scotch or Drambuie as the seed in step 6.

Kahlúa Seashore Fudge

Add ¼ cup of Kahlúa as the seed in step 6.

Kahlúa-Mocha Seashore Fudge

In step 1, add ¾ cup unsweetened cocoa, *or* add 3 squares (3 ounces) melted unsweetened chocolate *or* 3 packets premelted baking chocolate in step 9. In step 6, seed with ¼ cup Kahlúa.

Grasshopper Seashore Fudge

In step 6, seed with 1 ounce white creme de cacao and 1 ounce white creme de menthe. In step 9, streak with drops of green food coloring.

Other Flavor Possibilities

Almost any liqueur can be used as a seed—Cherry Heering, Triple Sec, Creme de Framboise or Bananas, for example—and combined with appropriate food coloring or even pieces of *candied* fruits, such as orange slices or jelly beans, added in step 9. However, beware of the new "creme" liqueurs, which contain real cream. They may also contain real preservatives to keep the cream from curdling . . . and your fudge from candying.

Summer Fudge

To me, fudge was always something you made in cold weather. The two went together—the candy, smooth and rich and thick and creamy and satisfying, ameliorating the harsh, impersonal bleakness of cold winter. Besides, you know how humidity and hot weather can sabotage the best fudge recipe. On the other hand, the desire for candy knows no season—at least not in my family; how about yours?

A brainstorm! Summer fudge. A candy that is to fudge what sherbet is to ice cream: light, airy, colorful, not too rich or too sweet, but not bland either. A cross between a fudge and a fondant. One that will cook up quickly and not have to ripen for twenty-four hours.

You will find the makings of literally dozens of summer fudges in the supermarket aisle with the Jell-O Brand Gelatin Desserts. Imagine, strawberry-banana, cherry, orange, lime, raspberry, and more. Add sugar and a low-fat dairy product, then cook, stir, and pour. They take thirty to forty-five minutes to make, from go to whoa, as they say in Australia. And they produce fudges in a most delightful range of bright pastel colors that are both appetizing and refreshing. You can even turn them into individual bonbons by pouring into foil-lined minimuffin pans. Or drop them by spoonfuls onto waxed paper, and have wonderful wafer candies. They freeze extremely well and don't need to be thawed before eating—really refreshing on a hot summer day.

Each batch makes 1 pound. Most require at least a 3-quart saucepan, but in some cases, even larger. Finish them by hand—they come up easy—or in less than a minute in a food processor, but for double batches, use an electric mixer. For the liquid, you can use whole milk, low-fat milk, reconstituted nonfat milk, even nonfat and regular yogurt, buttermilk, or sour cream. I've tried them with half-and-half and it's not bad, but to my mind, not worth the additional expense. Light and heavy cream do not work well. To intensify flavors, try the same flavor of yogurt, fruit extract, or fruit-based liqueur as the gelatin.

For a truly interesting combination, add Kool-Aid Brand Unsweetened Soft Drink mixes, but be sure to add ½ teaspoon more baking soda to neutralize some of the protective acids.

BASIC RECIPE

One 3-ounce package Jell-O Brand Gelatin Dessert

2¼ cups (1 pound) granulated white sugar

¼ to 1 teaspoon baking soda

   a. Use ¼ teaspoon for noncitrus flavors, such as raspberry, strawberry-banana, or apricot.

   b. Use ½ teaspoon for lemon, lime, orange, and other citrus flavors.

   c. Add ½ teaspoon more when using yogurt, sour cream, or buttermilk.

1 cup skim, 2 percent, or regular milk, light or regular yogurt, sour cream, buttermilk, reconstituted nonfat powdered milk

1 tablespoon ice-cold butter or ½ to 1 teaspoon flavoring

Optional:

   3–4 drops food coloring for a stronger color
   1 package (2-quart size) Kool-Aid Brand Unsweetened Soft Drink mix plus additional ½ teaspoon baking soda
   ½ cup chopped nuts
   ½ cup mini-marshmallows

STEP 1: PREPARE: Prewarm thermometer; use 3-quart saucepan unless using yogurt, sour cream, or buttermilk for liquid and/or orange, lemon, or lime gelatin, then use 6-quart saucepan. (Baking soda plus acid causes the batch to fluff up like cotton candy.) Measure all ingredients except seed butter or flavoring and optionals, and dump into saucepan; do *not* butter upper sides of saucepan. Grease and, if necessary, line a 5 × 10-inch pan. Freeze 1 tablespoon of butter. Fill glass with ice cubes and water and sink half-inch full of *hot* water (so gelatin does not set up prematurely).

STEP 2: DISSOLVE sugar, stirring constantly with wooden spoon over low heat until sugar is dissolved. Gritty sounds will cease, spoon will glide smoothly over bottom of pan. However, since you will see granules on the spoon, test by drawing finger—watch out, it may be very hot—through the spoon and feel to make sure it is not sugary. Increase heat to medium and bring to a boil.

STEP 3: BOIL after washing down any crystals that may have formed with pastry brush dipped in hot water from thermometer bath, using as little water as possible. Introduce prewarmed thermometer. Reduce heat while retaining boil. Stir almost constantly, especially around sides. Depending on the dairy product/gelatin combination you use, mixture may start to cook down and change color slightly.

STEP 4: TEST in ice-cold water when mixture thickens and bubbles become noisy. Ball, formed in ice water, should hold its shape until heat from your hand begins to flatten it and should be al dente— slightly chewy. Temperatures are very approximate; I had one batch ball at 222°F (105.5°C), another at 238°F (114.5°C), and others in between—so watch the bubbles and the thickening of the mixture. On the average, 236°F to 238°F (113.5°C to 114.5°C).

STEP 5: SHOCK by placing saucepan in sink.

STEP 6: SEED by adding, without stirring, frozen butter or flavoring, as well as any food coloring and Kool-Aid. Then allow to cool.

STEP 7: STIR when lukewarm and "skin" forms on top (110°F [43.5°C]). Return thermometer to its hot-water bath to soak clean. Stir fudge thoroughly but not vigorously by hand (gelatin may stick to bottom of pan so use scraping motion to free it), with electric mixer, or in food processor. Pause frequently to allow fudge to react.

STEP 8: WATCH for fudge to thicken, lose its sheen, become lighter in color or streaked with lighter shades, give off some heat, suddenly stiffen. If mixing by hand, fudge will "snap" with each stroke; by mixer, mixer waves will become very distinct; by food processor, fudge will flow sluggishly back to center when processor is stopped.

STEP 9: ADD any optional ingredients before fudge totally candies.

STEP 10: POUR, SCORE, AND STORE when cool in airtight container in refrigerator or at room temperature.

YIELD: 1 POUND. Recipe can be doubled if you have a large stockpot and if you process in your mixer. There's too much to process in one batch in food processor, and it's too hard on your arm to do by hand.

VARIATIONS

Gelatin–dairy product combinations: with citrus flavors, use milk to keep acid down; with noncitrus flavors, use milk (sets fastest) or yogurt (low, low fat) or sour cream (richer but treacherous). If you combine citrus flavors and yogurt or sour cream, be sure to add additional baking soda as specified in the basic recipe.

Black Cherry Summer Fudge

Use black cherry–flavored Jell-O, 8-ounce container black cherry yogurt, with or without fruit, and at least a 6-quart saucepan. Total amount of baking soda: ¾ teaspoon if yogurt has no fruit, 1 teaspoon for fruited yogurt. *Optional*: Use 1 teaspoon kirschwasser for seed instead of butter in step 6. You may also add 4 drops red food coloring.

Grand Marnier Soufflé Summer Fudge

Use strawberry-vanilla-flavored Jell-O, 1 cup sour cream, and at least a 6-quart saucepan. Total amount of baking soda: ¾ teaspoon. Because of reaction of baking soda and sour cream, the mixture foams up and bubbles like crazy. In step 6, seed with 2 teaspoons Grand Marnier (butter is optional).

Key Lime Summer Fudge

Use lime-flavored Jell-O, 6-ounce container key lime–flavored yogurt plus ¼ cup milk, and at least a 6-quart saucepan. Total amount of baking soda: ¾ teaspoon.

Lemonade Summer Fudge

Can you imagine a child asking Mommy for a piece of lemonade? It may well happen with this tartly refreshing summer fudge, especially if served frozen. Use lemon-flavored Jell-O, 2-quart-size unsweetened Kool-Aid Brand Lemonade Mix (in step 6), 2¼ cups sugar, 1 cup milk, 1 teaspoon baking soda (total), and at least a 6-quart saucepan. For a tart-tart lemonade taste, in step 6, seed with ½ teaspoon pure lemon extract instead of butter. For a sweeter lemonade fudge, increase sugar to 3 cups, milk to 1¼ cups.

Lemon-Licorice Summer Fudge

Use lemon-flavored Jell-O, 8-ounce container plain no-fat yogurt, and at least a 6-quart saucepan. Increase baking soda to 1 teaspoon (total). In step 6, eliminate butter but seed with ½ teaspoon real lemon extract. In step 9, add 3 drops yellow food coloring. Cut ½ cup licorice pieces into small pieces (⅛–¼ inch wide) and fold in.

Orange Sherbet Summer Fudge

Use orange-flavored Jell-O, 1 cup milk, 2-quart-size unsweetened Kool-Aid orange-flavored mix, and a 6-quart saucepan. Increase baking soda to 1 teaspoon (total). *Optional:* In step 6, seed with ½ teaspoon Cointreau instead of butter. Makes a soft fudge that has been compared to sherbet on a stick.

Rich Raspberry Summer Fudge

Use raspberry-flavored Jell-O, 8-ounce container raspberry-flavored yogurt (I use 150-calorie "light"), and at least a 4-quart saucepan. Increase baking soda to ¾ teaspoon (total).

Peaches 'n' Cream Summer Fudge

The name is misleading, although the fudge is creamy. Do not use cream, unless it's sour cream; peach-flavored yogurt lets flavor come through best. Use peach-flavored Jell-O and 8-ounce container yogurt. Use ¾ teaspoon baking soda (total). *Optional*: In step 6, add 1 table-spoon peach-flavored schnapps.

FIVE

Exceptional Exceptions

TRIPLE-RICH CARAMEL FUDGE
MIRACLE CARAMEL FUDGE

LAZY COOK'S FUDGE
LAZY COOK'S CHOCOLATE BROWNIE FUDGE
LAZY COOK'S CHOCOLATE-WALNUT BROWNIE FUDGE
LAZY COOK'S INTENSELY BUTTERSCOTCH FUDGE
LAZY COOK'S INTENSELY BUTTERSCOTCH-PECAN FUDGE
LAZY COOK'S INTENSELY BUTTERSCOTCH-RUM FUDGE
LAZY COOK'S INTENSELY CHOCOLATE CHIP BUTTERSCOTCH
FUDGE
LAZY COOK'S INTENSELY PEANUT BUTTER FUDGE

MILK CHOCOLATEY FUDGE

NUTTY FUDGE

CHOCOLATE CHIP NUTTY FUDGE
YOGURT CHIP NUTTY FUDGE

BUTTERSCOTCH CANDY BAR FUDGE

DOUBLE BUTTERSCOTCH CANDY BAR FUDGE
CHOCOLATE CANDY BAR FUDGE

THE BIG, BIG BASIC BATCH FUDGE

RICE CEREAL FUDGE

Everybody knows that old saying, The exception proves the rule. Herein are genuine exceptions, some to the methodology and some to the basic ingredients list.

Some of these fudges are more of a challenge to make than the basics, but others are less so. Several are commercial recipes converted to home use, others are family treasures, still others are the result of chance happenings.

Triple-Rich Caramel Fudge

This is one of the few commercial fudges made like homemade except that you don't shock it by placing it in cool water immediately after removing it from the heat, nor do you immediately seed it or wait until lukewarm to stir it. A thermometer is helpful, but not an absolute necessity although it is cooked to a higher ball than other fudges—as if it were a caramel.

It has not one but three kinds of sweetening, three types of liquid, three sources of butterfat. No wonder I call it Triple Rich. (Besides, I first tested it on Kentucky Derby Day, the first day of the Triple Crown.)

Commercial fudge-makers describe this fudge as a "straight, boiled, short, coarse-textured fudge"—a funny way of describing one of the richer, creamier fudges you'll ever taste.

The rather dark color of the fudge results from very slow cooling—from the firm-ball stage around 240°F (115.5°C) down to 165°F

(74°C). Don't try to speed this up by putting it over ice cubes—it cools down so fast, it gels, and you can't beat it in the usual way. If you do cool this fudge too quickly, all is not lost; see Miracle Caramel Fudge (pages 101–102).

> *3⅓ cups granulated white sugar*
>
> *⅓ cup light corn syrup*
>
> *⅓ cup honey*
>
> *⅓ cup water*
>
> *⅓ cup butter or margarine*
>
> *7 ounces (half a 14-ounce can) sweetened condensed whole milk*
>
> *½ cup heavy (whipping) cream*
>
> *¼ teaspoon salt*
>
> *1½ teaspoons vanilla, maple, or other flavoring*
>
> Optional: *½ cup nut meats or coconut*

STEP 1: PREPARE: Prewarm thermometer; use 3-quart saucepan; butter upper sides of saucepan; measure all ingredients except salt, flavoring, and optional ingredients, and dump into saucepan. Grease and, if necessary, line a 5 × 10-inch pan. Fill glass with ice cubes and water. Fill sink 1-inch full of water.

STEP 2: DISSOLVE sugar, stirring constantly with wooden spoon over low heat until butter melts, gritty sounds cease, spoon glides smoothly over bottom of pan. Increase heat to medium and bring to a boil.

STEP 3: BOIL after washing down any crystals that may have formed with pastry brush dipped in hot water from thermometer bath, using as little water as possible. Introduce prewarmed thermometer. Reduce heat as low as possible while retaining boil; this will keep the fudge a lighter color. Stir no more than necessary to prevent scorching.

STEP 4: TEST in ice-cold water when mixture thickens and bubbles become noisy. Ball, formed in ice water, should hold its shape except when firmly pressed and be more than slightly chewy. Approximately 240°F to 246°F (115.5°C to 119°C).

STEP 5: REMOVE FROM HEAT, BUT DO NOT SHOCK or take thermometer out. Let fudge cool on a trivet for twenty minutes, or until thermometer falls to 165°F (74°C). Then return thermometer to its hot-water bath to soak clean.

STEP 6: ADD salt and flavoring. Taste and correct flavorings.

STEP 7: STIR, after placing pan in sink filled with enough cold tap water to come up at least 1 inch on the sides. Stir fudge thoroughly but not vigorously by hand, with electric mixer, or in food processor (you will probably need to wrap a cold wet towel around the bowl). Pause frequently to allow fudge to react.

STEP 8: WATCH for fudge to thicken, lose its sheen, become lighter in color or streaked with lighter shades, give off some heat, suddenly stiffen. If mixing by hand, fudge will "snap" with each stroke; by mixer, mixer waves will become very distinct; by food processor, fudge will flow sluggishly back to center when processor is stopped.

STEP 9: ADD optional ingredients before fudge candies.

STEP 10: POUR, SCORE, AND STORE when cool in airtight container in refrigerator or at room temperature.

YIELD: 1 POUND. Recipe is easily doubled if you use a powerful electric mixer and can be frozen.

Miracle Caramel Fudge

Normally, I don't recommend cooling fudge over ice—this recipe is the exception. It came about as one of those fortunate accidents that happen in fudge-making. While testing the ice-cube theory of cooling, I thought I had ruined a batch of Triple-Rich Caramel Fudge. I tried rescuing it in the food processor and thought that a failure, too. Even after processing, it remained rich, smooth, luscious caramel. So I put it aside to use for something else. Imagine my surprise twenty-four hours later when it turned into the most interesting chewy yet creamy caramel fudge you can imagine. And the following day, it was fudge with a wondrous caramel flavor! A delicious failure!

Make Triple-Rich Caramel Fudge . . . but after the fudge is cooked, in step 5, set the pan over ice cubes and let it cool down rapidly, without stirring. When fudge has congealed into a thick layer all around the edges, scoop it out (it may be necessary to hold pan momentarily over your thermometer hot-water bath to warm the pan enough to get the caramel out) and put it in a food processor. Add 1½ teaspoons vanilla extract. Work it in the food processor, pulsing, for two to three minutes, or until caramel changes color and becomes lighter. It will not thicken the way it normally does. Spoon into a greased pan, top with coarsely chopped cashews if you wish, and chill. The first day it will be caramel; the next day it will become a fudgy caramel; the third day, if it lasts that long—I hid some just to see what would happen—it will have turned completely into fudge.

YIELD: 1½ POUNDS, ABOUT 4 DOZEN 1-INCH SQUARES. Store in airtight container in refrigerator. Will freeze but not for more than three months.

Lazy Cook's Fudge

The Lazy Cook's fudges don't follow that nice ten-step format we've been using. For one thing, they cook for literally hours . . . but they cook themselves with very little assistance from you. They're a nice fudge to make if you have something else to do at the same time, such as watching a videotape. (I've been known to put it on and run to the store to do errands.)

Each of the flavors of Lazy Cook's Fudges uses essentially the same ingredients but because of differences in butterfat and melting point, all but the chocolate need to be started off at a higher temperature to get the chips into solution. Although these fudges are seeded, they are really too fragile to shock. Instead, allow them to cool down slowly.

Lazy Cook's Chocolate Brownie Fudge

Think of the fudgiest brownie you've ever had—that's what this fudge tastes like. Intensely chocolate, moist, and very sugary—it proves the rule that chocolate fudge *wants* to grain. However, if you'd prefer it creamier, use the optional corn syrup and allow it to cool down very gradually, as per Lazy Cook's Intensely Butterscotch Fudge (page 105). Ideally, it should be stirred every half hour or so, concentrating on scraping down the chocolate that accumulates on the sides of the pan.

1⅔ cups superfine sugar

2 squares (2 ounces) unsweetened chocolate, grated or smashed

1 cup heavy (whipping) cream

6 tablespoons (¾ stick) soft butter

Optional: 1 tablespoon corn syrup

1 teaspoon vanilla extract

STEP 1: CHOOSE a 2- or 2½-quart saucepan—the heaviest you have. (Note: If it's too heavy, be prepared to turn the heat up about an hour into the cooking.) Combine all the ingredients but the vanilla. They will not be well blended, but don't worry. If you use the optional corn syrup, which inhibits candying, fill sink one-half inch full of warm water.

STEP 2: COOK for two hours on your lowest setting, letting mixture melt very slowly. Check it after half an hour or so and stir well, especially scrape down the edges . . . but if you forget, don't worry. If it isn't simmering after an hour, turn the heat up a hair. Stir again on the hour and half hour . . . but if you forget, it's okay. If you cook it an extra half hour, that's okay, too. This is a very forgiving fudge.

STEP 3: PREPARE thermometer and spray or butter 5 × 10-inch or loaf pan when two hours are almost up.

STEP 4: SCRAPE sides of pan, if necessary, with a knife if you haven't been stirring and scraping periodically before. If chocolate has totally solidified along the edges, wash down any crystals that may have formed with pastry brush dipped in hot water from thermometer bath, using as little water as possible. If it's really a mess or you're feeling extra lazy, pour into a clean pan. Increase heat to medium and bring to a boil.

STEP 5: BOIL. Introduce prewarmed thermometer. Reduce heat while retaining boil. Stirring occasionally, boil for about 10 minutes.

STEP 6: TEST in ice-cold water when mixture thickens and bubbles become noisy. Ball, formed in ice water, should hold its shape until heat from your hand begins to flatten it and be al dente—slightly chewy. Approximately 234°F to 244°F (112°C to 118°C).

STEP 7: COOL, returning thermometer to its hot water bath to soak clean. If you have used corn syrup, place pan in sink filled with warm water. Otherwise, place on heat-proof pad.

STEP 8: ADD vanilla.

STEP 9: STIR LAZILY every now and then. It will turn before you know it. In fact, I have made this without stirring at all. Without thinking, I poured the hot syrup into a *cold* pan, began drizzling vanilla over it, and before I was finished, boom! bang! fudge! Also, I must admit, it was not the creamiest of fudges. Very sugary in fact—but so chocolately, who cared!

STEP 10: POUR, SCORE, AND STORE in airtight container in refrigerator or at room temperature.

YIELD: 4 DOZEN 1-INCH SQUARES. Store in tightly closed plastic bags in refrigerator or at room temperature. Recipe is a doubtful doubler, but it can be frozen.

Lazy Cook's Chocolate-Walnut Brownie Fudge

Add ½ cup chilled and chopped walnuts just before you pour.

Lazy Cook's Intensely Butterscotch Fudge

Rich, rich, rich. Made like the Lazy Cook's Chocolate Brownie Fudge, but creamier. It also requires checking every 15 minutes or so because butterscotch chips seem more volatile. Because this version is stirred—but not vigorously—before pouring, it can be doubled. If you want to see the difference corn syrup makes in a fudge, make the chocolate first without the corn syrup, then this one with.

Follow Lazy Cook's Chocolate Brownie Fudge recipe with following exceptions: Substitute ½ cup (3 ounces) butterscotch chips for the unsweetened chocolate, and be sure to use 1 tablespoon light corn syrup. In step 2, cook for 15 minutes or so on medium-low heat until chips have melted. Then turn down to lowest setting and cook for 2 hours, checking it every 15 minutes or so and stirring well, especially along edges. Bring to a boil, stirring as little as possible. In step 6, ball, formed in ice water, should hold its shape until heat from your hand begins to flatten it and should be al dente—slightly chewy. Approximately 236°F to 244°F (113.5°C to 118°C). In step 8, seed with vanilla. Then shock slightly by placing saucepan on cool surface such as sink. In step 9, stir every couple of minutes. Mixture will become thicker, then light-streaked, and finally lose its sheen.

Lazy Cook's Intensely Butterscotch-Pecan Fudge

Follow directions for Lazy Cook's Intensely Butterscotch Fudge, but add ½ cup chilled pecans while mixture is still liquid in step 8.

Lazy Cook's Intensely Butterscotch-Rum Fudge

Follow directions for Lazy Cook's Intensely Butterscotch Fudge, but instead of vanilla extract, use ½ tablespoon rum in step 8.

Lazy Cook's Intensely Chocolate Chip Butterscotch Fudge

Follow directions for Lazy Cook's Intensely Butterscotch Fudge, but add ½ cup (3 ounces) chocolate chips in step 8 just before mixture turns. If you wish the chips to melt partially, use semisweet; if you wish them to remain very visible, use milk chocolate.

Lazy Cook's Intensely Peanut Butter Fudge

Follow directions for Lazy Cook's Intensely Butterscotch Fudge, but substitute peanut butter chips for the butterscotch. You'll truly enjoy stirring this one because, after an hour or so, you'll be treated to the smell of fresh roasting peanuts. Because of the higher fat content in the chips, this one must be stirred thoroughly every 15 minutes . . . and it takes longer to grain. However, my taste testers tell me it's worth the trouble. It's the peanuttiest without being cloying. You can even add ½ cup Spanish peanuts if you wish in step 8.

Milk Chocolatey Fudge

Ingredients make this fudge unique. It's an old-fashioned fudge made with unsweetened chocolate but tasting for all the world like milk chocolate, thanks to the use of powdered nonfat dry milk. Also, it is a cooked fudge made with confectioners' sugar, which is rare. Occasionally, it may take its time graining in the pan. As long as there are light-colored streaks present, it will turn into fudge.

1 square (1 ounce) unsweetened chocolate

2 tablespoons butter, divided in two

⅓ cup powdered nonfat milk

¼ teaspoon salt

3 cups (stirred and scooped) confectioners' sugar

½ cup water

1 tablespoon light corn syrup

1 tablespoon honey

1 teaspoon vanilla

Optional: ½ cup chopped walnuts or sliced almonds

STEP 1: PREPARE: Prewarm thermometer; use a 2-quart saucepan for making the sugary syrup and a 3-quart pan for the fudge itself. You will also need a heat-proof, micro-proof bowl or double boiler. Grease and, if necessary, line an 8 × 8-inch pan. Freeze 1 tablespoon butter. Fill glass with ice cubes and water and sink half-inch full of water.

STEP 2: MELT 1 tablespoon butter and the unsweetened chocolate in the heat-proof bowl over thermometer pan or in double boiler. (Or zap them separately in microwave: 1 minute on HIGH (100%) for chocolate, ½ minute on HIGH (100%) for butter.) Place in 3-quart saucepan. Chocolate will be grainy because of the water in the butter—don't worry about it. Mix in powdered milk and salt. Finally, add the confectioners' sugar. Mix as thoroughly as you can. It will be dry and look like a very pale cocoa.

STEP 3: HEAT, in 2-quart saucepan, water, corn syrup, and honey without stirring just to the boiling point—lazy bubbles will begin coming up slowly from the bottom. Pour hot syrup into mixture in fudge pan slowly, and mix well using a whisk. Reheat mixture over medium-low heat, stirring constantly, until gritty lumps melt, mixture becomes a little lighter and quite a bit thicker, then bring to a boil.

STEP 4: BOIL after washing down any crystals that may have formed with pastry brush dipped in hot water from thermometer bath, using as little water as possible. Introduce prewarmed thermometer. Reduce heat while retaining boil. Stir no more than necessary.

STEP 5: TEST in ice-cold water when mixture thickens and bubbles become noisy. Ball, formed in ice water, should hold its shape easily outside of the water and is definitely al dente—chewy. Approximately 236°F to 244°F (113.5°C to 118°C).

STEP 6: SHOCK by placing saucepan in sink.

STEP 7: SEED by adding, without stirring, vanilla and the tablespoon of frozen butter. Then allow to cool.

STEP 8: STIR when lukewarm and "skin" forms on top (110°F [43.5°C]). Return thermometer to its hot water bath to soak clean. Stir fudge thoroughly but not vigorously by hand, with electric mixer, or in food processor. Pause frequently to allow fudge to react.

STEP 9: WATCH for fudge to thicken, lose its sheen, become lighter in color or streaked with lighter shades, give off some heat, suddenly stiffen. If mixing by hand, fudge will "snap" with each stroke; by mixer, mixer waves will become very distinct; by food processor, fudge will flow sluggishly back to center when processor is stopped.

STEP 10: ADD any optional ingredients before fudge totally candies.

STEP 11: POUR, then bang pan smartly on countertop to get rid of air pockets. Score while lukewarm. Store when cool in airtight container in refrigerator or at room temperature.

YIELD: 1 POUND. Recipe is easily doubled and can be frozen.

Nutty Fudge

If you've been browsing through the many recipes in this book, you may have noticed that the most common optional ingredient is ½ cup nuts. Nuts to that! This recipe absolutely, positively, totally demands nuts. Use walnuts, almonds, hazelnuts, brazil nuts, any hard nut that can withstand a long cooking period. Avoid soft nuts, such as pecans and cashews.

2 cups granulated white sugar

1 cup water

2 cups chopped hard nuts

¼ cup light corn syrup

4 tablespoons (½ stick) butter

¼ teaspoon salt

5-ounce can evaporated milk

1 teaspoon vanilla extract

STEP 1: PREPARE: Prewarm thermometer; use 3-quart saucepan; butter upper sides of saucepan; measure all ingredients except evaporated milk and vanilla, and dump into saucepan. Grease and, if necessary, line a 5 × 10-inch pan. Fill glass with ice cubes and water and sink half-inch full of water.

STEP 2: DISSOLVE sugar, stirring constantly with wooden spoon over low heat until butter melts, gritty sounds cease, spoon glides smoothly over bottom of pan. Increase heat to medium and bring to heavy, violent boil. Add evaporated milk slowly so as not to break the boil.

STEP 3: BOIL after washing down any crystals that may have formed with brush dipped in hot water from thermometer bath, using as little water as possible. Introduce prewarmed thermometer. Reduce heat while retaining boil. Stir only enough to keep mixture from boiling over and nuts from sticking to bottom. Mixture will double and occasionally triple in volume. Cooking will seem to take forever, but since you don't have to stir constantly, it's not all that bad, and it does set up quickly. Eventually mixture will darken and thicken.

STEP 4: TEST in ice-cold water when mixture thickens and bubbles become noisy. Ball, formed in ice water, should hold its shape until heat from your hand begins to flatten it and should be al dente— slightly chewy. This fudge likes to ball at a low temperature, approximately 230°F to 238°F (111°C to 114.5°C).

STEP 5: SHOCK by placing saucepan in sink.

STEP 6: SEED by adding, without stirring, vanilla. Then allow to cool.

STEP 7: STIR when lukewarm and "skin" forms on top (110°F [43.5°C]). Return thermometer to its hot-water bath to soak clean. Stir fudge thoroughly but not vigorously by hand, with electric mixer, or in food processor. Pause frequently to allow fudge to react.

STEP 8: WATCH for fudge to thicken, lose its sheen, become lighter in color or streaked with lighter shades, give off some heat, suddenly stiffen. If mixing by hand, fudge will "snap" with each stroke; by mixer, mixer waves will become very distinct; by food processor, fudge will flow sluggishly back to center when processor is stopped.

STEP 9: ADD any optional ingredients for variations before fudge candies completely.

STEP 10: POUR, SCORE, AND STORE when cool in airtight container in refrigerator or at room temperature.

YIELD: 1 POUND. Recipe is not easily doubled, but it can be frozen.

VARIATIONS

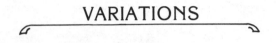

Chocolate Chip Nutty Fudge

Add ½ cup semisweet or milk chocolate chips in step 9. Although both chips will hold their shape, the milk chocolate ones will not soften.

Yogurt Chip Nutty Fudge

If you're fond of vanilla-flavored yogurt chips, this is the perfect environment for them, especially pastel ones. Simply add ½ cup or more in step 9.

Butterscotch Candy Bar Fudge

This fudge is exceptional in many ways. Making it is a challenge to your fudge-making skill, as it is the most complicated fudge in the book. However, it may well be the one that everyone remembers the longest, because it tastes very much like the nougaty center of the Three Musketeers bar. In fact, if you top it with melted milk chocolate chips, you'll have a close approximation of the candy bar.

It is also what I call a trade-off fudge: Because it is made with condensed milk and margarine, you have to stir almost constantly while cooking . . . but there's no beating afterward.

Also, it is one of the few fudges in the book that requires fondant, which is used in most factory fudges, to force the fudge to crystallize without getting coarse and lumpy while the marshmallow creme aerates the fudge and makes it a flexible, chewy-type of fudge. You may feel more comfortable using a candy thermometer with this fudge.

⅔ cup light corn syrup

6 tablespoons (¾ stick) margarine (or margarine spread)

14-ounce can sweetened condensed whole milk

1⅔ cups granulated white sugar

½ teaspoon salt

½ cup (⅔ pound) fondant (see chapter 8)

½ cup (3 ounces) butterscotch chips, melted (see page 112)

1 cup marshmallow creme

1 cup (6 ounces) milk chocolate chips or coating wafers, melted (see page 112)

STEP 1: PREPARE: Prewarm thermometer; use 3-quart saucepan; butter upper sides of saucepan; measure corn syrup, margarine, sweetened condensed milk, granulated sugar, and salt, and dump into saucepan. Grease and, if necessary, line an 8 × 8-inch or a 7 × 11-inch pan. Fill glass with ice cubes and water.

STEP 2: DISSOLVE sugar, stirring constantly with wooden spoon over low heat until sugar is dissolved. Margarine will have long since melted, but gritty sounds will cease and spoon will glide smoothly over bottom of pan. Increase heat to medium and bring to a boil.

STEP 3: BOIL after washing down any crystals that may have formed with pastry brush dipped in hot water from thermometer bath, using as little water as possible. Introduce prewarmed thermometer. Reduce heat while retaining boil. Stir almost constantly. If mixture should begin to scorch, stir vigorously to incorporate.

STEP 4: TEST in ice-cold water when mixture thickens and bubbles become noisy. Ball, formed in ice water, should hold its shape easily and firmly and taste quite chewy. Approximately 238°F to 246°F (114.5°C to 119°C).

STEP 5: REMOVE FROM HEAT, let cool for 10 minutes, or until temperature is 165°F to 170°F (74°C to 76.5°C).

STEP 6: SEED by adding fondant and mixing until fondant melts.

STEP 7: STIR in melted butterscotch chips (see below) and marshmallow creme. Mix thoroughly.

STEP 8: SPREAD fudge in pan. Bang pan smartly on countertop to get rid of air pockets. Let cool completely before coating with melted chocolate.

YIELD: 5 TO 6 DOZEN 1-INCH SQUARES. Cover with aluminum foil and store at room temperature.

To melt chips: Melt chips in double boiler or zap in microwave—1 minute at HIGH (100%), stir, 15 to 30 seconds on HIGH (100%) again if needed.

Milk chocolate chips, melted in this manner, won't have a sheen unless they're "tempered" (see chapter 10). For a better appearance, use pretempered coating wafers, melted in double boiler or on LOW (30%) in microwave.

VARIATIONS

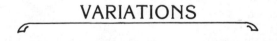

Double Butterscotch Candy Bar Fudge

For stronger butterscotch flavor, use 1 cup (6 ounces) chips in step 7.

Chocolate Candy Bar Fudge

For chocolate version, use ½ to 1 cup semisweet chips in place of the butterscotch chips in step 7.

The Big, Big Basic Batch Fudge

Most of the fudges in this book have been deliberately designed to make no more than one to two pounds. However, there are times when you'll want to make a big batch. So here's a quantity fudge recipe that won't give you fits because it uses ready-made frosting mix.

From this basic batch you can make two, three, four, even five different flavors of fudge or a single enormous batch of one flavor. Or you can make part fudge and part rice cereal candy (see page 116). I suggest that the first time you try it, you confine yourself to two flavors, such as chocolate and plain vanilla—varying these as the fudge shops do by adding nuts to half of each batch.

Don't feel you have to rush after fudge comes to a ball and you take it off the heat. The cooler the syrup is when blended with the ready-made frosting, the creamier the fudge and the faster it will set. *Important*: When cooling it in the sink, don't fill the sink more than one inch full. Also, stir this fudge frequently while cooling, especially around the sides so that edges don't set up before the center does. Here, again, you may find a long, thin candy thermometer helpful; if you are unable to clip it on the pan and still have the sensor down in the fudge, just rest the thermometer against the side of the pot.

½ cup light corn syrup

4½ cups (2 pounds) granulated white sugar

½ cup water

½ cup (4 ounces) margarine or margarine spread

7 ounces (half of 14-ounce can) sweetened condensed milk

1 teaspoon salt

1 tablespoon vanilla extract

Optional: *Two, three, or more 16-ounce containers ready-made (deluxe) frosting in choice of flavors*
Matching optional extracts:
  marshmallow creme
  chopped nuts
  shredded coconut

STEP 1: PREPARE: Prewarm thermometer; use at least an 8-quart stock-pot so that you won't be stirring constantly when it comes to a boil. Measure all ingredients except vanilla, the ready-made frosting, and any optionals, and dump into pot. Grease and, if necessary, line enough pans to handle 5 pounds of fudge: 5 × 10-inch pans for single pounds, 8 × 8-inch pans for 2 pounds. Have ready as many 1½-quart or larger heat-proof bowls as you're planning to have flavors. You'll also need a ½-cup ladle or a long-handled ½-cup measure (be sure to use a pot holder mitt; the handle, if metal, will get hot). Fill glass with ice cubes and water and sink half-inch full of water.

STEP 2: DISSOLVE sugar, stirring constantly with wooden spoon over *medium* heat until sugar is dissolved. Margarine will have long since melted, but gritty sounds will cease and spoon will glide smoothly over bottom of pan. Increase heat to *medium-high*, stir occasionally, and bring to a boil.

STEP 3: BOIL after washing down any crystals that may have formed with pastry brush dipped in hot water from thermometer bath, using as little water as possible. Introduce prewarmed thermometer. Reduce heat while retaining boil. Stir no more than necessary.

STEP 4: TEST in ice-cold water when mixture thickens and bubbles become noisy. Ball, formed in ice water, should hold its shape until heat from your hand begins to flatten it and should definitely be al dente—chewy. Approximately 236°F to 244°F (113.5°C to 118°C).

STEP 5: SHOCK by placing stockpot in sink.

STEP 6: SEED by adding vanilla. Stir frequently until fudge cools below 190°F (88°C), preferably closer to 175°F (79.5°C), which will take 15 to 20 minutes. Factory fudge-makers stir with the thermometer, checking temperatures all around the batch and stirring simultaneously.

STEP 7: PREPARE individual flavorings: Put frosting in individual fudge bowls and measure out optional ingredients as follows:
The proportions, per pound of fudge to be poured in one pan, are

1 cup fudge syrup to 1 cup (½ container) frosting plus optional ½ teaspoon flavoring to match frosting if other than vanilla or chocolate (strawberry, lemon, etc.)

approximately ½ cup marshmallow creme to make a tender, airier fudge (optional; reserve till step 11)

½ cup chopped nuts (optional; reserve till step 11)

½ to 1 cup shredded coconut (optional; reserve till step 11)

STEP 8: LADLE OUT cooled syrup over frosting (should be between 10 and 12 ladlesful total). Take your time. You want to melt frosting, not liquefy it.

STEP 9: STIR bowls gently in order you ladled out syrup, by hand or with portable mixer on lowest speed—you do not want to beat it.

STEP 10: WATCH for fudge to thicken, lose its sheen, become lighter in color or streaked with lighter shades, give off some heat, suddenly stiffen. If you are mixing by hand, fudge will "snap" with each stroke; by mixer, mixer waves will become very distinct. Particularly watch for loss of gloss. If bowl shows no signs of setting up after 5 minutes of stirring, return it to sink to cool some more.

STEP 11: ADD optional marshmallow creme, nuts and/or coconut before fudge totally candies.

STEP 12: POUR, SCORE, AND STORE when cool in airtight container in refrigerator or at room temperature.

YIELD: 5 POUNDS. Recipe can be frozen.

NOTE: If the syrup is too hot when you added it to the frosting, take heart. Although it may take as long as twenty-four hours for the fudge to set up or candy, it will do so eventually. When hot syrup is added to the frosting, the sugar crystals in the frosting are almost completely dissolved. But if you use a cool syrup, the crystals remain and encourage crystallization or candying.

VARIATIONS

You don't need to use frosting mix if you don't want to. Just divide batch and add as seed 1 teaspoon vanilla extract, plus ½ cup any flavor chips. Let cool to lukewarm before stirring.

Rice Cereal Fudge

If you think the traditional rice cereal candy is good, wait until you taste the combination of caramel fudge and crispy cereal surrounding pockets of fluffy marshmallow!

Make fudge as above without the frosting, shock, seed with vanilla, let cool to lukewarm, stir until just beginning to set, then add, for every 1 cup (2 ladlesful) syrup, 2 cups crispy rice cereal and ½ cup mini-marshmallows.

For a smaller batch, simply halve or quarter the ingredients.

To make the whole recipe into cereal candy, use 10 cups rice cereal, 2½ cups (1 package) mini-marshmallows, and buttered roasting pan or two buttered 8 × 12-inch dishes.

SIX

Exotic Fudges

LEMON BUTTER FUDGE
    UNCLE JACK'S POPPYSEED FUDGE
    MAPLE BUTTER FUDGE

CARROT FUDGE

DATE-NUT ROLL

APPLESCOTCH
    PINEAPPLESCOTCH

GOAT'S MILK FUDGE
    MAMA'S CHOCOLATE GOAT'S MILK FUDGE
    PEANUT BUTTER GOAT'S MILK FUDGE
    CREAMY MARSHMALLOW GOAT'S MILK FUDGE

Like the exceptional fudges, these fudges are different! And how! But in a delicious sort of way. Mostly they're different because of the unusual ingredients. And some of them will have definite appeal to the health-conscious among you. They are some of the more interesting fudges I've made.

Lemon Butter Fudge

This fudge is best made in your food processor if it's powerful enough, because there is a lot of butter to incorporate while stirring. Otherwise, use your electric mixer. Mix by hand only as a last resort, or if you have an arm-wrestling champ ready to help. Take it from me, if you like lemon, this is not merely good, it's glorious!

> 2 cups granulated white sugar
>
> ½ cup (or 5-ounce can) evaporated whole milk, unsweetened
>
> 1½ tablespoons lemon juice
>
> ¼ teaspoon salt
>
> 1 × 2-inch piece lemon zest
>
> 4 tablespoons (½ stick) butter (do not use margarine)
>
> Optional:
> ½ to 1 teaspoon lemon extract
> ½ cup chopped nuts
> 4 drops yellow food coloring

STEP 1: PREPARE: Prewarm thermometer; use 2-quart saucepan; butter upper sides of saucepan; measure all ingredients except butter, food

119

coloring, and optionals, and dump into saucepan. Grease and, if necessary, line a 5 × 10-inch pan. Freeze all the butter. Fill glass with ice cubes and water and sink half-inch full of water.

STEP 2: DISSOLVE sugar. Mixture may look curdled, but it will turn out fine. Stir constantly with wooden spoon over low heat until gritty sounds cease and spoon glides smoothly over bottom of pan. Increase heat to medium and bring to a boil.

STEP 3: BOIL after washing down any crystals that may have formed with pastry brush dipped in hot water from thermometer bath, using as little water as possible. Introduce prewarmed thermometer. Reduce heat while retaining boil. Stir no more than necessary.

STEP 4: TEST in ice-cold water when mixtures thickens and bubbles become noisy. Ball, formed in ice water, should hold its shape until heat from your hand begins to flatten it and should be al dente—slightly chewy. Approximately 236°F to 244°F (113.5°C to 118°C).

STEP 5: SHOCK by placing saucepan in sink.

STEP 6: SEED by adding, without stirring, frozen butter. Then allow to cool.

STEP 7: STIR when lukewarm and "skin" forms on top (110°F [43.5°C]). Return thermometer to its hot-water bath to soak clean. Add food coloring and check flavoring, adding optional lemon extract if desired. Remove zest, then agitate in food processor or with electric mixer and not by hand. Pause frequently to allow fudge to react.

STEP 8: WATCH for fudge to thicken, lose its sheen, become light in color or streaked with lighter shades, give off some heat, suddenly stiffen. If mixing in food processor, fudge will flow sluggishly back to center when processor is stopped (you may need to wrap wet towel around processor bowl to speed up process); by mixer, mixer waves will become very distinct; by hand, fudge will "snap" with each stroke.

STEP 9: ADD optional chopped nuts (pecans are good) just before you pour.

STEP 10: POUR, SCORE, AND STORE when cool in airtight container in refrigerator or at room temperature.

YIELD: 1 POUND. Recipe is not easily doubled but can be frozen.

VARIATIONS

Uncle Jack's Poppyseed Fudge

When my friend Jack Reznichek suggested a poppyseed fudge I was, to be honest, more than a little incredulous. Then the more I thought about it—well, to make a long story short, this is one of those he-who-laughs-last-laughs-best flavors. Let 'em laugh when you tell 'em you're planning to make it, then sit back and smile while they gobble it up. It's delectable.

Follow directions for Lemon Butter Fudge and, if you're fond of lemon, increase the flavoring to 2 teaspoons in step 7. Continue as above but in step 9, add ⅓ cup poppyseeds instead of nuts.

Maple Butter Fudge

Follow directions for Lemon Butter Fudge, omitting lemon juice and zest. In step 1, replace ⅓ cup granulated sugar with ¾ cup maple syrup. Alternate method: Follow recipe for Lemon Butter Fudge, omitting lemon juice and zest. Add ½ teaspoon maple concentrate in step 6 when you seed with butter.

Carrot Fudge

If you like carrot cake, you'll love this. It's creamy with just a hint of crunchiness from both the carrots and the walnuts.

>1½ cups peeled and grated carrots (5 or 6 long, thin ones—don't use old "woody" carrots, they won't cook down enough)
>
>3½ cups granulated white sugar
>
>½ cup sweetened condensed milk

½ *cup water*

½ *teaspoon lemon extract, not juice*

Optional: ½ *cup chopped walnuts (recommended)*

STEP 1: PREPARE: Prewarm thermometer; use 3-quart saucepan; butter upper sides of saucepan; measure all ingredients except lemon extract and optional nuts and dump into saucepan. Grease and, if necessary, line a 5 × 12-inch pan. Fill glass with ice cubes and water and sink half-inch full of water.

STEP 2: DISSOLVE sugar, stirring constantly with wooden spoon over low heat until gritty sounds cease and spoon glides smoothly over bottom of pan. Increase heat to medium and bring to a boil.

STEP 3: BOIL after washing down any crystals that may have formed with pastry brush dipped in hot water from thermometer bath, using as little water as possible. Introduce prewarmed thermometer. Reduce heat while retaining boil. Stir no more than necessary.

STEP 4: TEST in ice-cold water when mixture thickens and bubbles become noisy. Ball, formed in ice water, should hold its shape until heat from your hand begins to flatten it and should be al dente— slightly chewy. Approximately 234°F to 240°F (112°C to 115.5°C).

STEP 5: SHOCK by placing saucepan in sink.

STEP 6: SEED by adding, without stirring, lemon extract. Then allow to cool.

STEP 7: STIR when lukewarm and "skin" forms on top (110°F [43.5°C]). Return thermometer to its hot-water bath to soak clean. Stir fudge thoroughly but not vigorously either by hand or with electric mixer. (To retain the carrot-crunchiness, do not use food processor.) Whichever method you use, pause frequently to allow fudge to react.

STEP 8: WATCH for fudge to thicken, lose its sheen, become lighter in color or streaked with lighter shades, give off some heat, suddenly stiffen—I warn you, it goes fast. If mixing by hand, fudge will "snap" with each stroke; by mixer, mixer waves will become very distinct. (If fudge candies too quickly, just spoon it out as best you can and knead it with your hands; the heat from your hands will often bring it back together. If you're not using nuts, butter your fingers to give the top a nice shine. Or add nuts and push them down firmly into the top.)

STEP 9: ADD optional nuts before fudge totally candies.

STEP 10: POUR, SCORE, AND STORE when cool in airtight container in refrigerator or at room temperature.

YIELD: 1 POUND. Recipe is easily doubled and can be frozen.

Date-Nut Roll

The Date-Nut Roll is a candy with a long and admirable history. To stretch things a bit, I could say this candy harks back to the ancient Egyptian practice of combining dates and honey to make candy. More realistically, it can be dated back to A.D. 1470. German confectioners not only made gingerbread but "sweets"—sticky, sugary concoctions— from dried fruit, nut meats, sesame or poppy seeds, and spices, mixed and held together with honey. The sweets were then made into rolls and/or cut into pieces and rolled in flour, chopped nut meats, and poppy or sesame seeds to keep them from sticking together.

This version is simply nuts and dates bound together by a simple fudge . . . and yet it's so good, it rates raves.

8-ounce package of dates, well chilled
3 cups granulated white sugar
1 cup milk (low-fat works fine)
2 tablespoons (¼ stick) butter, at room temperature and divided in half
4 cups chopped pecans or walnuts
Optional: *confectioners' sugar*

STEP 1: PREPARE dates, chopping them finely. If they don't chop easily or are sticking too much, freeze them for 30 minutes, then chop. Prewarm thermometer; use 2-quart saucepan; measure sugar and milk, and dump with dates into saucepan; use 1 tablespoon butter to butter upper sides of saucepan, adding what's left to pot; freeze other tablespoon butter. Dampen two tea towels thoroughly. Fill glass with ice cubes and water and sink half-inch full of water.

STEP 2: DISSOLVE sugar, stirring constantly with wooden spoon over low heat until sugar is dissolved. Gritty sounds will cease and spoon will glide smoothly over bottom of pan. Increase heat to medium and bring to a boil.

STEP 3: BOIL after washing down any crystals that may have formed with pastry brush dipped in hot water from thermometer bath, using as little water as possible. Introduce prewarmed thermometer. Reduce heat while retaining boil. Stir no more than necessary.

STEP 4: TEST in ice-cold water when mixture thickens and bubbles become noisy. Ball, formed in ice water, should hold its shape until heat from your hand begins to flatten it and should be al dente—slightly chewy. Approximately 234°F to 240°F (112°C to 115.5°C).

STEP 5: REMOVE FROM HEAT and return thermometer to its hot-water bath to soak clean.

STEP 6: STIR IN BUTTER. When it has melted, add nuts.

STEP 7: MAKE ROLLS. Place both tea towels on counter, long edges parallel to counter edge (or do one at a time). Gradually pour half of mixture in a long, thick ribbon the length of the damp towel. Roll towel tightly away from you, and shape mixture into a roll approximately 10 inches long, 2 to 3 inches in diameter.

STEP 8: COOL at least 30 minutes in refrigerator.

STEP 9: UNWRAP and cut into thin slices. Dust with confectioners' sugar if desired. It will make roll less sticky, but it isn't necessary.

YIELD: 4 DOZEN SLICES OR MORE. Can be frozen.

Applescotch

Fruit and fudge are essentially incompatible, but they get along fine in this recipe. Neither appley nor butterscotchy, it makes for a very interesting flavor combination. People can't immediately identify it, but they like it. If you are using a thermometer, it must extend well down into the mixture. If the sensor is in the foam, you won't get an accurate reading. Because of the fruit, this fudge can take a while—sometimes several hours after you've poured it—to grain. So long as there are veins of light colors in the fudge, it will "candy" eventually.

1 cup sweetened applesauce (with least amount of preservatives you can find)

⅔ cup (half of a 14-ounce can) condensed sweetened milk

2 cups granulated white sugar

2 tablespoons (¼ stick) butter, ice cold

Pinch (⅛ teaspoon) of baking soda

1 teaspoon vanilla extract

Optional: *½ cup chopped pecans*

STEP 1: PREPARE: Prewarm thermometer; use 3-quart saucepan; butter upper sides of saucepan; measure all ingredients except butter, baking soda, vanilla, and optional nuts, and dump into saucepan. Grease and, if necessary, line a 5 × 10-inch pan. Freeze the butter. Fill glass with ice cubes and water and sink half-inch full of water.

STEP 2: DISSOLVE sugar, stirring constantly with wooden spoon over low heat until gritty sounds cease and spoon glides smoothly over bottom of pan. Increase heat to medium and bring to a boil. Add the baking soda and *watch out*, mixture will boil up. Stir as little as possible.

STEP 3: BOIL after washing down any crystals that may have formed with pastry brush dipped in hot water from thermometer bath, using as little water as possible. Introduce prewarmed thermometer. Reduce heat while retaining boil. Stir no more than necessary.

STEP 4: TEST in ice-cold water when mixture thickens and bubbles become noisy. Ball, formed in ice water, should hold its shape until heat from your hand begins to flatten it and should be al dente—slightly chewy. Approximately 234°F to 242°F (112°C to 116.5°C).

STEP 5: SHOCK by placing saucepan in sink.

STEP 6: SEED by adding, without stirring, vanilla and frozen butter. Then allow to cool.

STEP 7: STIR when lukewarm and "skin" forms on top (110°F [43.5°C]). Return thermometer to its hot-water bath to soak clean. Stir fudge thoroughly but not vigorously by hand, with electric mixer, or in food processor. Pause frequently to allow fudge to react.

STEP 8: WATCH for fudge to thicken, lose its sheen, become lighter in color or streaked with lighter shades—these are ultraimportant—give off some heat, suddenly stiffen. If mixing by hand, fudge will "snap" with each stroke; by mixer, mixer waves will become very distinct; by food processor, fudge will flow sluggishly back to center when processor is stopped.

STEP 9: ADD optional nuts before fudge totally candies.

STEP 10: POUR, SCORE, AND STORE when cool in airtight container in refrigerator or at room temperature.

YIELD: 1 POUND. Recipe is not easily doubled, nor does it freeze well.

VARIATION

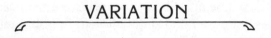

Pineapplescotch

This fudge has a very subtle flavor—more like a pineapple aftertaste—and is very mellow.

Follow the recipe for Applescotch, substituting pineapple pie filling (10-ounce jar) for the applesauce and increasing baking soda to ¼ teaspoon. In step 6, instead of seeding with vanilla extract, use ¼ teaspoon pure lemon extract. Of, if you prefer, use ½ teaspoon orange extract. Like Applescotch, this takes a while to grain. Watch for it to get very, very thick before you pour it.

Goat's Milk Fudge

This is an old-fashioned fudge that may remind you of the good old days, the days when a Sunday drive wasn't to the mall but out into the country, where you could actually drive a mile without seeing a house and the children could pass the time counting cows. Roadside signs advertised homemade preserves and pickles and honey, and "goat's milk fudge up ahead." Margaret Engel, author of *Food Finds*, remembers well that fudge from back in the 1950s and 1960s in the mid-Atlantic states. Then suddenly it disappeared, only to reemerge in the early eighties. She was kind enough to pass the word on to me, and I am delighted to pass it on to you. Shades of the early days of fudge.

These fudges are not only exotic but wholesome, too. In fact, many people are convinced goat's milk is better for you than cow's milk. For one thing, it provides more calcium, vitamin A, potassium, phosphorus, and niacin . . . and is lower in cholesterol. And for those allergic to cow's milk, especially children, this is the ideal dairy product.

More and more supermarkets are stocking goat's milk. Or try your local health-food store. If you can't get it there, write to Jackson-Mitchell Pharmaceuticals, P.O. Box 5424, Santa Barbara, CA 93150. They sell canned Meyenberg Evaporated Goat's Milk and a powdered product that allows you to reconstitute only as much as you need.

Mama's Chocolate Goat's Milk Fudge

Based on a recipe developed by Christine Fuller, mother of one of the distributors of Meyenberg Evaporated Goat's Milk.

2 squares (2 ounces) unsweetened chocolate, grated or smashed

¾ cup reconstituted dry or evaporated goat's milk

2 cups granulated white sugar

1 teaspoon light corn syrup

1 teaspoon vanilla extract

2 tablespoons (¼ stick) butter or margarine

Optional: *½ cup broken nuts*

STEP 1: PREPARE: Prewarm thermometer; use 2½-quart saucepan; butter upper sides of saucepan; measure all ingredients except butter, vanilla, and optional nuts, and dump into saucepan. Grease and, if necessary, line an 8×8-inch pan. Freeze butter. Fill glass with ice cubes and water and sink half-inch full of water.

STEP 2: DISSOLVE sugar, stirring constantly with wooden spoon over low heat until chocolate melts, gritty sounds cease, and spoon glides smoothly over bottom of pan. Increase heat to medium and bring to a boil.

STEP 3: BOIL after washing down any crystals that may have formed with pastry brush dipped in hot water from thermometer bath, using as little water as possible. Introduce prewarmed thermometer. Reduce heat while retaining boil. Stir no more than necessary.

STEP 4: TEST in ice-cold water when mixture thickens and bubbles become noisy. Ball, formed in ice water, should hold its shape until heat from your hand begins to flatten it and should be al dente— slightly chewy. Approximately 234°F to 240°F (112°C to 115.5°C).

STEP 5: SHOCK by placing saucepan in sink.

STEP 6: SEED by adding, without stirring, vanilla and frozen butter. Then allow to cool.

STEP 7: STIR when lukewarm and "skin" forms on top (110°F [43.5°C]). Return thermometer to its hot-water bath to soak clean. Stir fudge thoroughly but not vigorously by hand, with electric mixer, or in food processor. Pause frequently to allow fudge to react.

STEP 8: WATCH for fudge to thicken, lose its sheen, become lighter in color or streaked with lighter shades, give off some heat, suddenly stiffen. If mixing by hand, fudge will "snap" with each stroke; by mixer, mixer waves will become very distinct; by food processor, fudge will flow sluggishly back to center when processor is stopped.

STEP 9: ADD optional nuts before fudge totally candies.

STEP 10: POUR, SCORE, AND STORE when cool in airtight container in refrigerator or at room temperature.

YIELD: 1 POUND. Recipe is easily doubled and can be frozen.

Peanut Butter Goat's Milk Fudge

1 cup firmly packed light brown sugar

1 cup granulated white sugar

¾ cup evaporated goat's milk

1 tablespoon light corn syrup

Pinch (⅛ teaspoon) of salt

½ cup creamy peanut butter

1 tablespoon butter

½ teaspoon vanilla extract

Optional: 1 cup chopped peanuts, freeze-dried or cocktail

STEP 1: PREPARE: Prewarm thermometer; use 1-quart saucepan; butter upper sides of saucepan; measure all ingredients except peanut butter, butter, and vanilla, and dump into saucepan. Grease and, if necessary, line an 8×8-inch pan. Freeze butter. Fill glass with ice cubes and water and sink half-inch full of water.

STEP 2: DISSOLVE sugar, stirring constantly with wooden spoon over low heat until gritty sounds cease, spoon glides smoothly over bottom of pan. Increase heat to medium and bring to a boil.

STEP 3: BOIL after washing down any crystals that may have formed with pastry brush dipped in hot water from thermometer bath, using as little water as possible. Introduce prewarmed thermometer. Reduce heat while retaining boil. Stir no more than necessary.

STEP 4: TEST in ice-cold water when mixture thickens and bubbles become noisy. Ball, formed in ice water, should hold its shape until heat from your hand begins to flatten it and should be al dente—slightly chewy. Approximately 234°F to 240°F (112°C to 115.5°C).

STEP 5: SHOCK by placing saucepan in sink.

STEP 6: SEED by adding, without stirring, peanut butter, butter, and vanilla. Then allow to cool.

STEP 7: STIR when lukewarm and "skin" forms on top (110°F [43.5°C]). Return thermometer to its hot water bath to soak clean. Stir fudge thoroughly but not vigorously by hand, with electric mixer, or in food processor. Pause frequently to allow fudge to react.

STEP 8: WATCH for fudge to thicken, lose its sheen, become lighter in color or streaked with lighter shades, give off some heat, suddenly stiffen. If mixing by hand, fudge will "snap" with each stroke; by mixer, mixer waves will become very distinct; by food processor, fudge will flow sluggishly back to center when processor is stopped.

STEP 9: ADD any optional ingredients before fudge totally candies.

STEP 10: POUR, SCORE, AND STORE when cool in airtight container in refrigerator or at room temperature.

YIELD: 1 POUND. Recipe easily doubles and can be frozen.

Creamy Marshmallow Goat's Milk Fudge

Because of the marshmallow in this fudge and all the seeding you're going to do, it doesn't need to be candied. However, it does have to be chilled so that the marshmallows will firm up and then kept re-frigerated so they don't soften again.

2 cups granulated white sugar

5 ounces evaporated goat's milk

16 large marshmallows

¼ teaspoon salt

1 cup (6 ounces) butterscotch or semisweet chocolate chips

4 tablespoons (½ stick) butter

1 teaspoon vanilla extract

Optional: *½ cup chopped nuts*

STEP 1: PREPARE: Prewarm thermometer; use 3-quart saucepan; butter upper sides of saucepan; measure all ingredients except chips, butter, vanilla, and optional nuts, and dump into saucepan. Grease and, if necessary, line an 8 × 10-inch pan. Freeze butter. Fill glass with ice cubes and water and sink half-inch full of water.

STEP 2: DISSOLVE sugar, stirring constantly with wooden spoon over low heat until marshmallows melt, gritty sounds cease, and spoon glides smoothly over bottom of pan. Increase heat to medium and bring to a boil.

STEP 3: BOIL after washing down any crystals that may have formed with pastry brush dipped in hot water from thermometer bath, using as little water as possible. Introduce prewarmed thermometer. Reduce heat while retaining boil. Stir no more than necessary.

STEP 4: TEST in ice-cold water when mixture thickens and bubbles become noisy—about 5 minutes after bubbles have covered entire surface of pan. Ball, formed in ice water, should hold its shape until heat from your hand begins to flatten it and should be al dente—slightly chewy. Approximately 234°F to 240°F (112°C to 115.5°C). Return thermometer to its hot-water bath to soak clean.

STEP 5: SEED with chips, butter, vanilla, and optional nuts.

STEP 6: STIR immediately and until chips are completely melted.

STEP 7: SPREAD mixture into pan.

STEP 8: CHILL until firm. Keep refrigerated until ready to serve.

YIELD: 1 POUND. Recipe is not easily doubled; freezing changes the texture.

SEVEN

Quick 'n' Easies

MICROWAVE MASTER RECIPE
    DOUBLE-CHIP MICROWAVE FUDGE
    BUTTERSCOTCHY MICROWAVE FUDGE

EVEN QUICKER MICROWAVE FUDGE
    CHOCOLATE-MINT EVEN QUICKER MICROWAVE FUDGE
    ROCKY ROAD EVEN QUICKER MICROWAVE FUDGE
    PEANUT CUPS EVEN QUICKER MICROWAVE FUDGE
    MULTICOLORED EVEN QUICKER MICROWAVE FUDGE
    CHOP-CHOP CHIP-CHIP EVEN QUICKER MICROWAVE FUDGE

FREEZER FROSTING FUDGE
    BANANA FREEZER FROSTING FUDGE
    CANDY CANE FREEZER FROSTING FUDGE
    CHERRY-VANILLA FREEZER FROSTING FUDGE
    COCONUT CREAM FREEZER FROSTING FUDGE

GOOBIES FREEZER FROSTING FUDGE
LEMON FREEZER FROSTING FUDGE
MELT-IN-YOUR-MOUTH FREEZER FROSTING FUDGE
ORANGE FREEZER FROSTING FUDGE
SANDWICH FREEZER FROSTING FUDGE
CHOCOLATE-CHOCOLATE FREEZER FROSTING FUDGE
CHOCOLATE-MALT FREEZER FROSTING FUDGE
CHOCOLATE MARSHMALLOW FREEZER FROSTING FUDGE
CHOCOLATE-ORANGE FREEZER FROSTING FUDGE
CHOCOLATE–PEANUT BUTTER FREEZER FROSTING FUDGE
GRASSHOPPER FREEZER FROSTING FUDGE
KAHLÚA FREEZER FROSTING FUDGE
DOUBLE-COCONUT-PECAN FREEZER FROSTING FUDGE
CHOCOLATE COCONUT-PECAN FREEZER FROSTING FUDGE
STRAWBERRY-BANANA FREEZER FROSTING FUDGE
LEMON ICE TEA FREEZER FROSTING FUDGE

PUDDING FUDGE

FRENCH VANILLA PUDDING FUDGE
BANANA CREAM PUDDING FUDGE
COCONUT CREAM PUDDING FUDGE
PISTACHIO PUDDING FUDGE
LEMON PUDDING FUDGE
MILK CHOCOLATE PUDDING FUDGE
BUTTERSCOTCH PUDDING FUDGE
VANILLA PUDDING FUDGE

THREE-LAYER THREE-MINUTE PERFECTION

QUICK POTATO CANDY FUDGE

QUICK PEANUT BUTTER POTATO CANDY FUDGE
QUICK COCONUT POTATO CANDY FUDGE
QUICK MOCHA POTATO CANDY FUDGE
QUICK CHOCOLATE POTATO CANDY FUDGE
QUICK PEANUT BUTTER PINWHEEL POTATO CANDY FUDGE

WHOLESOME PEANUT CANDY

NO-COOK CREAM CHEESE FUDGE

BUTTERSCOTCH NO-COOK CREAM CHEESE FUDGE
BUTTER-RUM NUTTY NO-COOK CREAM CHEESE FUDGE

COCONUT NO-COOK CREAM CHEESE FUDGE
MAPLE SYRUP NO-COOK CREAM CHEESE FUDGE
PEANUT BUTTER NO-COOK CREAM CHEESE FUDGE

If you've a craving for a homemade sweet but aren't in the mood to preside over the traditional fudge pot, these recipes are for you. Many use ingredients you already have on the shelf, many offer you the opportunity to use your creativity, many are ideal for keeping young children amused on a rainy day. And although they are not quite so good as traditional cooked fudge, all offer you something different in the way of a sweet. Among others, there's Freezer Frosting Fudge, Pudding Fudge, No-Cook Cream Cheese Fudge, Quick Potato Candy Fudge, plus, of course, that perennial favorite in two versions: fast and faster microwave fudge.

The beauty of microwaved candy is that it does not need to be stirred during the early stages of cooking, nor frequently thereafter. However, unless you have a microwave-safe thermometer that registers up to 240°F to 250°F (115.5°C to 121°C), getting the candy to the right stage at the right time can be a little tricky. Even if you have an instant, probe-type micro-thermometer, you need to put it in as soon as you open the oven door, otherwise the reading will be inaccurate. Again, our ice-cold-water test comes to the rescue.

The following master recipe can be used to create various flavors of fudge. Just remember, sugar attracts microwave energy, so the mixtures boil high. Therefore, be absolutely, positively sure to *thoroughly* butter the interior of the container/casserole you use.

To convert another recipe to microwave use, make sure you have a large enough container . . . and an oven large enough to hold it. Generally speaking, the microwave-proof container should be one quart larger than the saucepan called for. However, if your casserole and/or oven are too small, it's easy to make half or three-quarters of a microwave recipe. If you do cut back on a recipe, use 1 tablespoon corn syrup for every cup of granulated white sugar to control the graining. Also, as cream, particularly heavy cream, curdles easily in microwave ovens, do not cook recipes containing cream on HIGH

(100%). Just cut back the power to MEDIUM (50%) and double the cooking time. *Or*, rather than cutting back on cooking power, substitute milk for the cream (see page 40) and add extra butter when you seed. Also, before you convert a recipe, you really ought to try it the regular way so that you know what to look for.

Microwave Master Recipe

2 tablespoons (¼ stick) butter

2 cups granulated white sugar

1 cup milk

2 squares (2 ounces) unsweetened chocolate

2 tablespoons light corn syrup

Pinch (⅛ teaspoon) of salt

1 teaspoon vanilla extract

Optional: ½ cup chopped nuts

STEP 1: BUTTER thoroughly the interior of a 3-quart micro-proof casserole, preferably see-through, with a cover (improvise with an upside-down micro-proof pie plate). Grease and, if necessary, line a 5 × 10-inch pan. Freeze butter. Fill glass with ice cubes and water and sink half-inch full of water.

STEP 2: MEASURE all other ingredients but vanilla and optional nuts, and dump in casserole. Cover casserole.

STEP 3: MICROWAVE on HIGH (100%) for 5 minutes.

STEP 4: STIR to melt chocolate.

STEP 5: MICROWAVE, uncovered for 10 minutes on HIGH (100%), stopping and stirring twice: after 4 minutes, after 7 minutes, and again when 10 minutes are up. If mixture is runny, continue to microwave in 60-second increments until mixture thickens.

STEP 6: TEST in ice-cold water when mixture thickens. Ball, formed in ice water, should hold its shape until heat from your hand begins to flatten it and should be al dente—slightly chewy. Approximately 234°F to 240°F (112°C to 115.5°C).

STEP 7: SEED by adding, without stirring, vanilla and frozen butter. Then allow to cool for 10 minutes.

STEP 8: PLACE in sink.

STEP 9: STIR when lukewarm and "skin" forms on top (110°F [43.5°C]). Stir fudge thoroughly but not vigorously by hand—it turns so quickly there's no need to dirty your mixer or food processor. Pause frequently to allow fudge to react.

STEP 10: WATCH for fudge to thicken, lose its sheen, become lighter in color or streaked with lighter shades, give off some heat, suddenly stiffen. If mixing by hand, fudge will "snap" with each stroke.

STEP 11: ADD any optional ingredients before fudge totally candies.

STEP 12: POUR, SCORE, AND STORE when cool in airtight container in refrigerator or at room temperature.

YIELD: 1 POUND. Recipe is easily doubled if you have large enough casserole and oven and can be frozen.

VARIATIONS

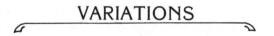

Double-Chip Microwave Fudge

In step 1, reduce butter to 1 tablespoon. In step 2, use ½ cup (3 ounces) semisweet chocolate in place of unsweetened chocolate. In step 11, stir in ½ cup (3 ounces) milk chocolate chips to get a dark fudge with nuggets of light chocolate.

For a light fudge with dark nuggets, in step 1, premelt the milk chocolate chips for 1 minute on HIGH (100%), stir, microwave another 30 seconds, then add other ingredients and continue with the recipe. In step 11, add ½ cup (3 ounces) semisweet chocolate chips.

Butterscotchy Microwave Fudge

Follow Master Recipe but in step 1, reduce butter to 1 tablespoon and add 1 cup (6 ounces) butterscotch chips in step 11.

Even Quicker Microwave Fudge

Understand that to purists, these are not truly fudges. To children, they sure taste like fudge. But as the microwave giveth quick cooking, so doth the refrigerator taketh its time chilling the batch. You win a little, you lose a little. On the other hand, clean-up is easy—you can even use the same quart container to make consecutive batches if you do as the slab fudge-makers do: begin with light flavors and go to dark.

1¼ cups (8 ounces) unsweetened chocolate or butterscotch chips

7 ounces (half of 14-ounce can) condensed sweetened milk

1 tablespoon butter, cold

1½ teaspoons vanilla extract

Optional: *½ cup chopped nuts*

STEP 1: MICROWAVE chips in 1-quart glass measuring cup for 1 minute on HIGH (100%), stir, microwave another 30 seconds, stir again (depending on chip used, you may need to microwave another 30 seconds or so).

STEP 2: BLEND in condensed milk.

STEP 3: TOP with butter, cut in two or three pieces to facilitate melting.

STEP 4: MICROWAVE on HIGH (100%) another 45 seconds or until butter melts. Add vanilla and nuts, stirring only until well mixed.

STEP 5: POUR into a greased 5 × 10-inch disposable pan or wax paper–lined small loaf pan.

STEP 6: DON'T spread with spatula if you can avoid it; the less you touch the surface after pouring, the shinier the fudge will look.

STEP 7: CHILL in refrigerator for at least 2 hours before cutting. Store in refrigerator.

YIELD: 1 POUND. Can be frozen and doubled if microwave is large enough.

VARIATIONS

Chocolate-Mint Even Quicker Microwave Fudge

Use 10-ounce package of chocolate-mint chips and cut vanilla back to 1 teaspoon. Makes a particularly good Rocky Road fudge if poured over ¾ to 1 cup of mini-marshmallows.

Rocky Road Even Quicker Microwave Fudge

After adding vanilla in step 4, fill the quart measuring cup almost full of mini-marshmallows (1 to 1½ cups) and fold in before pouring in step 5.

Peanut Cups Even Quicker Microwave Fudge

Make fudge with semisweet chocolate chips, then, in step 4, add ½ cup peanut butter chips and 1 teaspoon vanilla; *or* add vanilla, then swirl in ½ to ¾ cup creamy peanut butter. Pour immediately.

Multicolored Even Quicker Microwave Fudge

Candy coating wafers or discs are available in candy supply stores and some supermarkets in an array of colors: pink, blue, red, yellow, orange, green, orchid—but only one flavor, which I call fatty vanilla and the rest of the world calls "white chocolate." In step 1, use 1 cup discs, microwave on LOW (30%) for 30 seconds, stir, repeat, and continue repeating until melted. Stir in scant ½ can condensed sweetened milk, top with 1 tablespoon butter, melt on HIGH (100%) for 30 seconds, add 1 teaspoon or more extract (orange, pistachio, cherry, and so on, but use artificial vanillin for white fudge). In step 4, you can add ½ cup chopped nuts or candied fruit (I use the end of packages of other flavors of chips and morsels, all jumbled together).

Chop-Chop Chip-Chip Even Quicker Microwave Fudge

In separate pint containers, microwave on HIGH (100%) 1 cup (6 ounces) each butterscotch and semisweet chocolate chips. Pour both over 1 large can (5 ounces) chow mein noodles. If you're ambidextrous and can pour two-handed, children are really impressed. Mix quickly and not too thoroughly. Pour or scoop into a pan and cool at room temperature or, if you're impatient, in the refrigerator.

Freezer Frosting Fudge

Quick to prepare, this fudge must be chilled for several hours—I not only chill it in the freezer, I store the fudge there since it won't freeze solid. Straight from the freezer, it makes for a very refreshing candy with an interesting taste sensation: cold yet creamy.

> 1 cup confectioners' sugar, lump-free
>
> 1 teaspoon cream or milk, cold
>
> 1 container ready-made creamy (preferably deluxe) frosting
>
> ½ to 1 teaspoon extract in complementary flavor

STEP 1: MOOSH confectioners' sugar to make sure it's lump-free. (To moosh: stir the sugar well, scoop out a cup, pour into a sealable plastic bag, and use your hands or a rolling pin to break up any lumps.) Or sift it.

STEP 2: STIR sugar, milk, and frosting together, and add the flavoring of your choice. Real juice or premelted chocolate or peanut butter may require additional confectioners' sugar to get the right, thick consistency. Pour and place in freezer.

YIELD: 1 POUND. Although Freezer Frosting Fudge will not freeze solid, it can be stored in the freezer up to four months without loss of quality.

VARIATIONS

Frostings are available in more than ten flavors. So the sky's the limit when it comes to creating Freezer Frosting Fudge.

With vanilla, cream cheese, or sour cream frosting:
Banana Freezer Frosting Fudge

Add 1 teaspoon banana extract. If you wish, you can add yellow food coloring. I don't—I think it's more interesting to get that banana taste in a white fudge.

Candy Cane Freezer Frosting Fudge

Use peppermint extract to taste. Streak, if desired, with 4 to 5 drops red food coloring, or crush some real peppermints—good use for tired candy canes.

Cherry-Vanilla Freezer Frosting Fudge

Using vanilla frosting mix, add 24 chopped, *well-drained* maraschino cherries (red and/or green), and/or chopped walnuts. If you have some maraschino liqueur, add ½ teaspoon. For sour cream or cream cheese frosting, add ½ teaspoon or more vanilla extract.

Coconut Cream Freezer Frosting Fudge

Add ½ teaspoon coconut flavoring and ½ cup toasted coconut.

Goobies Freezer Frosting Fudge

Add ½ cup or more chocolate-covered peanuts.

Lemon Freezer Frosting Fudge

Use 1 teaspoon lemon extract plus ½ to 1 tablespoon grated zest (optional) and 3 to 4 drops yellow food coloring.

Melt-in-Your-Mouth Freezer Frosting Fudge

Add ½ to 1 cup M&M's.

Orange Freezer Frosting Fudge

Use orange juice to taste, beginning with a tablespoon, *or* use 1 teaspoon orange extract.

Sandwich Freezer Frosting Fudge

Chop 5 or 6 chocolate sandwich cookies into *large* pieces and mix in. Strengthen vanilla taste by adding ½ teaspoon extract.

With plain, dark Dutch, milk, or chocolate chip frosting:

Chocolate-Chocolate Freezer Frosting Fudge

To begin with, you may find that most chocolate frostings are simply not chocolatey enough . . . at least not for fudge. Add 2 tablespoons cocoa *or* 1 packet premelted baking chocolate, *or* zap ¼ cup (1½ ounces) chocolate chips in the microwave on HIGH (100%)—approximately 15 seconds for milk chocolate, 30 seconds for semisweet. (You just want to soften them.) Then add chips to frosting. Be careful not to get chocolate too hot, or it will keep fudge from hardening for a long time.

Chocolate-Malt Freezer Frosting Fudge

Add up to 3 tablespoons malted milk mix to taste.

Chocolate Marshmallow Freezer Frosting Fudge

Stir in ½ cup of mini-marshmallows.

Chocolate-Orange Freezer Frosting Fudge

Add ½ teaspoon orange flavoring, *or* use 1 teaspoon orange-based liqueur (Cointreau or Grand Marnier).

Chocolate–Peanut Butter Freezer Frosting Fudge

Add ⅓ cup creamy peanut butter, stirring in completely or marbleizing, *or* use ½ cup peanut butter chips.

Grasshopper Freezer Frosting Fudge

Add ½ teaspoon peppermint flavoring *or* 1 teaspoon creme de menthe.

Kahlúa Freezer Frosting Fudge

Use 1 to 2 teaspoons extra-strong coffee (if you like crunch in your fudge, add same amount of instant without dissolving), *or* add 1 ounce Kahlúa, or to taste.

With fruit-flavored frostings, coconut-pecan, lemon, and strawberry:

Double-Coconut-Pecan Freezer Frosting Fudge

Add ½ cup more coconut, and ½ cup chopped pecans.

Chocolate Coconut-Pecan Freezer Frosting Fudge

Add ½ cup chocolate chips. For a crunchier fudge, use as is, or melt in microwave on HIGH (100%) for 90 seconds, stirring after every 30 seconds.

Strawberry-Banana Freezer Frosting Fudge

Add ½ teaspoon or more banana extract.

Lemon Iced Tea Freezer Frosting Fudge

Dissolve 1 teaspoon instant iced tea mix in cream and microwave for a few seconds on DEFROST (30%), then chill before adding to lemon frosting.

Pudding Fudge

This is a no-cook fudge that you can really get your hands into . . . literally. The persnickety might think it's a bit messy but not the kids—they'll love it.

2 large egg whites, slightly beaten

1 tablespoon milk

3½-ounce package instant pudding and pie filling mix

About 2 cups confectioners' sugar, mooshed until semi-lump-free

Decorations, nuts, chips, whatever your imagination desires

STEP 1: BUTTER or grease a 5 × 10-inch pan.

STEP 2: BEAT egg whites until frothy but not stiff.

STEP 3: ADD milk and pudding mix and mix well.

STEP 4: DUMP in 1½ cups of sugar and work in.

STEP 5: KNEAD on a sugared board, using "the baker's friend," either your right or left hand. It's a little awkward, but do try to keep one hand clean to sprinkle more sugar as needed. The object is to work in as little as necessary of the remaining ½ cup (not all of it, so fudge doesn't get too sweet). Keep kneading until it forms a ball.

STEP 6: WORK in any optional ingredients.

STEP 7: FOLD in on itself as if a piece of bread dough so that no sugar shows. Then pat into pan.

STEP 8: CHILL for 15 minutes and it's ready to go.

YIELD: 1 POUND. Can freeze but not for more than a month.

VARIATIONS

French Vanilla Pudding Fudge

Use vanilla-flavored instant pudding mix. It's yellow-ly lovely with multicolored nonpareils sprinkled on top.

Banana Cream Pudding Fudge

Use banana-flavored instant pudding mix. Chill and coat with softened chocolate chips for a Boston Banana Cream Fudge Pie.

Coconut Cream Pudding Fudge

Accentuate the coconut flavor of coconut instant pudding mix by adding ½ cup shredded and toasted coconut in step 6.

Pistachio Pudding Fudge

Heighten the flavor of pistachio instant pudding mix by adding ½ teaspoon pistachio extract (optional) and ½ cup coarsely chopped pistachio nuts in step 6.

Lemon Pudding Fudge

You can do so many things with lemon instant pudding mix: In step 6, add ½ cup seedless raisins, chopped glacé pineapple, or chopped dates and figs, or really intensify the flavor by adding ½ cup chopped citron.

Milk Chocolate Pudding Fudge

In step 6, add ½ cup (3 ounces) semisweet chocolate chips or vanilla yogurt chips, or give milk chocolate instant pudding mix a double whammy with ½ cup (3 ounces) milk chocolate chips.

Butterscotch Pudding Fudge

Give butterscotch instant pudding mix some crunch with more butterscotch chips, or make it sm-o-o-oth with mini-marshmallows. Some chopped nuts wouldn't hurt, either, nor would salted cocktail nuts or even plain peanuts.

Vanilla Pudding Fudge

Make French Vanilla Pudding Fudge, and instead of patting it out into a pan, use it to stuff dates or dried apricots. Or make pecan sandwiches, using ½ teaspoon of fudge as filling between pecan halves.

Three-Layer Three-Minute Perfection

Three layers, three ingredients, total cooking time three minutes! The end result, a candy lover's dream.

½ cup nuts to match candy bars, or *chopped or whole walnuts or unsalted peanuts*

2 cups mini-marshmallows

One 16-ounce package, snack-size chocolate candy bars, your choice (I like Almond Joys)

STEP 1: BUTTER an 8 × 8-inch baking pan.

STEP 2: SPREAD nuts in bottom, marshmallows on top.

STEP 3: UNWRAP snack-size candy bars and place in a single layer in glass pie plate.

STEP 4: MICROWAVE 1½ to 2 minutes on HIGH (100%), stir briefly.

STEP 5: POUR over marshmallow-nut layers. Fold together until candy blends into mixture. Do not worry if fudge does not look well combined.

STEP 6: COOL, then cut into pieces. Depending on candy bar used, it will be creamy or chewy.

YIELD: 1 POUND. Can be frozen. I do not recommend doubling. If you want a larger quantity, do several batches.

Quick Potato Candy Fudge

This very creamy fudge is good the first day but better the second since it loses all the potato taste and becomes pure peanutty. This fudge has a long and noble history dating back, supposedly, to frontier times. Its history is hard to document since, like gravy, there seemed no need for a formal recipe. One simply combined leftover potatoes with whatever was on hand. However, it finally made the recipe books in the 1907 edition of *Woman's Favorite Cookbook*. There it was called simply "potato candy."

Historically, Potato Candy Fudge waxes and wanes in popularity depending on famines and world wars. Whenever butter, sugar, and/or chocolate are scarce, mothers rediscover potato fudge. You can use leftover potatoes and mash them, or boil 1 large, real, honest-to-goodness potato and mash it. But for a quickie, use instant potato flakes.

Quick Peanut Butter Potato Candy Fudge

2 servings instant mashed potatoes (equals ½ cup leftover mashed potato or 1 large baked potato)

¼ teaspoon salt

⅔ cup creamy peanut butter

2¼ cups (1 pound) confectioners' sugar (or more depending on heat and humidity)

Optional: ½ cup salted peanuts

STEP 1: PREPARE potato. If using instant potatoes, use as little milk and water (or all milk or all water) as necessary to bind potatoes together and begin to fluff them.

STEP 2: BEAT in salt and peanut butter, beating until well incorporated, using whisk or portable mixer on low.

STEP 3: ADD unsifted confectioners' sugar in ½-cup increments, beating constantly. Continue beating until mixture is thick and forms very distinctive ribbons in bowl.

STEP 4: PAT into buttered 5 × 9-inch pan, garnish with salted peanuts, if desired. Chill before cutting. Fudge mellows with age, tasting more peanutty the second day.

YIELD: 1 POUND. Do not double—it's too hard to incorporate sugar. Does not freeze well.

VARIATIONS

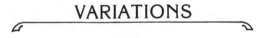

Whatever variations you decide on, choose *strong* flavors that will overwhelm the potatoes in the beginning and then mellow as time goes on. Quantities given are based on using instant potato flakes.

Quick Coconut Potato Candy Fudge

Decrease instant mashed potatoes to ½ cup. Use piña colada mix or cream of coconut for the water-milk called for on the instant potato package. Add 1 cup shredded and/or toasted coconut instead of peanut butter.

Quick Mocha Potato Candy Fudge

Make the instant potatoes with strong black coffee. Instead of peanut butter, add chocolate chips.

Quick Chocolate Potato Candy Fudge

Instead of peanut butter, add 3 squares (3 ounces) melted unsweetened chocolate.

Quick Peanut Butter Pinwheel Potato Candy Fudge

Instead of mixing peanut butter with the mashed potatoes, put it to one side and be sure it's at room temperature. Combine mashed potatoes, salt, confectioners' sugar, and add 1 teaspoon vanilla. Mix well and spread into a rectangle on waxed paper or plastic wrap. Spread with peanut butter. Roll as for jelly roll, beginning at long side of rectangle. (*Optional:* Press chopped salted peanuts over the roll.) Wrap tightly and chill for 3 hours. You may wish to dust outside of roll with confectioners' sugar before cutting into ¼-inch slices.

YIELD: 2 DOZEN SLICES.

Wholesome Peanut Candy

This recipe came my way via a very health-conscious young mother, who patronizes the local health-food store. She insists that you use nonhydrogenated peanut butter; I have used supermarket brands satisfactorily. You need a food processor for this.

½ cup creamy peanut butter
½ cup honey (light or golden)

1 cup powdered nonfat milk

1 teaspoon vanilla extract

Optional (*quantities approximate*):
   ½ cup sesame seeds
   ½ cup granola
   1 cup rice cereal
   ½ cup finely chopped nuts

STEP 1: CREAM peanut butter and honey in food processor equipped with a metal blade.

STEP 2: POUR in nonfat milk gradually. Mixture will become granular looking. Stop and scrape down sides at least once during processing.

STEP 3: ADD vanilla and process until candy suddenly forms a ball.

STEP 4: PLACE ball in center, lengthwise, of a 2-foot-long piece of wax paper or plastic wrap. Work candy into long, thin roll. The more you handle it, the easier it will be, if you wish, to coat the outside with seeds, nuts, or cereal.

STEP 5: COAT: Spread topping lengthwise along top third of the paper. Using the paper, flip the peanut roll away from you and on top of the coating. Press down to firmly coat that side. Open paper and spread balance of topping on third of the paper closest to you. Now roll candy onto that. Wrap with another piece of plastic wrap or wax paper.

STEP 6: CHILL before cutting into pieces.

YIELD: 1½ TO 2 POUNDS. Keeps well in the refrigerator but does not freeze well.

No-Cook Cream Cheese Fudge

This is the most famous of all the "no-cook" fudges and enjoyed quite a vogue a few years ago. No self-respecting fudge book would exclude it. It is one of the few "fad" fudges that is worthy of your attention.

It is quick, easy, and delicious, but its texture is different from that of a cooked fudge.

Take advantage of its ease of preparation and go whole hog, utilizing every shortcut you can. Use packets of premelted baking chocolate. Microwave chips. If you use a food processor, you don't have to worry about lumps in the confectioners' sugar, but you can only do 1-pound batches at a time. If you're into quantity no-cook fudge-making, be sure to use an electric mixer (by hand is impossible) and "moosh" your sugar first to make sure it's lump-free.

2 squares (2 ounces) unsweetened baking chocolate, or 2 packets premelted chocolate

2 cups stirred and scooped confectioners' sugar

4 ounces (half of 8-ounce package) cream cheese, room temperature

1 tablespoon milk, half-and-half, or cream

1 teaspoon vanilla extract

Optional:

   ½ cup nuts

   1 cup coconut

   1 cup another flavor chips

STEP 1: PREPARE chocolate. If using packets, warm them for a few minutes in bowl of hot tap water. To melt chocolate in microwave, zap on MEDIUM (50%) for 90 seconds, stirring every 30 seconds. Butter or spray 5 × 10-inch disposable pan.

STEP 2: STIR sugar and place in container of food processor with metal blade.

STEP 3: ADD cream cheese and softened baking chocolate.

STEP 4: PROCESS until lumpy and granular. Scrape down sides.

STEP 5: ADD milk and pulse until mixture is smooth and creamy.

STEP 6: STIR in extract and optional(s).

STEP 7: POUR into pan.

STEP 8: CHILL several hours before cutting.

   YIELD: 1 POUND. Can freeze.

VARIATIONS

Butterscotch No-Cook Cream Cheese Fudge

Use 1 cup (6 ounces) butterscotch chips. Microwave on HIGH (100%) 60 seconds, stir, microwave another 30 seconds, then add to sugar/cream cheese in step 3.

Butter-Rum Nutty No-Cook Cream Cheese Fudge

Instead of vanilla extract, use 1½ teaspoons rum and ¾ cup pecans.

Coconut No-Cook Cream Cheese Fudge

In place of chocolate, use "white baking pieces" or white candy coating, but microwave on medium-low (DEFROST—30%) or low for 90 seconds, stirring every 30 seconds until soft and liquid. Add to sugar and cream cheese in food processor in step 3. Increase liquid to 1½ tablespoons milk in step 5, or use 2 tablespoons cream of coconut or ⅔ teaspoon coconut oil flavoring in step 6, along with 1 to 1½ cups shredded coconut.

Maple Syrup No-Cook Cream Cheese Fudge

Use one 3-ounce package cream cheese; reduce confectioners' sugar to 1½ cups; eliminate chocolate, milk, and vanilla; add ½ cup maple syrup in step 5. Goes well with whole or chopped pecans.

Peanut Butter No-Cook Cream Cheese Fudge

Use one 3-ounce package cream cheese. Replace chocolate with either ⅓ cup creamy peanut butter or 1 cup (6 ounces) peanut butter chips, microwaved to melt. Add salted peanuts if desired.

EIGHT

Fondantly Speaking

ADULT PLAY DOUGH: BASIC FONDANTS
CLASSIC FONDANT
READY-TO-USE FONDANT
FONDANT FOR FUDGE
FONDANT FLAVORINGS
    EXOTIC
    GRASSHOPPERS
    ROYAL RASPBERRY
    CRUNCHY COFFEE
    GRAND GRAND MARNIER
    SCOTCHIES
WORKING FONDANT
    CHERRY-VANILLA CHERRY CORDIALS
    ALL-CHOCOLATE CHERRY CORDIALS
    CORDIAL CHERRIES
    THE BENNINGS' FAVORITE FONDANT

CANDYING FONDANTS
   SIMPLE SYRUP METHOD
   JELL-O BRAND GELATIN METHOD

HOMEMADE BUTTER CREAMS

UNCOOKED FONDANT ITALIANO

RIGI PEAKS

"**F**ondant?" you may ask. "What's fondant, and why would it be in a book on fudge?" Fondant tastes bland, the epitome of sugar-sweet. To the bite, it is creamy but swiftly dissolving. It is a versatile, amenable candy, gladly taking on other forms, shapes, and tastes to suit our preference. It serves as the center for chocolate creams, as the coating for petit fours and bonbons, as the flowers and frosting adorning a wedding cake. The first and oldest of the "candied" sweets—those using sugar syrup, cooked to the ball, then forced to grain under controlled conditions—it has earned a chapter for itself in any book on candy. But particularly so in a book on fudge. For when the technique of making fondant was married, rather spontaneously, to the ingredients of caramel, the offspring was fudge!

Until recently, confectioners considered fondant the most important yet most difficult sweet to master. The invention of the food processor has changed all that. Using a food processor, it can take you less time to make fondant from start to finish than to make the trip to a store to buy it ready-made. (Don't try it with an electric mixer; you might just burn out the motor. However, you can always do it the classic way, with a scraper or spatula and good strong arm.)

Whichever way you make it, you're in for an awe-inspiring sight. Unlike fudge, which may dawdle along before changing or pull a fastie, fondant is predictably wondrous to watch. I, for one, never tire of seeing the miraculous transformation of a sugar-water syrup from clear to cloudy to pure white right before my eyes. Additionally, as you'll discover when you read on, one basic fondant recipe (I give three) can be doctored to yield several different looking and tasting candies.

Speaking of doctoring fondant, it is also the "fudge doctor," the ultimate failure-fixer of all time. Simply remelt your botched fudge batch, bring back up to the soft-ball stage, and introduce the candy version of Elmer's Glue—fondant. If that sounds unappetizing, let me assure you, any fudge, even failed fudge, tastes best when made with fondant.

The commercial world, which can't afford failure, uses other products, such as glucose or corn syrup, chemically inverted sugar or real honey, and sweetened condensed whipping cream, to prevent graininess and premature candying. But almost all factory fudges are made with fondant, the universal fudge seed. And when fondant is combined with a frappe (the commercial term for marshmallow creme), there occur the chemical reactions that force fudge to do what you want: candy.

The following rules will make fondant preparation much less of a hassle and assure success not just with fondants, but frequently with fudge also.

1. Avoid stirring or disturbing candy that is meant to be clear. You can stir before it boils, but not afterward. Sugar can be boiled all the way up to the crack and remain clear if not stirred. If, however, it is disturbed either by dipping nuts into it or stirring, it will become cloudy and may go back to sugar.

2. Introduce an acidic ingredient, such as vinegar or some other fruit acid (lemon juice or even cream of tartar), which will act as a lubricant, prevent clouding, and allow forceful handling.

3. Never, when pouring out boiled candy, scrape your kettle or pan into the batch or allow any of the scrapings to fall into it.

4. Always use a thick enameled or, preferably, a heavy copper kettle to boil the sugar.

5. Use the best and purest granulated sugar you can get. If it has formed hard lumps, crush them thoroughly before using the sugar. Do this with a heavy rolling pin, or mix it with the water for the batch and set aside to soften.

6. To retard or prevent granulation, use cream of tartar in clear or pulled candy to acidulate or grease it.

7. Never allow crystals to remain on the side of the pan; keep them wiped off with a wet cloth, damp sponge, or wet pastry brush.

8. Never shake or move the kettle while syrup is boiling or the batch may grain.

9. Prepare fondant a day ahead of your fudge cooking or before you proceed with other candies as it needs time to mellow and ripen.

10. Always have everything ready before beginning a batch. You'll need 1- to 2-quart saucepans (smaller than for fudge), tight-fitting lid for pan, wax paper for making that lid fit even tighter, pot holders for handling that lid.

11. To make fondant the classic way, you'll need a candy scraper or a stiff, wide putty knife and a shiny working surface that won't absorb heat and hold it in. The surface must be nonporous so it doesn't absorb candy. Use jelly-roll pans or cookie sheets for thick liquids (those cooked to crack or beyond).

12. If fondant grains from being boiled too long, add water and boil again.

13. Just as you use only the best-quality granulated sugar for boiling, use only the best confectioners' sugar for kneading.

14. Cool by setting in a cool, dry place—*not* a refrigerator.

Adult Play Dough: Basic Fondants

All fondants are not alike. A slight change in ingredients yields a different type of fondant. But all fondants are made the same way (see Basic Fondant Instructions, page 162).

Classic Fondant

A firm fondant that needs to be remelted before using. Remember to stir constantly while remelting, otherwise fondant will return to syrup.

> *2 cups granulated white sugar*
> *½ cup water*
> *Pinch (⅛ teaspoon) of cream of tartar*

YIELD: 2 CUPS, OR 1⅔ POUNDS.

Ready-to-Use Fondant

A tender fondant that can be used to make most candies without the need to remelt it.

> 2 cups granulated white sugar
> 2 tablespoons light corn syrup
> ½ cup water

YIELD: 2 CUPS, OR 1⅔ POUNDS. (Halve recipe if using a food processor.)

Fondant for Fudge

This can't-fail fondant with the taste of honey needs little additional flavoring. It's the one to use to make fudge crystallize without beating your arms to death. Best made by food processor.

> 1 well-rounded cup granulated white sugar
> 2 tablespoons light corn syrup
> 1 generous tablespoon of honey
> ¼ cup water

YIELD: 1 CUP, OR ¾ POUND.

BASIC FONDANT INSTRUCTIONS

They should seem familiar to you, as this is much the same method used for fudge.

STEP 1: PREPARE: Prewarm thermometer; and decide on your work surface, a 1½ × 2-foot cookie sheet, marble slab, Formica countertop, even roasting pan. Get out food processor. Fill glass with ice cubes and water and sink 1 to 2 inches full of cold water. Place all ingredients in heavy 1½-quart pan that has a tight-fitting lid.

STEP 2: DISSOLVE sugar, stirring constantly with a wooden spoon over low heat. Liquid will become clear instead of opaque, gritty sounds will cease, spoon will glide smoothly over bottom of pan. Increase heat to medium and bring to a boil.

STEP 3: BOIL: Cover pan with wax-paper square and lid, steam 1 to 2 minutes to dissolve sugar crystals. (Listen to make sure pot doesn't boil over.) Remove lid. If crystals still cling to side, wash down with brush dipped in hot water from thermometer bath. If scum appears, skim it. Introduce prewarmed thermometer. Reduce heat while retaining boil *but do not stir.*

STEP 4: TEST in ice-cold water when mixture thickens and bubbles become noisy. Ball, formed in ice water, should hold its shape until heat from your hand begins to flatten it and should be al dente—slightly chewy. Approximately 234°F to 240°F (112°C to 115.5°C).

STEP 5: REMOVE FROM HEAT without undue splashing and return thermometer to its water bath to soak clean.

STEP 6: CREAM, using either classic or modern methods (see steps 6a and 6b).

STEP 6a: CREAM BY CLASSIC METHOD OF PREPARATION
   1. Sprinkle water over work surface.
   2. Pour syrup on surface but *don't scrape pan.* Sprinkle syrup with more cold water.
   3. Other than pushing syrup back into center to keep it from running over, let it rest until lukewarm (110°F [43.5°C]), a skin is formed on top, and a finger poked in it leaves a deep semipermanent depression.
   4. Work syrup with putty knife (food scraper or metal spatula or sturdy pancake turner will also work but not as well). Begin by pushing blade-full away from you and into center, flip fondant over, then spread it back toward you. It will take 15 to 20 minutes and you will develop muscles, but eventually the mass will turn thick and gooey and sugar-white! It may also turn rock-hard, but don't worry.
   5. Place in 1½- to 2-quart casserole, top with damp towel, and

cover with lid. Let rest several hours or overnight in cool place. *Do not put in refrigerator unless kitchen is sweat bath.*

STEP 6b: CREAM BY MODERN METHOD OF PREPARATION

1. Pour syrup into food processor bowl equipped with metal blade. *Don't scrape pan.*

2. Place food processor bowl in kitchen sink with enough cold tap water in it to come up 1 inch around the bowl.

3. Let syrup rest until temperature drops to 100°F to 110°F (38°C to 43.5°C) (use instant-reading microwave probe thermometer to check if you have one—otherwise, a skin should have formed on the surface of the syrup). It is better to be too cool than too warm, but it must be lukewarm.

4. Wet a tea towel to wrap about the sides of the processor bowl.

5. Put processor top in place but remove pusher from feed tube so steam can escape. Process fondant by pulsing for approximately 2 minutes. Use 1-second pulse, 2-to-3-second pause, then repeat. (It should go from clear to cloudy or opaque and have thickened quite a bit.)

6. Remove lid (and clean if necessary) and dry it off. The bowl will have become extremely warm to the touch as a result of the heat released by the chemical change in the fondant.

7. You may need to rewet the tea towel and let fondant cool down again. Small batches will turn white almost before your eyes; with larger batches, you may need to process again for 2 minutes but wait 4 to 5 minutes to be sure fondant cools to lukewarm. Be sure to remove, clean, and dry lid while letting fondant cool. Repeat as needed until fondant turns pure white and very thick.

8. Pour into plastic resealable bag (I place bag in pint measuring cup or freezer container to hold it upright). Leave bag open until fondant is cool and has hardened. Then top with damp paper towel and seal. Let rest several hours or overnight in cool place. *Do not put in refrigerator unless kitchen is sweat bath.*

STEP 7: KNEAD, if necessary, for 10 to 15 minutes the next day through the bag to soften. Fondant made by food processor usually doesn't need to be kneaded. It remains soft and ready to be flavored.

STEP 8: STORE in tightly closed plastic bags in refrigerator or pat plastic wrap down on surface and store in covered container at room temperature. I have kept it for weeks on my kitchen counter with plastic wrap in place, or for months with a damp paper towel enclosed. It seems to live forever in the refrigerator.

TO CURE HARDENED FONDANT

If the bag is kept sealed, fondant will stay fairly soft for several weeks at room temperature. It won't spoil, so don't toss it away if it hardens rock-solid. Simply soften it by putting it in top of double boiler over hot (not boiling) water and adding Simple Sugar Syrup (see page 246) a tablespoonful at a time.

INTRODUCING FONDANT TO FUDGE

Although very few recipes in this book actually call for fondant, it greatly improves almost any of the basic recipes (except Summer Fudge). Use ½ cup fondant as a seed for every 2 to 2¼ cups of sugar called for in recipe.

When adding fondant to fudge for the purpose of seeding (getting the fudge to form the right-size—small, fine, almost microscopic—crystals), here are some things to remember:

1. The smoother-grained your fondant is, the smoother your fudge will be, too.

2. Fondant cannot be added when the fudge is too hot, otherwise fondant will simply melt instead of acting as a candy cement and binding crystals together. Instead, shock, let cool for 10 minutes or until temperature registers 165°F to 170°F (74°C to 76.5°C), then seed in step 6 with fondant. Add any flavorings after you stir in fondant.

3. Do not rely on fondant alone, without stirring, to achieve the smoothness you want.

4. Fondant must be made far enough in advance of fudge-making so that it will be cold when added to fudge; a hot fondant will cause spotty fudge.

HAVE A FONDANT FLAVORING PARTY!

It's fun to make lots of different flavors, especially if you have children around. On a rainy day, refrigerate fondants after making them so they don't absorb moisture and go soft.

If you are using oil-based flavorings, substitute 1 drop oil for ¼ teaspoon extract (¼ teaspoon oil per teaspoon of regular extract).

FLAVOR COLORING CHART

Fondants will have more appeal if they're appropriately colored—besides, this is the only way to tell some apart. Flavor to taste: For ½ cup fondant, add 2 drops oil or ½ teaspoon flavoring to begin with.

FONDANT FLAVORINGS	SUGGESTED COLOR	DROPS OF COLOR REQUIRED			
		GREEN	YELLOW	RED	BLUE
Anise	Black	1	3	3	1
Apricot	Light Orange		2	1	
Banana	Yellow		3		
Butterscotch/rum	Light Brown		1	4	3
Cherry	Red			3	
Cinnamon	Red			3	
Lemon	Yellow		3		1
Licorice	Black	1	3	3	1
Orange	Orange		3	1	
Peppermint	Marbled Red*			2	
Pistachio	Pale Yellow Green	3	1		
Raspberry	Blue Red			3	1
Spearmint	Pale Green	3			

*Swirl food coloring through the white fondant to get a marbled effect.

EXOTIC FLAVORINGS

All the following recipes are based on using ½ cup of soft or softened fondant. That way you can make two to four different candies from one batch.

YIELD PER RECIPE: AT LEAST 1 DOZEN CANDY CUPS, depending on the amount of optional ingredients used.

Grasshoppers

¼ teaspoon white creme de cacao
¼ teaspoon green creme de menthe
1 drop green food coloring

Royal Raspberry

2 teaspoons Chambord liqueur
Optional: 4 drops red food coloring
4 drops blue food coloring
Fresh raspberries, if available, to pour over

Crunchy Coffee

Make without heating the fondant or after melted fondant has cooled back down to room temperature. This way the instant coffee does not melt until it gets in your mouth.

2 teaspoons Tía Maria or Kahlúa
2 teaspoons instant coffee
Optional: 2 drops yellow food coloring

Grand Grand Marnier

2 teaspoons Grand Marnier

Small strawberries, whole but hulled, one placed in bottom of each candy cup

4 drops yellow or orange food coloring

Scotchies

4 teaspoons Drambuie

½ cup chopped nuts, sprinkled on top

WORKING FONDANT

Ingredients:

> 1 or more cups of Classic Fondant or Ready-to-Use Fondant (Fondant for Fudge has too much of a honey taste)
> heavy cream, chilled
> Simple Sugar Syrup (see page 246)
> confectioners' sugar, lump-free
> flavoring
> food coloring

Equipment needed:

> cutters
> cutting board
> molds (plastic)
> funnel (½-cup capacity or larger)
> wooden spoon with handle to fit securely in funnel tube
> paper candy cups or cases, 2-teaspoon capacity

CLASSIC METHOD OF WORKING FONDANT:
Use this method to coat fruit with fondant or make fondant centers for bonbons: Put fondant in saucepan over warm (not hot) water and

melt, adding 1 teaspoon heavy cream. Then add flavoring and optional coloring (see page 166). If fondant is very dried out, add a little Simple Sugar Syrup. If fondant is too thin, add 1 to 3 tablespoons (or more) confectioners' sugar to thicken it. Remelting fondant "cements" the sugar crystals together, and when the fondant cools down and hardens, it is creamy but firm.

SIMPLIFIED METHOD IF FONDANT IS SOFT AND FRESH:
Put fondant in bowl, add flavoring and optional coloring (see page 166), mash together with sturdy spoon. Flavorings, especially liqueurs or alcohol-based extracts, dilute fondant sufficiently. If fondant becomes soupy, you may need to add confectioners' sugar to thicken it.

MAKING CANDIES: Knead fondant on board. Add confectioners' sugar until it stops being sticky. Pat out to ½-inch thickness. Dip mini-cookie cutter in confectioners' sugar before cutting out shapes. Place in paper candy cups immediately. Add decorations if desired, such as candied violets, jimmies, silver balls, and so on. Resulting candy will not be as glossy as poured fondant.

To roll into balls around whole nuts or stuff dried fruit: Keeping hands well dusted with confectioners' sugar, knead fondant until it stops being sticky. Break off small pieces and work around nuts or insert in fruit. Place in paper candy cases. Fondant will not be as glossy as poured fondant so you may wish to finish balls by rolling in chopped nuts or coconut.

METHOD I RECOMMEND: Instead of kneading, pour fondant into paper candy cups using a funnel with a wooden spoon handle inserted in tube. To fill, stand funnel, spoon in place, in cup or glass. To pour, use spoon handle as plunger, pulling and pushing it, in and out, to regulate flow of fondant into cups. If poured candies are slow to harden, refrigerate.

Cherry-Vanilla Cherry Cordials

2 teaspoons vanilla "cream" liqueur mixed with ½ cup fondant

Ready-made, store-bought chocolate cups, or candy cups coated with melted chocolate (see page 246)

Maraschino cherries, squeezed gently to get rid of excess liquid, one placed in bottom of each candy cup

After filling cups with vanilla-flavored fondant let stand at least 24 hours (2 or 3 days is even better) while cherry liquefies center of fondant.

All-Chocolate Cherry Cordials

1 packed premelted baking chocolate (use as much as you like; about ½ packet suits me fine) mixed with ½ cup fondant plus 1 teaspoon white creme de cacao (optional)

Ready-made, store-bought chocolate cups, or candy cups coated with melted chocolate (see page 246)

Maraschino cherries, squeezed gently to get rid of excess liquid, one placed in bottom of each candy cup

After filling cups with chocolate fondant let stand at least 24 hours (2 or 3 days is even better) while cherry liquefies center of fondant.

Cordial Cherries

Use homemade brandied cherries (fresh, with stems, brandied in a mixture of 6 parts brandy to 1 part sugar. Place in jar with really good screw top, refrigerate, turning the jar over once a week. Use in three to four months). Or use fresh or maraschino cherries (with stems).

Be sure the cherry skin is absolutely dry, or the fondant will slide off. Use the classic method of working fondant (see page 168), diluting ½ cup fondant with 1 teaspoon kirschwasser or cherry juice instead of cream. If fondant is not fluid enough, add more kirsch or juice. Holding cherries by their stems, dip them into fondant, let them drip well, and then place one cherry in each candy cup. This same method can be used with strawberries, grapes, or other fruit, either fresh or brandied.

The Bennings' Favorite Fondant

Very simple, very elegant: Add 2 teaspoons Dutch vanilla liqueur per ½ cup soft fondant—liqueur will make it pourable; pour into chocolate-coated cases. If you're feeling really ritzy, place a whole cashew in each cup before pouring. Let sit until firm.

CANDYING FONDANTS

Simple Syrup Method

Bring Simple Sugar Syrup (see page 246) to a boil and allow it to cool partially, just until it won't melt fondant centers when they're dipped into it. Dip kneaded fondant balls into syrup. After candy dries, the syrup on the outside of the fondants will become unsaturated and crystallize, giving candy a crusty look.

Jell-O Brand Gelatin Method

Bring Simple Sugar Syrup (see page 246) to a boil, then cool to lukewarm. Add ½ (or to taste) of 3-ounce package Jell-O Brand Gelatin Dessert, which brings the syrup out of solution immediately. Dip kneaded fondant balls into the syrup. Let dry until crusty.

Homemade Butter Creams

There are fondants made with water and fondants made with milk, and then there are "cream" fondants. Rich? You know it. And when surrounded by chocolate, these are as good as any expensive butter creams you can buy! You can make different flavorings from a single batch, see step 7. By the way, this fondant can't be remelted.

> *2¼ cups (1 pound) granulated white sugar*
>
> *2 tablespoons light corn syrup*
>
> *¾ cup light (table) cream*
>
> *¼ teaspoon salt*
>
> *½ pound (2 sticks) butter, at room temperature*
>
> *1 cup (6 ounces) semisweet chocolate chips*
>
> Optional: *½ pound coarsely ground walnuts*
>
> *Individual candy cups*
>
> Optional flavorings: *see pages 166–168, suggestions for basic fondants*

STEP 1: PREPARE: Prewarm thermometer; use 2½- to 3-quart saucepan with tight-fitting lid; measure all ingredients except butter, chocolate, and nuts, and dump into saucepan; butter upper sides of saucepan. Fill glass with ice cubes and water and sink half-inch full of water.

STEP 2: DISSOLVE sugar, stirring constantly with wooden spoon over low heat until gritty sounds cease and spoon glides smoothly over bottom of pan. Increase heat to medium and bring to a boil.

STEP 3: COVER pan with wax paper square and lid, steam 1 to 2 minutes to dissolve sugar crystals. (Listen to make sure pot doesn't boil over.) Remove lid. If crystals still cling to side, wash down with pastry brush dipped in hot water from thermometer bath.

STEP 4: BOIL, after introducing prewarmed thermometer, stirring constantly.

STEP 5: TEST in ice-cold water when mixture thickens and bubbles become noisy. Ball, formed in ice water, should hold its shape except under pressure and should definitely be al dente—quite chewy. Approximately 236°F to 244°F (113.5°C to 118°C). Remove from heat and return thermometer to hot-water bath to soak clean.

STEP 6: WORK, by classic method (see step 6a, page 163), or in food processor. (I recommend the latter because butter can be hard to work in otherwise.)

TO CREAM IN FOOD PROCESSOR:

1. Pour syrup into food processor bowl equipped with metal blade. *Don't scrape pan.* Leave food pusher in feed tube.

2. Place food processor bowl in kitchen sink with enough cold tap water in it to come up 1 inch around the bowl.

3. Let syrup rest, moving bowl in sink every five minutes or so, until temperature drops to 100°F to 110°F (38°C to 43.5°C) (use instant-reading microwave thermometer to check if you have one). Bowl should be absolutely cool to the touch and a skin should have formed on the surface of syrup. It is better to be too cold than too warm. It will take about 30 minutes.

4. Remove pusher from feed tube so steam can escape. Stir fondant with wooden spoon to make sure food processor blade can move freely. Process fondant by pulsing for approximately 2 minutes. (It should lighten in color and have thickened quite a bit.)

5. Add butter, about 2 tablespoons at a time, almost continuously, to keep from overworking motor.

STEP 7: PLACE butter cream into plastic resealable bag (use a quart measuring cup or freezer container to hold the bag upright). If you wish to make several flavors from this batch, divide now into individual plastic bags and add flavorings and colorings.

STEP 8: CHILL in refrigerator until it has hardened, several hours or place in freezer for 30 minutes or so. If it gets too hard, simply knead it—through the bag—to soften.

STEP 9: MELT chocolate in double boiler over hot, not boiling, water, or in microwave (1 minute on HIGH [100%], stir, 30 seconds on HIGH) and keep warm by placing over thermometer bath or heating pad on low setting.

STEP 10: SHAPE, when fondant is hard, into small balls with small end of melon baller, or roll between your hands. Dip in chocolate (use a dipping fork if you have one or a regular fork with wide-set prongs). Drop chocolate-covered fondant into nuts, if desired (roll or not as you choose with second fork). Invert candy cup over each to pick it up and to keep nuts on top of unrolled candies. If you get tired of making balls, stop, refrigerate balance, and make the rest another day. Or add nuts to balance of fondant in plastic bag, knead together to blend, then snip corner of bag and squeeze out into candy cups. Or pour into greased, wax paper–lined small loaf pan and cut into squares when chilled. Top with more nuts.

YIELD: 2 CUPS FONDANT, OR 4 DOZEN BUTTER CREAMS. Chill in refrigerator. Since these lack the preservatives of commercial candies, store in refrigerator; do not freeze.

Uncooked Fondant Italiano

This uncooked fondant is simple to make but not half as fascinating to watch being made as doing the real thing. Eaters won't know the difference, and these will bring you raves.

> 1 large or extra-large egg white, at room temperature
>
> 3 cups sifted confectioners' sugar
>
> 4 tablespoons (½ stick) butter, softened
>
> Green food coloring
>
> ¼ teaspoon peppermint extract
>
> ½ teaspoon vanilla extract
>
> 1 tablespoon cocoa
>
> ½ cup finely chopped walnuts or almonds

STEP 1: BEAT egg white in small bowl of electric mixer until soft peaks form.

STEP 2: ADD confectioners' sugar, 1 cup at a time, alternating with 2 tablespoons butter. Continue to beat until mixture comes away from beaters and is as fluffy as possible.

STEP 3: REMOVE ⅔ mixture and divide between 2 small bowls. To one bowl, add 2 drops green food coloring and ¼ teaspoon peppermint extract. To the other, add ⅜ teaspoon vanilla extract.

STEP 4: ADD to remaining third in mixer bowl 1 tablespoon cocoa and ⅛ teaspoon vanilla extract. May need to beat it to fully incorporate cocoa.

STEP 5: WRAP each third individually and loosely in a 12×12-inch piece of plastic wrap, and knead candy through plastic into an approximate 3×9-inch rectangle.

STEP 6: CHILL in refrigerator for 30 minutes or so and then rework while still inside plastic wrap into 5×12-inch or larger rectangles. Chill for another 15 minutes or so for ease of handling. Remove wrap.

STEP 7: STACK one layer on top of the other (I put chocolate on bottom, then vanilla, then peppermint) atop a large piece of wax paper.

STEP 8: ROLL, jelly-roll style, starting on long side and using wax paper to help. Press nuts onto finished roll and wrap in plastic wrap.

STEP 9: CHILL overnight. Slice crosswise into ¼-inch-thick slices.

YIELD: 4 DOZEN SLICES. Can be frozen but not doubled.

NOTE: Traditionally, entire batch is flavored with 1 teaspoon vanilla, then divided into thirds with one portion left white, a second colored red, and the third colored green to duplicate the colors of the Italian flag.

Rigi Peaks

From Switzerland naturally, this candy-topped cookie is a confectioner's version of a snow-covered alp.

1 cup white candy coating wafers

¼ pound (1 stick) butter, softened (not margarine)

½ cup fondant

1 teaspoon vanilla liqueur, or ½ teaspoon vanilla extract

1 square (1 ounce) semisweet chocolate, melted and cooled,
or 1 packet premelted baking chocolate, at room temperature

½ teaspoon kirschwasser

24 vanilla wafers, or pound cake cut with cookie cutter into 24 pieces

Optional: silver balls for decorations

STEP 1: SOFTEN candy wafers in top of double boiler (or metal bowl over saucepan) filled with hot, *not* boiling, water. Water should not touch base of upper pan. When candy wafers have softened around edges, remove pan from heat. Stir candy wafers well to melt them all.

STEP 2: BEAT softened butter and fondant until light and fluffy in small bowl of electric mixer.

STEP 3: ADD melted candy wafers 1 tablespoon at a time, beating each addition well.

STEP 4: DIVIDE mixture, putting half back into double boiler top to keep it soft and malleable. Add vanilla to this.

STEP 5: ADD melted chocolate and kirsch to the other half.

STEP 6: PIPE chocolate mixture onto vanilla wafers or pound cake using a star tube and forcing mixture to spread out across base. (It should look like a topped Christmas tree.) With star tube, pipe vanilla mixture on top of chocolate, pulling it up to a peak. Finished candy should stand 1½ inches high.

STEP 7: TOP with optional silver balls. Can be stored at room temperature for several days, but not if you use cake as a base. Cover with aluminum foil and refrigerate to keep cake fresh.

Optional: Make the peaks all vanilla or all chocolate or use colored candy wafers and have green peaks with white "snow" covering.

YIELD: 2 DOZEN CANDY COOKIES. Do not double or freeze.

NINE

Something to Chew On: Caramel

SIMPLE ONE-STEP CARAMEL
> SIMPLE ONE-STEP ROCKY ROAD CARAMEL
> SIMPLE ONE-STEP CHOCOLATE CARAMEL
> SIMPLE ONE-STEP CHOCOLATE CHEWY CARAMEL
> SIMPLE ONE-STEP COCONUT CARAMEL
> SIMPLE ONE-STEP RUM-RAISIN CARAMEL

CLASSIC TWICE-COOKED CARAMEL
> CLASSIC VANILLA TWICE-COOKED CARAMEL
> CLASSIC INTENSIVE VANILLA TWICE-COOKED CARAMEL
> CLASSIC CHOCOLATE TWICE-COOKED CARAMEL
> CLASSIC BUTTERSCOTCH TWICE-COOKED CARAMEL
> CLASSIC INTENSIVE BUTTERSCOTCH TWICE-COOKED
>   CARAMEL
> CLASSIC MAPLE SYRUP TWICE-COOKED CARAMEL
> CLASSIC COFFEE-FLAVORED TWICE COOKED CARAMEL

CLASSIC MOCHA TWICE-COOKED CARAMEL
CLASSIC COCONUT TWICE-COOKED CARAMEL
CLASSIC CHOCOLATE-ORANGE TWICE-COOKED CARAMEL
CLASSIC PEANUT BUTTER TWICE-COOKED CARAMEL

SUPER DUPER DELUXE THREE-STAGE CARAMEL

SUPER DUPER DELUXE CHOCOLATE CARAMEL
SUPER DUPER DELUXE PEANUT BUTTER CARAMEL
SUPER DUPER DELUXE LEMON CARAMEL

CARAMEL APPLES

TOFFEE

BUTTERSCOTCH TOFFEE BRITTLES

At last, we meet the other progenitor of fudge, the one that initially supplied the ingredients that got botched. Ladies and gentlemen, may I present Madame la Caramel, named for Count Albufage Caramel of Nismes.

Not to be confused, of course, with that other citizen of France, caramelization, the process of melting sugar until it goes from yellow to burnt to black . . . from thick and richly sweet to bitter and acrid. Caramelization, particularly at the dark end, is omnipresent in the world of commerce, where it is used extensively as a natural food coloring. Without it such things as soy sauce or gravy mixes would be rather pale.

The caramel I present to you is the one that melts in the mouth, tempting us to chew even though it means cutting our pleasure short. It is the one that surrounds apples and tops a sundae or, in the case of a recalcitrant fudge, is what you and I accidentally produce when we had something else in mind.

Most cookbook authors who cover caramel seem determined to talk you out of ever attempting it. For example, one warns against making caramel in a tin-lined pan because tin's melting point is "below that of caramel." I promise you pure sugar liquefies some 125 degrees below tin's melting point. Furthermore, you'd have a blackened mess of decomposing sugar long before your tin was in danger of melting. Predictions of caramel's uncontrollable candying, or graining, are also scarifying. However, to my delight, I have found the threats of uncontrollable candying about as true as the folktales about the rigors of making fudge.

Obviously, that doesn't mean you're going to go out of your way to deliberately candy the caramel. On the other hand, using large quantities of corn syrup is your best guarantee that you'll end up with caramel instead of fudge.

I recommend certain precautions. I do believe in buttering the sides of your saucepan so no sneaky little sugar crystal can creep up the sides and lurk, just waiting to get to work crystallizing the whole batch. And since caramel cooks to a higher temperature and thus for a longer time than fudge, you will undoubtedly get the candy equivalent of ring-around-the-caramel. Which will have to be cleaned up eventually, either during cooking or during cleaning. It's easier to do it during cooking, especially with any batch containing chocolate; so scrub away with a pastry brush dipped in the hot water from the thermometer bath. Do remember, please, that excess water on that brush will just prolong the evaporation process you're going through.

If it will make you feel better, when the mixture comes to a boil, steam down the sides by covering the saucepan with a square of wax paper and a tight-fitting lid for 2 to 3 minutes.

If you're frugal, you might be tempted to scrape out the pan. Don't. For one thing, there may be scorched things down there you don't want in your caramel. For another, scraping could just set the caramel to candying—defeating our purpose.

Have I scared you, too? Forgive me and allow me to make amends by letting you in on a secret. The hardest thing I have found about making caramel is getting the stuff out of the dish once it has set and cooled. I strongly suggest that you use a disposable pan and butter it thoroughly. If you can't, then line your pan with wax paper, and butter that, too, thoroughly but lightly. If it persists in sticking to the wax paper, turn it over (onto a greased surface) and apply a hot dish towel to the wax paper side of the caramel. You can usually peel the paper right off.

By the way, most of these caramel recipes are set up to go into an 8 × 10-inch, 7 × 11-inch, or a 9 × 9-inch pan. Anything smaller and the caramel will be much thicker and take longer to cool. You can also use a big jelly-roll pan for a thin layer that sets up fast.

One more thing. All those fudge recipes you've been reading? You can make caramel out of most of them provided:

1. the recipe contains a crystallizing inhibitor, such as corn syrup, which you should increase so that the proportions are 3 parts sugar (white, brown, or any combination thereof) to 1 part corn syrup. Time out for a good word for sugar: It does more than add sweetness, it tenderizes caramel. If you use more corn syrup and less sugar, a candy's toughness increases. However,

you must use enough corn syrup to prevent caramels from becoming grainy. During the summer, for example, factory fudge-makers use half sugar, half corn syrup in order to improve storage quality.

2. the recipe calls for heavy cream or sweetened condensed milk. Those calling for evaporated milk will work also providing they contain more than 2 tablespoons of butter; if not, increase the butter to at least 2 tablespoons, preferably 4 tablespoons. You need a large percentage of fat in caramels, not just for taste but to increase the chewiness. Moreover, high-butterfat caramels don't stick to wrappers . . . most of the time.

3. you're willing to cook the fudge even longer—until it reaches one of the two stages of caramel. The first, a firm ball that holds together readily out of ice water, gives a bit under pressure and is very definitely chewy to the bite, at approximately 242°F to 248°F (116.5°C to 120°C). If you don't cook the caramel firm enough, it has to be stored in the refrigerator. Even so, for this stage or softer, conscientious cooks can wrap each caramel individually. On general principles known as impatience and old age, I am against individually wrapped caramels unless done commercially or by someone younger whom I can con into it. If your conscience insists you wrap, twisted ends go much faster than the envelope style, but the latter are neater.

For a harder caramel, cook until the ball feels hard in the ice water and, when taken out, has to be almost forced into a ball. Chewy to the bite? You bet! Temperature range? About 245°F to 255°F (118.5°C to 124°C).

As you can see, with caramel, even more than fudge, you have a wide latitude for the candy to ball at. Remember, it will come in two degrees lower in winter than summer. Also, if you have to make a choice, go for the harder ball, it's easier to handle later.

Actually, there is still a third type of caramel, which, when loaded up with butter, is known as toffee (also known as English toffee). There is much confusion, even among cookbook writers, as to the difference among caramel, toffee, taffy, and brittle; frequently, the names are used interchangeably. Dictionaries, for example, treat taffy and toffee as synonymous, but they're not. In an attempt to differentiate between them, you'll sometimes see writers use the term "butter-toffee." I define them thus: Taffy and brittle, like fondant, are basically sugar-water confections, while caramel and toffee are fudge-like in that they contain butterfat.

Good-quality toffees have a crunchy texture but should contain about 40 percent butter and 60 percent sugar. Lower grades have less butter, about 33 percent. Toffees are cooked at least to the hard-ball stage, which, because of the butter, is about 250°F to 267°F (128°C to 131°C), or even to the soft-crack stage, 270°F to 290°F (132°C to 143°C). At this stage they form hard threads in water that will stretch.

Despite all this, believe me, compared to making fudge, caramel is a cinch! Besides, if your caramel is too soft, you can always load it up with nuts and call it a chew; if it is too hard, load it up with nuts and call it a toffee; if it is woefully overcooked, load it up with nuts and call it a brittle.

Now that you know everything you ever wanted to know about caramels but were too uninterested to ask, let's go to work!

I promise you the work is worth it. If your idea of a caramel was a square thing from the supermarket, you're in for a treat.

Simple One-Step Caramel

Let's begin at the beginning, with a caramel that is simply an extension of the fudge-making you've been doing all along. This makes for a somewhat chewy caramel, but isn't that what a caramel is supposed to be? You can tenderize it by not overcooking it: Stop at the first hint of the firm-ball stage. While it is best to use only heavy cream and real butter, it's not truly necessary because the proportion of sugar to corn syrup is high.

1½ cups granulated white sugar

¼ cup butter-margarine blend or butter

½ cup light corn syrup

1½ cup half-and-half or light or heavy cream

Pinch (⅛ teaspoon) of salt

1½ teaspoons vanilla extract

Optional: 1 cup chopped nuts, coconut, mini-marshmallows

STEP 1: PREPARE: Prewarm thermometer; cut wax paper into approximately 3 × 4-inch pieces if you intend to wrap caramels individually; *lightly* grease an 8 × 10-inch pan and line with buttered aluminum foil (wax paper sticks); butter upper sides of 2-quart saucepan. Fill glass with ice cubes and water. Measure all but flavorings and optionals, and dump in pan.

STEP 2: DISSOLVE sugar, stirring constantly with wooden spoon over low heat. Butter will have melted, gritty sounds will cease, spoon will glide smoothly over bottom of pan. Increase heat to medium and bring to a boil.

STEP 3: BOIL. Cover with wax-paper square and tight-fitting lid. Steam for 1 to 3 minutes to dissolve sugar crystals. Wash down any crystals that may have formed with brush dipped in hot water from thermometer bath. Introduce prewarmed thermometer. Reduce heat while retaining boil. Stir as little as possible.

STEP 4: TEST in ice-cold water when mixture thickens and clings to spoon. Ball, formed in ice water, should hold its shape unless pressure exerted against it and should be quite chewy. Approximately 242°F to 245°F (116.5°C to 118.5°C).

STEP 5: REMOVE FROM HEAT. Return thermometer to its water bath to soak clean.

STEP 6: STIR IN any flavoring or optional ingredients.

STEP 7: POUR, COOL, SCORE, AND STORE when cool in airtight container at room temperature or in refrigerator. Cut with sharp knife.

YIELD: 1 POUND, OR ABOUT 78 PIECES. Recipe is easily doubled, and can be frozen.

VARIATIONS

Simple One-Step Rocky Road Caramel

If you've ever wondered where the name Rocky Road came from, this recipe will demonstrate it (although to my Philadelphia-trained eyes, it looks more like a cobblestone road). Replace ½ cup white sugar with ½ cup light brown sugar, firmly packed, and use half-and-half. In step 3, add 1½ squares (1½ ounces) unsweetened chocolate, grated or smashed, when mixture begins to boil. Place 1½ cups (or more) mini-marshmallows on the greased pan to cover, but not pack, the surface. When you pour the caramel over them, they'll turn a light chocolate color, swell a bit, and look like a section of chocolate-brick road.

Simple One-Step Chocolate Caramel

Follow the directions for Simple One-Step Rocky Road Caramel but omit the marshmallows. However, you might want to add some nuts.

Simple One-Step Chocolate Chewy Caramel

Instead of putting the marshmallows in the pan as in Simple One-Step Rocky Road Caramel, add 1 cup miniature marshmallows (8 to 10 large ones, quartered) in step 3 at the same time you add the chocolate. The result will be a smooth but very chewy caramel.

Simple One-Step Coconut Caramel

Stir in ½ to 1 cup toasted coconut (use straight from the package— not toasted—for chewier caramel) into Simple One-Step Caramel just before pouring.

Simple One-Step Rum-Raisin Caramel

To Simple One-Step Caramel, add ½ cup rum-soaked raisins (or figs, dates, or any combination thereof) in step 6, just before pouring.

Classic Twice-Cooked Caramel

This is the ne plus ultra of caramels. It is cooked, in the classic manner, twice (literally, double-boiled)! After you bring the syrup up to the ball stage, you add additional ingredients, which lower the temperature, and then bring the caramel back up to the ball stage again. Yes, it takes more time but only ten to fifteen minutes more, and the results are delectable. You know what happens when you remelt fudge or add fondant to it (which, in effect, is what you are doing here): The results are more tender, more delicious, more delicate than any single-cooked candy.

In these recipes, you withhold half the liquid until the mixture has come to the ball once, then, without breaking the boil, you add the liquid slowly. This method accomplishes many things. One, it means you don't have to stir as much—the action of adding the liquid stirs the mixture by convection. Two, it forces rapid evaporation. Three, it introduces more butterfat at a time when it will be less likely to scorch. Four, because of the recooking, you do not need as much butterfat to achieve a smooth texture. Fifth, it gives you some flexibility in terms of converting a basic recipe into variations, such as changing the master recipe to maple or chocolate or coconut or whatever. The result? Over 72 melt-in-your-mouth caramels!

> 1 cup granulated white sugar
>
> 1 cup cream (divided); use heavy (the best), light, half-and-half, or even evaporated milk
>
> ¾ cup plus 2 tablespoons light corn syrup
>
> Pinch (⅛ teaspoon) of salt
>
> ¼ pound (1 stick) butter or butter-margarine blend
>
> 1 teaspoon vanilla extract
>
> Optional: ½ to 1 cup chopped nuts (pecans, walnuts, whatever)

STEP 1: PREPARE: Prewarm thermometer; cut individual wrapping papers into approximate 3 × 4-inch pieces; *lightly* grease an 8 × 10-inch or 7 × 11-inch pan and line with greased wax paper; butter upper sides of 2-quart saucepan. Fill glass with ice cubes and water. Measure all ingredients but ½ cup of cream, flavoring, and nuts, and dump in pan.

STEP 2: DISSOLVE sugar, stirring constantly with wooden spoon over low heat. Butter will have melted, gritty sounds will cease, spoon will glide smoothly over bottom of pan. Increase heat to medium and bring to a boil.

STEP 3: BOIL, reducing heat while retaining boil. Introduce prewarmed thermometer. Stir as little as possible.

STEP 4: TEST in ice-cold water after 15 to 20 minutes when mixture thickens considerably and clings to spoon. Ball, formed in ice water, should hold its shape unless pressure exerted against it and should be quite chewy. Approximately 242°F to 248°F (116.5°C to 120°C).

STEP 5: POUR other ½ cup cream into mixture slowly so as not to break boil. Temperature may go down as much as 10 degrees. Bring back to firm-ball stage, which will be *lower* than before as technically mixture is recooking. Return thermometer to its water bath to soak clean.

STEP 6: STIR in flavoring and/or optional ingredients.

STEP 7: POUR caramel but don't attempt to spread; it will level out.

STEP 8: COOL in a cool place with pan on a cool surface, if possible.

STEP 9: SCORE, WRAP, AND STORE in airtight container in refrigerator or at room temperature.

STEP 10: SOAK cooking utensils immediately in hot water.

YIELD: 1 POUND. Recipe is easily doubled. Freezes well; thaw in refrigerator.

VARIATIONS

Classic Vanilla Twice-Cooked Caramel

Instead of adding flavoring in step 6, add 2-inch piece of vanilla bean when you add the ½ cup cream in step 5. When you pour the caramel, the bean will come to the surface and can be easily removed.

Classic Intensive Vanilla Twice-Cooked Caramel

Use half-and-half instead of cream, replace butter with ⅔ cup (6 ounces) of white chocolate (stir constantly and don't rush its melting). In step 5, add ¼ cup Irish Creme Liqueur along with balance of half-and-half. Check flavoring at second ball stage; if not vanilla enough, add up to 2 teaspoons vanilla extract in step 6.

Classic Chocolate Twice-Cooked Caramel

In step 5, add 1½ to 2 squares (1½ to 2 ounces) unsweetened chocolate, grated or smashed, when you add the other ½ cup liquid. Or use premelted baking chocolate packets—amount depends on how chocolatey you like it.

Classic Butterscotch Twice-Cooked Caramel

Replace granulated sugar with packed light brown sugar, use cream and butter only, use either vanilla extract or ¾ teaspoon butterscotch oil flavoring.

Classic Intensive Butterscotch Twice-Cooked Caramel

Follow Classic Butterscotch Twice-Cooked Caramel recipe, using vanilla extract, but add ½ cup premelted butterscotch morsels in step 5 when you add ½ cup cream.

Classic Maple Syrup Twice-Cooked Caramel

Instead of using cream, use 1 cup maple syrup in step 1, and, in step 5, add one 7-ounce can evaporated milk.

Classic Coffee-Flavored Twice-Cooked Caramel

Substitute one 12-ounce can evaporated milk for the cream. Add 6 ounces in step 1, then, in step 5, add ¼ cup strong black coffee (or 2 heaping teaspoons instant coffee) plus rest of evaporated milk.

Classic Mocha Twice-Cooked Caramel

To Classic Coffee-Flavored recipe, add 1 square (1 ounce) unsweetened chocolate, grated or smashed, *or* 1 packet premelted baking chocolate.

Classic Coconut Twice-Cooked Caramel

Use ½ cup cream only and add it all in step 1. Then, in step 5, add ½ cup coconut cream. For a chewier caramel, stir in 1 cup flaked and shredded coconut in step 6, *or* toast coconut and spread, in step 7, on bottom of pan and again on top of caramel in layered effect.

Classic Chocolate-Orange Twice-Cooked Caramel

Substitute evaporated milk for the cream and use butter only. In step 5, add ½ cup orange juice and 1 ounce unsweetened chocolate (grated, smashed, or premelted) plus the other ½ cup of evaporated milk.

Classic Peanut Butter Twice-Cooked Caramel

Use half-and-half or evaporated milk and only ¼ cup (½ stick) butter-margarine blend. In step 5, add ½ cup premelted peanut butter chips *or* generous ¼ cup creamy peanut butter.

Needless to say, you can add nuts to any of these caramels. I suggest pecans for more delicate ones; cashews go great with Classic Intensive Vanilla. Almonds or hazelnuts are fine with stronger flavors, and walnuts, peanuts, and brazil nuts can hold their own against the strongest flavors.

Super Duper Deluxe Three-Stage Caramel

For the cook who has tried everything and has all the time in the world, this is the *crème de la crème*, literally, of caramels. It is cooked thrice! But don't let it frighten you, because it is very similar in ingredients and procedure to Classic Twice-Cooked Caramel. The big difference is that you cook to the soft-ball stage as you would for fudge, but do it three times.

2 cups granulated white sugar

3 cups heavy cream (divided into 1-cup portions)

1¾ cups light corn syrup

Pinch (⅛ teaspoon) of salt

1 teaspoon flavoring

Optional: ½ to 1 cup chopped nuts (pecans, walnuts, whatever)

STEP 1: PREPARE: Prewarm thermometer; cut individual wrapping papers into approximate 3 × 4-inch pieces; *lightly* grease an 8 × 10-inch or 7 × 11-inch pan and line with greased wax paper; butter upper sides of 2-quart saucepan. Fill glass with ice cubes and water. Measure all ingredients but 2 cups cream, flavoring, and nuts, and dump in pan.

STEP 2: DISSOLVE sugar, stirring constantly with wooden spoon over low heat. Butter will have melted, gritty sounds will cease, spoon will glide smoothly over bottom of pan. Increase heat to medium and bring to a boil.

STEP 3: BOIL. Introduce prewarmed thermometer. Reduce heat while retaining boil. Stir as little as possible.

STEP 4: TEST in ice-cold water after 15 or 20 minutes when mixture thickens and bubbles become noisy. Ball, formed in ice water, should hold its shape until heat from your hand begins to flatten it and should be al dente—slightly chewy. Approximately 236°F to 242°F (113.5°C to 116.5°C).

STEP 5: POUR second cup cream into mixture slowly so as not to break boil. Temperature may go down as much as 10 degrees. Bring back to soft-ball stage, which will be *lower* than before since technically mixture is recooking.

STEP 6: REPEAT step 5 with third cup cream, bringing it back once more to the soft-ball stage. Return thermometer to water bath to soak clean.

STEP 7: STIR in flavoring and/or nuts.

STEP 8: POUR caramel but don't attempt to spread; it will level out.

STEP 9: COOL in a cool place with pan on a cool surface, if possible.

STEP 10: SCORE, WRAP, AND STORE in airtight container in refrigerator or at room temperature.

STEP 11: SOAK cooking utensils immediately in hot water.

YIELD: 1 POUND. Recipe is easily doubled. Freezes well but thaw in refrigerator.

VARIATIONS

Like any of the other caramels, it is possible to vary this basic recipe. The trick is knowing when to add the other flavorings. As a rule, add flavors you want to intensify with second cup of cream in step 5. But add flavors that can be overpowering with third cup of cream in step 6. For mild or subtle flavors that rely strictly on extracts and flavorings, add after candy is removed from heat in step 7.

Super Duper Deluxe Chocolate Caramel

Some people can't get enough chocolate, so this one you would want to intensify. Add 2 squares (2 ounces) unsweetened chocolate, grated or smashed, in step 5.

Super Duper Deluxe Peanut Butter Caramel

For many people, a little peanut butter goes a long way. So add ⅔ cup premelted peanut butter chips in step 6.

Super Duper Deluxe Lemon Caramel

A delicate flavor if there ever was one. Add 1 teaspoon lemon extract plus 2 tablespoons grated lemon zest (optional) after removing from heat in step 7.

Caramel Apples

Although many people prefer to melt packaged caramels in a double boiler over simmering water to use for dipping apples, homemade caramel has more taste. However, if you insist on packaged caramels, at least the techniques for dipping the apples will come in handy. By the way, this recipe is not only easily doubled, it can be quadrupled if you have a large-enough stockpot.

6 medium or 4 large apples, such as Granny Smith, Rome, or Delicious

8 ounces (half of 16-ounce bottle) light corn syrup

1 cup firmly packed light brown sugar

½ cup granulated white sugar

¼ cup water

⅞ cup (7-ounce can) evaporated skim milk

3½ tablespoons butter

⅛ teaspoon salt

½ teaspoon vanilla extract

½ pound salted peanuts, chopped into ⅛-inch pieces

4 to 6 craft sticks (they look like notched Popsicle sticks)

STEP 1: PREPARE: Prewarm thermometer in a water bath. Wash apples and dry them thoroughly. *Lightly* grease a cookie sheet on which to put finished apples. Butter upper sides of 3-quart saucepan. Fill large, heat-proof, preferably metal bowl half full of ice cubes as well as glass with ice water. Measure corn syrup, sugars, and water and place into saucepan.

STEP 2: DISSOLVE sugar, stirring constantly with wooden spoon over low heat. Gritty sounds will cease, spoon will glide smoothly over bottom of pan. Increase heat to medium and bring to a boil.

STEP 3: ADD evaporated skim milk in a slow steady stream so as not to break the boil. Introduce prewarmed thermometer. Reduce heat while retaining boil. You will need to stir almost constantly, especially after mixture reaches 200°F (93.5°C) because milk solids tend to fall to the bottom and scorch. If mixture begins to look curdled, don't worry; it comes back.

STEP 4: TEST in ice-cold water when mixture thickens and clings to spoon. Ball should hold together readily out of ice water but give under pressure and be chewy to the bite, at approximately 240°F to 248°F (115.5°C to 120°C). It is better to overcook than undercook.

STEP 5: REMOVE FROM HEAT, replace thermometer in water bath, and put pot on hotpad or trivet.

STEP 6: STIR IN butter, salt, and vanilla, and watch caramel smooth out.

To Dip Apples

Don't rush, you have lots of time. In fact, the caramel will cling to the apples better when it's cooler, and you won't risk cooking the apples.

STEP 1: ADD enough cold water to bowl of ice cubes to fill three-quarters full. Put chopped nuts into dish suitable for rolling apple in.

STEP 2: INSERT craft stick at least one-third of way into apple. Craft sticks hold better than plain sticks.

STEP 3: DIP apple into caramel, twirling it about and spooning caramel over it if necessary to cover it completely.

STEP 4: PLUNGE apple into ice water and give it at least one complete twirl. When you remove apple, caramel coating will be cool enough for you to handle and manipulate to cover any uncoated areas.

STEP 5: DIP apple into ground nuts, using your hands to press nuts into caramel and to reshape coating if necessary.

STEP 6: PLACE coated apple on lightly greased cookie sheet.

STEP 7: SERVE at room temperature but store in refrigerator, removing at least 30 minutes before serving to allow caramel to soften; otherwise the caramel is brittle and will shatter and/or separate from the apple when you bite into it or cut it.

Toffee

Last but not least, we have toffee, the hardest caramel of them all. Not hardest in terms of making, but hardest in terms of cooking the longest. In making toffee, the thing to avoid is burning the butter. Good English toffee like this can retail for almost thirty dollars a pound, so it makes for a wonderfully appreciated gift. However, don't try to wrap individual pieces. Place the toffee in a box and separate layers with wax paper or baking parchment sheets. On page 265 you will find a recipe for the famed Treacle Toffee with a molasses taste.

Butterscotch Toffee Brittles

1 pound (4 sticks) unsalted butter

2½ cups superfine sugar

2 tablespoons plus 2 teaspoons honey

½ cup whole raw almonds

¾ teaspoon salt

1 teaspoon vanilla extract

1 cup (6 ounces) semisweet chocolate chips or chocolate candy coating wafers

Optional: 4-ounce package ground almonds

STEP 1: PREPARE: Prewarm thermometer; butter jelly-roll pan and upper sides of 2-quart saucepan. Fill glass with ice cubes and water. Cut butter into chunks and dump in pan.

STEP 2: MELT BUTTER over low heat to prevent browning, then add sugar and honey, stirring constantly with wooden spoon over low heat until sugar is dissolved. Gritty sounds will cease, spoon will glide smoothly over bottom of pan. Increase heat to medium and bring to a boil.

STEP 3: BOIL, after washing down any crystals that may have formed with brush dipped in hot water from thermometer bath, *using as little water as possible.* Introduce prewarmed thermometer. Reduce heat while retaining boil. Stir as necessary to prevent scorching and heat to about 260°F (126.6°C).

STEP 4: ADD whole almonds.

STEP 5: CONTINUE COOKING and stirring until batch takes on consistency similar to stiff jelly.

STEP 6: TEST in ice-cold water. When hitting the water, individual strands should be hard but not brittle. When stretched they should give. About 290°F (143.3°C), depending on the quality of the butter.

STEP 7: ADD salt and vanilla.

STEP 8: SPREAD on greased jelly-roll pan, leveling off with metal spatula to evenly distribute nuts throughout batch.

STEP 9: FINISH in one of two ways: Scatter semisweet chips or chocolate candy wafers on the top, letting them sit a moment or two—they'll melt—and then spreading. Over this, you can sprinkle ground roasted almonds if desired. Then break toffee. Or first cut toffee and break toffee into pieces, then dip the pieces into the melted chocolate chips, either plain or mixed with ground, roasted almonds.

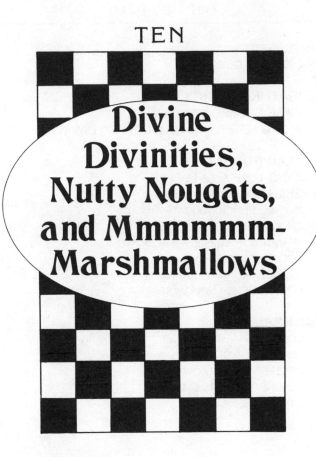

TEN

Divine Divinities, Nutty Nougats, and Mmmmmm-Marshmallows

DIVINITY FUDGE
  BASIC DIVINITY
    THE FAMED CHRISTMAS DIVINITY
    CHOCOLATE DIVINITY
    ORANGE DIVINITY
    COFFEE DIVINITY
    MOCHA DIVINITY
    HONEY DIVINITY
    MAPLE SYRUP DIVINITY
    RUM-RAISIN DIVINITY
  BASIC SEA-FOAM DIVINITY
    RUM-RAISIN SEA-FOAM DIVINITY
    CHERRY-WALNUT SEA-FOAM DIVINITY
  FRUIT-FLAVORED DIVINITIES
  CHEWY STRAWBERRY DIVINITY

MARGUERITES
MICROWAVE DIVINITY

NOUGATLIKE DIVINITY
DOUBLE-COOKED DIVINITY
THE TWO SISTERS' DOUBLE-COOKED DIVINITY

REGULAR NOUGAT
NOUGAT LOAF ALLA NAPOLI
FRENCH NOUGATS
   MOCHA FRENCH NOUGATS
   CHOCOLATE FRENCH NOUGATS
   PEANUT BUTTER FRENCH NOUGATS
   COCONUT FRENCH NOUGATS
   ORANGE FRENCH NOUGATS
   LEMON FRENCH NOUGATS

MARSHMALLOWS
COCONUT MARSHMALLOW
ORANGE-FLAVORED MARSHMALLOW
MOCHA MARSHMALLOW
ALMOND/NUT MARSHMALLOW
OTHER POSSIBILITIES

Why include divinities, nougats, and marshmallows in a book on fudge?

It does seem a little incongruous until you realize that divinity began as a fudge. Only later was it handled like an egg white–based nougat. And marshmallow, which looks as if it is made of egg whites, uses gelatin to get divinity's fluffiness.

That's why, today, describing divinity is a little like having six blind men examine six different parts of an elephant—you come away with a snakelike, ropelike, tree-shaped, befanged, floppy, enormous something. So it is with divinity. It can be heavily fudgelike or Italian meringue-crusty or chewy nougaty or even meltingly marshmallowy. You can spread it like fudge or drop it like kisses or bake it like meringues.

No one knows where it originated or when, but everyone agrees that divinity, too, is an American confection, and at least one author claims it to be Kentucky-bred. Like "fudge," its name is a mystery. Giving a candy a name with such strong religious connotations seems frivolous, unless there once was some theological connection we are not aware of now. Then again, considering the amount of stirring involved in making divinity in the early days of hand-beaten candies, only a saint with unselfish, divine devotion to her family would make this confection. Using my method, you can make it in less than an hour, start to finish.

In any event, the earliest dictionary reference to it I found was in 1913 as "divinity fudge." According to one cookbook, it was a special-occasion fudge made with egg whites. Flavored with vanilla or mint, it was served at teas. When made with red and green candied cherries, it was reserved for the Christmas season.

Again, like fudge, a change in ingredients from white sugar to brown results in a name change. Where fudge becomes penuche, divinity made with brown sugar becomes sea-foam. If it is made successfully, it is light as foam; if it fails, it makes a darn good substitute for glue.

It is a candy that even gourmets either love or loathe. Craig Claiborne, in his *A Feast Made for Laughter* (Doubleday, 1982), puts it in the fudge category when he reminisces about his childhood: "There are dozens of dishes come to my mind when I think of my mother's kitchen [in Sunflower, Mississippi]—fantastic caramels, divinity fudge, a luscious coconut cake with meringue and fresh coconut topping . . ." Unfortunately, Mrs. Claiborne's recipe for divinity fudge was not included in the cookbook she passed on to her son, but he tells me that hers was made with nuts.

James Beard confessed, in his book *American Cookery* (Little, Brown, 1972), "I loathed divinity fudge when I was young, and I still have no taste for it." Still, he includes a recipe for it, one made with candied cherries.

I have mixed emotions. I love its delicate taste and much prefer it chilled than at room temperature; I loathe the waiting on bad-divinity-making days, which is any hot and/or humid day if you don't have air-conditioning. If you do, temperature is not really a factor; however, the beating will take longer on humid days. Also, be sure, unless you run your air conditioner twenty-four hours a day, that you store divinity in airtight packages if you don't refrigerate it—it is extremely water-absorbent.

DIVINITY FUDGE

What better way to learn a new type of candy than with one that makes use of techniques you've already mastered: the cooking of a syrup, fondantlike, followed by agitating until, fudgelike, it loses its gloss? The difference is that, right smack in the middle, you add the syrup, meringuelike, to egg whites . . . and this fudge takes real beating! However, the combination of techniques results in one very light, very luscious divinity.

Because the early divinities didn't use corn syrup, the sugar syrup had to be watched very carefully to make sure that no crystallizing took place. You know the rote: cover pan and steam, wash down sides, wipe down before pouring, and so on. And these are still wise precautions for any divinity recipe you are not familiar with or one made without corn syrup.

By the way, with divinity fudge, if you goof and don't cook the syrup to a high enough temperature, you'll end up with a delicious divinity caramel.

Basic Divinity

2 cups granulated white sugar

½ cup light corn syrup

½ cup water

Pinch (⅛ teaspoon) of salt

2 large egg whites

1 teaspoon vanilla extract

Optionals: 1 cup chopped nuts, cherries, orange peels, etc.

STEP 1: PREPARE: Prewarm thermometer; separate eggs, allowing whites to come to room temperature in large bowl of electric mixer. (Return yolks to refrigerator, cover with small amount of water and/or plastic wrap so they don't dry out.) Fill glass with ice cubes and water. To make dropped divinities, you'll need 2 cookie sheets, topped with greased wax paper. For squares, use a greased and wax paper–lined 8 × 8-inch pan. Measure sugar, corn syrup, water, and salt, and dump into a heavy 2-quart saucepan with tight-fitting lid.

STEP 2: DISSOLVE sugar, stirring constantly with wooden spoon over low heat. Syrup will become clear, gritty sounds will cease, spoon will glide smoothly over bottom of pan. Increase heat to medium and bring to a boil.

STEP 3 (OPTIONAL): COVER pan with square of wax paper and lid, pushing down firmly. Steam 2 to 3 minutes to dissolve sugar crystals. (Listen to make sure pot doesn't boil over. To double-check, remove lid, leaving wax paper in place.)

STEP 4: WASH down any crystals clinging to sides with brush dipped in hot water from thermometer bath. Introduce prewarmed thermometer. No need to stir.

STEP 5: BEAT egg whites until stiff but not dry. If your mixer is heavy-duty, you can wait until the bubbles in the syrup become very large and airy before beating the egg whites. Otherwise, do now when thermometer in syrup registers 240°F (115.5°C).

STEP 6: TEST syrup when thermometer registers 246°F (119°C). Continue testing until it reaches the firm-ball stage, 246°F to 260°F (119°C to 126.5°C). Syrup will be hard to scrape up in ice water. It will have to be forced into a ball, but once formed, it should hold its shape well but give under pressure. Return thermometer to hot water bath to soak clean.

STEP 7: DRIBBLE syrup into egg whites in a slow, steady stream, beating at slow speed. Tilt syrup pan to get the last drop but do not scrape pan. Once syrup is completely incorporated, change to a flat whip if you have one.

STEP 8: HAVE PATIENCE and continue beating. The amount of time you spend mixing depends on the power of your mixer. Although mine is not a commercial one, I have been able to put the pedal to the medal or "punch it!" and at full speed ahead make divinity in less than 5 minutes. With a less powerful machine, it has taken 20 minutes. The important thing is to beat it at the highest speed your machine is capable of. (If you've always been told to use medium speed, forget it unless you have the patience of a saint. It will work but takes forever.) Remember, if you've chosen a bad divinity day, it's going to take longer no matter what speed you use.

STEP 9: TEST the divinity. The first and most important test occurs when you lift the beaters. If the candy falls back in ribbons that immediately merge back into the batter, it isn't done. Eventually, a stationary column will form between beaters and bowl. Candy will lose its sheen/gloss and stop being sticky; teaspoonful dropped onto wax paper will hold its shape, even a peak. If your machine is laboring and the candy is not quite there yet, you have two choices: Pour anyway and put in frost-free freezer to set up . . . or finish by hand.

STEP 10: FOLD in flavoring and nuts and/or other optional items using mixer or, if very thick, wooden spoon.

STEP 11: DROP OR SPREAD divinity either on wax paper–covered cookie sheets or in buttered pan. Dropping it teaspoon by teaspoon is harder work for you, but it ripens quicker and is ready to eat sooner. (A neat trick: Instead of dropping, pipe it, using a cake decorating bag, or put divinity in plastic storage bag and cut a hole in one corner and pipe it out.) If you spread it in a pan, which is easier and less time-consuming, you have to wait awhile before it's firm enough to cut. However, some people think divinity is better after 24 hours, having mellowed. Others warn against letting it dry out. Cool by placing pan in refrigerator. Store in airtight container at room temperature or in refrigerator, which is my preference.

YIELD: 1 POUND BUT LOOKS LIKE MORE. Recipe cannot be doubled; it can be frozen, but not for extended periods of time.

VARIATIONS

The Famed Christmas Divinity

The very one loathed by James Beard. In step 10, use ½ cup chopped candied red cherries and ½ cup green, or ¼ cup of each and ½ cup chopped or slivered blanched almonds or pistachios.

Chocolate Divinity

When divinity has solidified, in step 10, stir in 1 to 2 squares (1 to 2 ounces) unsweetened chocolate, melted and cooled, or similar pre-melted packets. One ounce gives a very subtle flavor; chocoholics may prefer three. Chocolate divinity will look very dull as compared to others.

Orange Divinity

In step 10, add ⅓ cup grated orange rind *or* ½ cup chopped candied orange peel plus 1 teaspoon orange extract.

Coffee Divinity

Instead of water, use ½ cup black coffee.

Mocha Divinity

Instead of water, use ⅓ cup strong black coffee and 1 to 2 packets premelted baking chocolate warmed under the faucet.

Honey Divinity

Replace light corn syrup with honey.

Maple Syrup Divinity

Replace 1 cup granulated white sugar with ¾ cup maple syrup, and use only ⅓ cup water.

Rum-Raisin Divinity

In step 10, add ½ cup chopped raisins soaked for ½ hour in ¼ cup rum, then drained. Use 1 tablespoon of drained rum in place of vanilla.

Basic Sea-Foam Divinity

Replace 1 cup white sugar with 1 cup light brown sugar *or* light corn syrup with dark corn syrup.

Rum-Raisin Sea-Foam Divinity

For a bit more tang, make Rum-Raisin Divinity but replace light corn syrup with dark.

Cherry-Walnut Sea-Foam Divinity

In step 10, fold in 1 cup chopped candied cherries and 1 cup chopped walnuts to Basic Sea-Foam Divinity.

Fruit-Flavored Divinities

Fruit-flavored divinities are lighter and airier than regular divinities. To make them, use the same basic divinity recipe with a few modifications plus 1 package (3 ounces) of any flavor Jell-O Brand Gelatin Dessert.

Follow steps 1 through 4 but use a 9×9-inch pan. In step 5, do not beat egg whites until the syrup has come to a firm ball, 246°F to 260°F (119°C to 126.5°C). Syrup will be hard to scrape up in ice water. It will have to be forced into a ball, but once formed, it should hold its shape well but give under pressure. Remove syrup from heat, place pan on a heat-proof pad or trivet, and immediately add 1 package any flavor Jell-O Brand Gelatin Dessert. Stir it in and, as it dissolves in hot syrup, begin to beat egg whites until stiff but not dry. By the time the egg whites are stiff, the gelatin will have dissolved. Check to be sure. Then return to step 7 of basic recipe. In step 9, the divinity will not lose its sheen, but remain glossy.

■ ■ ■

As for flavorings. In most cases, you won't need to add any, not even vanilla. But you can always intensify flavors by adding complementary extracts, like orange to Strawberry Jell-O. Or you can add 2 teaspoons of any liqueur, but do it while the divinity is still hot so alcohol evaporates.

If you wish, you can add the Jell-O in step 1. However, it takes twice as long, there's much more stirring to do, you have to adjust temperatures to prevent scorching, and the gelatin tends to bubble over (use at least a 3-quart saucepan).

Do not try to add the Jell-O after you add the sugar syrup to egg whites; you'll just get a grainy divinity.

Chewy Strawberry Divinity

This recipe tastes so much like old-fashioned Turkish Taffy, you won't believe it; however, it should be kept refrigerated.

Replace corn syrup with ¼ teaspoon cream of tartar. Follow steps 1 to 6. Add 1 cup (8 ounces) strawberry preserves (drained if very runny) to syrup and recook to firm-ball stage. Then add to stiffly beaten egg whites. Beat mixture on medium speed (seemingly forever) until it becomes very elastic. Pour into 5 × 10-inch greased pan and chill. Score before it becomes completely cold, otherwise you will have a devil of a time cutting it. At first bite, it will be hard and brittle, then it will slowly grow chewy and finally melt in your mouth. You can add nuts, but I don't recommend it; I prefer it plain.

Marguerites

These are more like cookies than candies.

1 cup granulated white sugar
⅓ cup water

1 teaspoon white vinegar
1 large egg white
¾ cup chopped walnuts
18 to 24 saltine crackers

Follow Basic Divinity recipe, except that in step 11, instead of dropping or pouring, spread generously on saltines and bake, meringuelike, on greased cookie sheet in preheated moderate oven (325°F to 350°F) until light brown.

Microwave Divinity

Divinity works well in the microwave because it requires less stirring than fudge, and one doesn't need to watch over it like a mother hen. On the other hand, it must be cooked to a higher temperature, which makes timing a little tricky. Remember, if you get it up at least to firm-ball stage, it will continue cooking outside of the oven.

2½ cups granulated white sugar

½ cup light corn syrup

½ cup water

Pinch (⅛ teaspoon) of salt

2 large egg whites

1 teaspoon vanilla

Optional: *½ to 1 cup chopped nuts*

STEP 1: COMBINE in 3-quart micro-proof casserole sugar, corn syrup, water, and salt.

STEP 2: MICROWAVE on HIGH (100%) for 5 minutes.

STEP 3: STIR well.

STEP 4: MICROWAVE on HIGH (100%) another 7 to 13 minutes, depending on power of your microwave, testing after every 2 to 3 minutes.

STEP 5: REMOVE casserole, using oven mitts, and stir well.

STEP 6: TEST a small amount in ice-cold water. It should be difficult to scrape up and have to be forced into a ball, but once formed, it should hold its shape but give under pressure, or measure 246°F to 260°F (119°C to 126.5°C) on micro-probe.

STEP 7: BEAT egg whites until stiff peaks form.

STEP 8: POUR syrup slowly, ladling at first, over egg whites while beating at high speed with electric mixer. Continue beating 4 to 5 minutes, or until mixture holds its shape and starts to lose its gloss.

STEP 9: ADD vanilla and fold in chopped nuts, if desired.

STEP 10: DROP heaping teaspoonfuls quickly onto wax paper or spread into a lightly buttered 10 × 6-inch dish and cut when cool into pieces.

YIELD: 5 DOZEN 1-INCH PIECES. Does not freeze well. Do not double.

Nougatlike Divinity

In divinities made like nougats, the syrup is cooked and added in two stages. The result is chewier and more substantial than divinity fudge. While it takes longer to do, it is also known by divinity-makers as "no-fail divinity," because it is almost 100 percent guaranteed to work.

Double-Cooked Divinity

2½ cups granulated white sugar

1½ cups water

1½ cups light corn syrup

Pinch (⅛ teaspoon) of salt

2 large egg whites

1 teaspoon vanilla extract

1 cup chopped nuts

Follow steps 1 through 4 for Basic Divinity.

STEP 5: BEAT egg whites with electric mixer until stiff but not dry when syrup reaches 230°F (110°C).

STEP 6: TEST, when thermometer reaches 234°F (112°C), to see if it forms soft ball in ice-cold water. (Ball should hold its shape outside of water and only flatten from heat of your hands.) Return thermometer to hot water bath to stay warm while you proceed to step 7.

STEP 7: DRIZZLE about half the boiling mixture into egg whites, beating slowly. Increase speed to medium and continue beating.

STEP 8: RETURN syrup to heat, replacing thermometer, which you have wiped dry—be careful, it will be hot.

STEP 9: BOIL syrup 2 minutes longer, or until mixture reaches firm-ball stage (246°F to 260°F [119°C to 126.5°C]). Syrup will be hard to scrape up in ice water. It will have to be forced into a ball, but once formed, it should hold its shape well but give under pressure.

STEP 10: ADD balance of syrup to mixture. Increase speed to high and continue beating until mixture holds its shape (when you lift beaters, continuous stationary column will form between beaters and bowl). Candy should start to lose its gloss.

STEP 11: FOLD in vanilla and chopped nuts.

STEP 12: POUR into buttered 8×8-inch pan and cut into squares, or quickly drop heaping teaspoonfuls onto wax paper.

YIELD: 64 1-INCH PIECES. Do not double; do not freeze.

VARIATIONS

For variety, add a few drops of food coloring while beating or pour out part and color the rest.

You can make any of the basic variations (see pages 203–204) with Double-Cooked Divinity. In addition, the second stage of cooking allows you to add such things as peanut butter (¼ to ⅓ cup), or ½ cup of any of the chips—butterscotch, chocolate-mint, peanut butter, semisweet chocolate—premelted.

The Two Sisters' Double-Cooked Divinity

It has been a tradition for two Philadelphia sisters, Ruth Cake and Mary Jane Peters, to get together at the beginning of the holiday season to make these divinities. Gossip has it that it took them all day . . . but I think it was more the gossip than the cooking that took so long. I hope some of you will continue the tradition of making the Two Sisters' Double-Cooked Divinity.

This batch of divinity is larger than any of the other recipes and will test your electric mixer's motor and capacity. You will need a 2-quart saucepan for the first batch of syrup and the smallest one you have for the second batch, as well as at least a 4-quart mixing bowl.

3 cups granulated white sugar

1 cup light corn syrup

⅔ cup water

3 large egg whites

1 cup sugar

½ cup water

1 tablespoon vanilla

1 cup chopped or broken nuts

Follow steps 1 through 7 of Basic Divinity using first four ingredients. After syrup has been incorporated—the mixture will swell up and threaten to overflow the mixing bowl—switch to the flat whip if you have one. In step 8, continue beating at medium speed while you cook second batch of syrup from 1 cup sugar and ½ cup water, in smallest saucepan you have, to hard-ball stage—240°F to 260°F (119°C to 126.5°C)—you may have to tilt pan occasionally to get an accurate thermometer reading.

STEP 9: BARELY DRIBBLE this second batch into the first mixture.

STEP 10: INCREASE speed and beat as hard and as fast as you can. It may take 15 to 20 minutes or more until mixture solidifies and loses its gloss.

STEP 11: ADD vanilla and nuts.

STEP 12: POUR into greased 9 × 13-inch pan. Let stand until firm before cutting into small squares.

YIELD: APPROXIMATELY 60 PIECES. Do not double or freeze.

NOUGAT

One would think that in cooking, at least, the world would speak the same language, most usually French, as in sauté instead of fry. But why one man's praline is another's fudge pecan patty is a Frenchman's ground almond paste is a German's nougat, that I don't understand.

Nevertheless, the traditional nougat recipe originated in the French town of Montelimar, situated in the southern Rhone Valley, and the confection by that name is still very popular. Originally it was made from honey and whipped egg whites, mixed with chopped nuts and preserved fruit.

Ingredientwise, honey is what differentiates a nougat from a divinity, at least in America and at best most of the time. As for methodology, nougats have an extra step: You recook the candy after you incorporate the syrup into the egg whites.

GENERAL DIRECTIONS

For a lighter nougat, increase the number of eggs slightly. The main thing is to see that the eggs are well beaten and then that the batch is evaporated (but not boiled) to the proper degree. A candy thermometer can be very helpful when making nougats.

ADDITIONAL TESTS FOR DONENESS

Beyond the soft-ball, firm-ball, and so on tests, you must check further to be sure that the candy has been properly evaporated. Does it "snap" if a small amount is taken off on the blade of a spatula, flattened out, and placed in or under cold water? If you can "snap" it off with your finger, it is done. If it is soft and tough and does not snap, it must be evaporated a little longer.

Second test: Tap it with the back of your hand. It's done when it does not stick.

Regular Nougat

This recipe looks like a lot of work but it really isn't. Besides, the candy is worth it: It tastes great and lasts for weeks in the refrigerator. I really suggest you double the recipe (quantities given in parentheses).

1 cup granulated white sugar	(2 cups)
⅓ cup clear honey	(⅔ cup)
⅓ cup light corn syrup	(⅔ cup)
3 large egg whites	(6 whites)
¾ cup plus 2 tablespoons confectioners' sugar	(1¾ cups)
1 cup chopped nuts	(2 cups)
1 teaspoon vanilla	(2 teaspoons)

STEP 1: PREPARE a makeshift double boiler (storebought ones are too deep and narrow); choose a shallow heat-proof bowl large enough to whip the eggs in and any size pan to go underneath that will provide a secure foundation for the bowl. Prewarm thermometer; use 1½-quart sauce-pan, unbuttered, with tight-fitting lid; measure granulated sugar, honey, and corn syrup, and dump into saucepan. Grease and line, with very lightly buttered wax paper coated with confectioners' sugar, a 5 × 9-inch loaf pan or 6 × 12-inch pan. Fill glass with ice cubes and water.

STEP 2: DISSOLVE sugar, stirring constantly with wooden spoon over low heat until gritty sounds cease and spoon slides smoothly over bottom of pan. Increase heat to medium and bring to a boil.

STEP 3: COVER with a square of wax paper and tight-fitting lid, then boil 1 to 2 minutes to wash down sugar crystals. Introduce prewarmed thermometer. Then continue cooking (be careful honey doesn't burn).

STEP 4: BEAT egg whites to stiff peaks in your "double-boiler top" or large mixing bowl when sugar dissolves and syrup reaches 225°F (107°C).

STEP 5: TEST in ice-cold water when mixture thickens and bubbles become noisy (246°F to 260°F [119°C to 126.5°C]). Ball, formed in ice water, will be hard to scrape up and have to be forced into a ball, but once formed, it should hold its shape well but give under pressure.

STEP 6: REMOVE ½ cup hot syrup. Continue cooking rest to 270°F (132°C).

STEP 7: DRIBBLE ½ cup syrup into egg whites, beating constantly, and continue beating at lower speed to keep mixture moving while rest of syrup cooks.

STEP 8: RETEST syrup in clean water when it reaches 270°F (132°C). Between here and 290°F (143.5°C), syrup will reach soft-crack stage— that is, when syrup is dropped into water, it separates into strands that can be stretched when removed from the water. Return thermometer to its water bath to soak clean.

STEP 9: POUR balance of syrup—slowly—into egg whites, still beating constantly.

STEP 10: STIR in powdered sugar.

STEP 11: EVAPORATE excess moisture from mixture by placing bowl over hot water in your makeshift double boiler and stirring until nougat "snaps."

STEP 12: FOLD in chopped nuts and vanilla.

STEP 13: POUR into prepared pan. For a 1-inch-thick nougat, use standard 5 × 9-inch loaf pan. For a thinner nougat, use a 7 × 10-inch pan.

STEP 14: COVER nougat with wax paper and weigh it down. (I place another loaf pan of the same size inside the first, and use a brick or 5-pound bag of sugar as the weight.) Let sit overnight at room temperature, then refrigerate. This nougat keeps forever and travels well.

YIELD: 3 DOZEN THICK PIECES, 5 TO 6 DOZEN THIN ONES. Do not freeze.

Nougat Loaf alla Napoli

This nougat improves with age and can be stored at room temperature. It's a slightly soft nougat that will firm up over a day or two, so don't give up on it. Try slicing it and serving it with ice cream as a dessert.

½ cup honey, or ¼ cup honey and ¼ cup light corn syrup

1 cup granulated white sugar

¼ cup water, divided

2 large egg whites, at room temperature

Pinch (⅛ teaspoon) of salt

3 packets premelted unsweetened chocolate, or ¾ cup cocoa melted with ¼ cup margarine or solid vegetable shortening

1 egg yolk

½ cup finely ground nuts

1 cup plain crumbled cookies or leftover yellow cake, in small pieces

Optional: another ½ cup finely ground nuts to roll candy in

STEP 1: HEAT honey and sugar together with 1 tablespoon water in heavy saucepan or skillet, stirring occasionally, until they begin to turn brown, or caramelize.

STEP 2: BEAT egg whites with salt in a small electric mixer bowl until stiff.

STEP 3: POUR caramelized mixture slowly into egg whites until smoothly blended.

STEP 4: COMBINE chocolate with 3 tablespoons water in small saucepan (or microwave on MEDIUM [50%] for 30 seconds, stir, and repeat until smooth).

STEP 5: ADD chocolate to egg whites, and stir in egg yolk and half of the nuts, blending well.

STEP 6: FOLD in cookies or cake.

STEP 7: SPRINKLE half of remaining nuts on the bottom of a greased and wax paper–lined loaf pan (let wax paper extend up the ends).

STEP 8: POUR nougat into loaf pan. Top with balance of nuts. Cover that with more wax paper and weigh down by placing second loaf pan inside first and brick or sack of flour inside of that. Let sit at room temperature until bottom is completely cool, then refrigerate at least overnight. Slice into cubes and roll in optional nuts.

YIELD: 1 POUND. Can freeze; do not double.

French Nougats

This is one of the easiest, most fail-proof, fastest-cooking, bestest candy recipes I know. It makes a chewy, traditional nougat with most of the work done by machine and lends itself to all sorts of variations. It cannot, however, be easily doubled since the egg whites expand so.

2¼ cups granulated sugar

1 cup light corn syrup

½ cup water

3 large egg whites, at room temperature

8 teaspoons (⅙ cup) lightest honey you can find

3 tablespoons butter at room temperature

⅓ teaspoon salt

½ cup slivered almonds

1 teaspoon or more instant coffee granules

Optional: *¼ cup or more confectioners' sugar*

STEP 1: PREPARE thermometer. Put ice water in glass. Measure sugar, corn syrup, and water and place in 2-quart saucepan.

STEP 2: DISSOLVE sugar, stirring frequently with wooden spoon over medium heat until sugar is dissolved and mixture loses its opacity. Increase heat to medium-high and bring to a boil.

STEP 3: INTRODUCE prewarmed thermometer. Continue cooking without stirring (follow step 4 while waiting) at medium-high to high heat until mixture reaches soft crack (270°F to 275°F [132°C to 135°C]):

a small amount poured into ice water will form separate strands that stick together; when removed from water, the mass is stretchy. Replenish ice water in glass; you're going to need it to test the nougat later on.

STEP 4: BEAT egg whites in largest bowl of electric mixer until stiff while sugar syrup is cooking.

STEP 5: HEAT honey until boiling. Easily done in microwave-proof measuring cup in microwave and takes approximately 1 minute on HIGH (100%).

STEP 6: ADD honey slowly to whipped whites, beating continuously. Continue beating until whites double approximately in bulk. (If sugar syrup is not yet ready, continue beating at slighty slower speed until sugar is ready.)

STEP 7: RETURN thermometer to its water bath and add sugar syrup to egg whites in slow steady stream while beating on high speed. *Do not scrape saucepan* to get last drops. Continue beating until mixture is very light.

STEP 8: TEST egg white mixture in cold water. If it is stiff, not light and chewy, beat in ½ teaspoon at a time of hot water from thermometer bath to reduce stiffness.

STEP 9: STIR in softened butter; mixture will deflate immediately. Add in salt, almonds, and coffee. Taste nougat to see if honey-taste is too strong; if so add more coffee. Remember, when cold, all flavorings are less overpowering.

STEP 10: POUR into a greased and wax paper–lined (grease that, too) 8 × 10-inch pan (for thicker nougat use smaller pan) or onto oiled cookie sheets (you will need two, since mixture spreads). When cool, place in refrigerator to chill, preferably overnight. When cold, if still sticky, turn out onto board dusted with ⅛ cup of confectioners' sugar, remove wax paper, and sprinkle balance of sugar on nougat, coating it well. If using immediately, cut to size, wrap individually if you like, or return to pan and store in refrigerator; otherwise, store in pan, cutting pieces as needed.

YIELD: 6 DOZEN 1-INCH SQUARES. Does not freeze well.

VARIATIONS

This is the most versatile nougat recipe of all those I experimented with. Easily made, it lends itself to variations since the butter, flavoring, and almonds can all be replaced and/or eliminated.

Mocha French Nougats

Replace butter with 2 ounces (2 squares) unsweetened chocolate, melted and cooled.

Chocolate French Nougats

Replace butter with 2 ounces unsweetened chocolate, melted and cooled. Add ½ to 1 teaspoon vanilla extract instead of coffee.

Peanut Butter French Nougats

Replace butter with room temperature peanut butter. Can retain coffee granules or replace with ½ to 1 teaspoon vanilla extract. Eliminate salt and use salted peanuts instead of almonds.

Coconut French Nougats

Replace almonds with ½ cup or more coconut flakes. Can retain coffee granules or use ½ to 1 teaspoon vanilla extract or coconut extract.

Orange French Nougats

Replace coffee granules with 1½ teaspoons orange extract (may want to add some food coloring). Instead of nuts, use chopped gum drops.

Lemon French Nougats

Replace coffee granules with 1½ teaspoons pure lemon extract. Replace almonds with chopped candied fruit, such as cherries or citron.

MARSHMALLOW

Now, finally, I have found a candy whose name is traceable, pin-downable, real! And fortunately, the candy is delicious enough to live down the very connotations of its name, derived as it is from the mucilaginous root of a plant found in marshes and wetlands.

Mary Poppins must have had this candy in mind when she sang about a spoonful of sugar making the medicine go down, for the sugar is already incorporated in this honest-to-goodness pharmaceutical, the "marshmallow." For centuries, decoctions of marshmallow root were made into sweet aerated pieces and used for the treatment of chest complaints. The recipe has been handed down to the confectioner much as it was originally with one exception: It is no longer made from the marshmallow root; now it is made from unflavored gelatin.

Why would anyone want to make his or her own marshmallows when store-bought ones are so convenient and inexpensive?

Good question. Initially the only answer I could come up with was because store-bought only gives you one choice of flavors: bland, blander, and blandest.

Then I began making my own. Oh, what a difference! The ones you make are tender, buttery (even those without a pat of butter in them), delicate, truly melt-in-your-mouth . . . and if you have an electric mixer, they almost make themselves. I promise you this, once you've made your own, those other bland things that are all chewy, sugary air will be saved for cooking or—a fitting fate—scorching over a fire.

Like most of the other sweets, marshmallow has numerous variations but is based on a common formula that resembles nougat but with a higher moisture content and no egg whites or fats.

Two things are important to guarantee success: (1) Sugar must be in solution, otherwise the marshmallows will be sandy; and (2) you mustn't let marshmallows dry out while making them, otherwise they are difficult to whip and may even ferment. Also, underwhipped marshmallow gives a product that sets slowly. A batch also sets slowly when it is too warm when poured, and setting is delayed if the batch contains too much moisture.

Marshmallows

Although this is made with coffee, no one would guess it. The result has a buttery flavor.

¼ cup cornstarch

¼ cup confectioners' sugar

2 envelopes (2 tablespoons or ½ ounce) unflavored gelatin

¾ cup cold black coffee, not too strong, or 1 teaspoon instant coffee, dissolved (see step 2)

1½ cups granulated white sugar

1 cup light corn syrup

¾ cup water

Pinch (⅛ teaspoon) of salt

1½ teaspoons vanilla

STEP 1: MIX cornstarch and confectioners' sugar and place in a sifter or sieve. For ½-inch-thick marshmallows, lightly butter or oil sides of two 8 × 8-inch pans. Line with greased wax paper. Using sifter, cover bottom of each pan with a generous layer of cornstarch-confectioners' sugar mixture (1 heaping tablespoon per pan). Reserve rest for later.

STEP 2: SOAK gelatin in cold coffee (or dissolve 1 teaspoon instant coffee in 2 tablespoons hot water, adding ice to cool and enough cold water to measure ¾ cup) in heat-proof dish or measuring cup. Let stand until liquid is absorbed, 5 to 10 minutes. In the meantime, prewarm thermometer. Then dissolve gelatin by heating over hot water or microwaving for 45 to 60 seconds on MEDIUM (50%). Place in large bowl of electric mixer.

STEP 3: COMBINE granulated sugar, corn syrup, water, and salt in heavy 2-quart saucepan with tight-fitting lid, stirring constantly with wooden spoon over low heat until sugar dissolves, gritty sounds cease, spoon glides smoothly over bottom of pan. Increase heat to medium and bring to a boil.

STEP 4: COVER with a square of wax paper and tight-fitting lid, then boil 1 to 2 minutes to wash down sugar crystals. If necessary after removing lid, wash down any crystals that may have formed with pastry brush dipped in hot water from thermometer bath, using as little water as possible. Introduce prewarmed thermometer and continue cooking without stirring.

STEP 5: TEST syrup when mixture thickens and clings to spoon (approximately 270°F [132°C]). Between here and 290°F (143.5°C), syrup will reach soft-crack stage: When syrup falls into water, it separates into strands that can be stretched when removed from the water. Return thermometer to its hot water bath to soak clean.

STEP 6: ADD hot syrup—*very slowly*—to gelatin, beating at lowest speed possible. It will splatter at first. Increase speed slightly and beat for several minutes, or until froth covers the top. Increase speed to medium and beat at least 10 minutes, or until mixture becomes light and shiny and fluffy and holds its shape on a spoon.

STEP 7: FOLD in vanilla.

STEP 8: SPREAD in sugared pans and refrigerate until firm—at least an hour, but the marshmallow is easier to handle after 3 or 4 hours.

STEP 9: TURN OUT, when firm, upside-down onto wax paper covered with the balance of the cornstarch–confectioners' sugar mixture.

STEP 10: CUT with sharp knife dipped in cold water (or use round cookie cutters, dipped in cornstarch-sugar mixture). Roll marshmallow edges in more of the mixture. Store in airtight container in cool place or refrigerator. Toughens up after several days.

YIELD: 48 TO 72 1¼-INCH SQUARES. Cannot be doubled or frozen.

VARIATIONS

Coconut Marshmallow

In step 2, eliminate coffee—dissolve gelatin in ¾ cup cold water—and increase vanilla to 1 tablespoon in step 7. Spread 1½ cups coconut in jelly-roll pan and toast in preheated 350°F oven, stirring every 5 minutes, until lightly brown. Fold in in step 7 or divide, putting half in bottom of pan, sprinkling balance on top of marshmallow mixture.

Orange-Flavored Marshmallow

In step 1, add finely grated zest from 1 orange to the cornstarch-sugar mixture. In step 2, soak gelatin in ½ cup orange juice (eliminate coffee), diluting it with ¼ cup water. Eliminate all other flavoring.

Mocha Marshmallow

In step 1, add ¼ cup cocoa to cornstarch-sugar mixture. In step 2, triple the amount of instant coffee (still add 1½ teaspoons vanilla). In step 10, roll cut edges in more cocoa.

Almond/Nut Marshmallow

Soak gelatin in plain water. Eliminate vanilla and, in step 7, add 2 teaspoons almond extract and ½ cup slivered blanched almonds. Or add almond extract but dust top with ground almonds and roll marshmallow edges in more ground nuts.

Other Possibilities

Spread coconut/nuts in bottom of greased and dusted pan or chocolate shot (jimmies) or cocoa directly on greased wax paper.

ELEVEN

Fudge Failures and How to Fix Them

FAILURES . . . CAUSES AND CURES
WEEPING FUDGE
GRAINY FUDGE
CARAMELY FUDGE
SOFT AND CHEWY FUDGE
TOO-SUGARY FUDGE
SPOTTED FUDGE

MARSHMALLOW-BASED FAILED FUDGES

FANTASTIC FLOPPEROOS
DRIZZLE BARS
TAFFY-APPLE BARS
FAILED-FUDGE BROWNIES
FAILED-FUDGE CEREAL TREATS

FUDGAMON BUNS
NO-GOOD NOUGAT
ONE FAILED FUDGE = ONE MAGNIFICENT MOUSSE
FAILED-FUDGE BAVARIAN CREAM
FAILED-FUDGE FROSTING
MOCK PECAN PIE A.K.A. FAILED-FUDGE PIE

Don't be discouraged by a failure. It can be a positive experience.
Failure is, in a sense, the highway to success, inasmuch as every
discovery of what is false leads us to seek earnestly after what
is true, and every fresh experience points out some form of error
which we shall afterwards carefully avoid.

—JOHN KEATS

How true, how true! On the other hand, failure need
not mean flop. Instead, we may just end up with something other
than what we expected. For example, we can thank a clumsy soda
jerk for the ice cream soda. He accidentally dropped a scoop of ice
cream in a glass of soda pop. *Fizz-bang*, a whole new drink was in-
vented.

As you will recall, fudge itself began life as a failure or accident:
A batch of caramel accidentally grained and produced fudge. This is
one reason why fudge can be so cantankerous and difficult to make:
It is difficult to reproduce an accident. So remember that you're trying
to create an accident. If it doesn't come out, you didn't fail, you were
just too successful for your own good.

What is remarkable is that industry has just as much difficulty
making fudge as we do. One Chicago-based candy manufacturer is
reported to have spent a year and nearly a quarter of a million dollars
in research into making a commercial fudge. The company
failed . . . on a grand scale.

Actually, my research shows that the problems factory fudge-
makers and homemakers face are direct opposites. Factory fudgemen
give symposiums and read reports on how to prevent graining and
retain moisture to prolong shelf life, which is why they use so much
corn syrup and other invert sugars. But homebodies complain about
fudge soup—they can't get their fudge to solidify. As to keeping it
edible for months on end, what fudge ever lasted that long in a house
with kids?

So, to every maker of fudge soup and other failed fudges, I dedicate
this chapter. In it you will learn what I have learned from all those
recipes that failed. Like Keats, I learned far more from my failures
than from my successes, beginning with the fact that many, many
fudge recipes contain inherent problems. No one, but no one, could
make them work. Some, obviously, were cooked up at a typewriter.

Others rely on boiling for a specific amount of time without stating what degree of boil. Some give a single temperature as a goal when in fact the temperature of the ball will change from hour to hour, day to day.

Then, if the recipe is sound, you must still consider the fact that it may be too hot outside or in; the humidity may be too high (it's never too low); your air conditioner may not pull enough moisture out of the air. In the home, there are a zillion things that can make a fudge fail without the cook lifting a finger. However, fortunately for us fudge-makers, a fudge failure is rarely fatal. And all those failures have challenged me to figure out how to use up a lot of fudge.

In this chapter I'll explain how to soften hard fudge and recook soft fudge, and what to do when all else fails. Some of these dishes are worth deliberately sabotaging a batch of fudge. I also include a checklist for analyzing fudge recipes from other sources to see if the problem is in the recipe, not the fudge pot.

FAILURES ... CAUSES AND CURES

IF FUDGE WHILE COOLING WEEPS

Cause: Too much humidity in room is creating condensation.

Cure: Pour off excess liquid and proceed with recipe.

IF FUDGE TURNS TOO QUICKLY AND BECOMES COARSE AND GRAINY

Cause: Beaten too long or too hard, probably with electric mixer.

Cure 1: Soften it if it's just a bit hard.

Try kneading it with your hands. Frequently the heat from your hands will be sufficient to melt the sugar crystals enough so that you can bind the fudge together. Buttering your fingers will not only help bind the fudge but will also give it a gloss.

Cure 2: Soften it if it won't submit to a helping hand.

Simply wet a paper towel (not dripping or sopping but wet-wet) and place it in a rescalable plastic bag along with the pan of fudge. Leave the bag at room temperature until the next day. If the paper towel dries out and the fudge is still hard, repeat.

Cure 3: Melt rocks, so to speak. When it is rock-hard, you can try giving it a water bath.

Separate the fudge from the sides of the pan by running a knife along it and wiggling it back and forth. Then pour ¼ cup cold water around the edge of the pan, letting it flow down to the bottom. Allow it to sit for 2 to 3 minutes until the fudge (remember, it's hygroscopic and absorbs moisture readily) has taken up as much moisture as it will. Drain well and let the fudge sit for a few minutes, then test its softness. Still not sticking together? Try bathing it for another minute.

Cure 4: Recook it, except if it contains marshmallow (see page 230 for that).

Add 1 cup water and ½ tablespoon corn syrup per cup of sugar (any kind) in the original recipe, then follow original recipe, adding any fresh flavoring to taste except peanut butter, coconut, or chocolate.

Note: Because the sugar has already come up to soft-ball stage once, it will do so at a lower temperature on recooking. This is particularly true of peanut butter fudge. Modern peanut butters have so many additives to control their consistency that you will have to go by trial and error. However, peanut butter fudge should froth up and then smooth out with large bubbles imploding here and there when it is near the soft-ball stage, which can occur as low as 208°F (97.5°C). Be sure to cook at least to medium firm-ball stage.

Cure 5: Make something else out of it. (See recipes beginning on page 231.)

IF FUDGE TURNS TO CARAMEL

Cause: You didn't beat it before it cooled completely, or it cooled too fast (for example, over ice cubes).

Cure 1: Force it to become fudge.

Work it in a food processor for 1 minute without stopping, then spoon it into a pan and chill. On the first day it will be rich, smooth, luscious caramel, but 24 hours later it will have turned into the most interesting caramel fudge you can imagine. A delicious failure!

Cure 2: Enjoy . . . just pretend you were making caramel all along.

Cure 3: Recook it, and end up with a better fudge than originally planned—I promise you!

Check the original recipe and add water equivalent to half the original major liquid component. For example, use ½ cup water for a recipe that calls for 1 cup evaporated milk regardless of the fact that it also calls for ¼ cup each corn syrup and honey. Melt fudge over low heat until it is completely dissolved. If you have added pecans or cashews or other soft nuts, you'll have to remove them to retain their delicate flavor. (You don't have to remove walnuts, brazil nuts, or pistachios.) To remove a small amount of nuts, use a slotted spoon. (Loaded with nuts? Pour the fudge through a large sieve or colander into a heat-proof bowl.) Using a wet cloth or paper towel, wipe clean the pour area on the side of your cooking pan. If you are working with a milk-based fudge, butter the sides before returning the batch to the cooking pan. Add the drained nuts later, when the original recipe calls for them. Recook to soft-ball stage—see Note on page 227.

Cure 4: Make something else out of it. (See recipes beginning on page 231.)

IF FUDGE DOESN'T HARDEN COMPLETELY BUT IS STICKY AND CHEWY

Cause: It was not cooked to the right ball, not beaten enough, weather conditions weren't right, too much corn syrup or honey was used, flavoring was old, or you used a creme-based liqueur.

Cure 1: Do nothing.

Sometimes it takes a fudge several hours to grain. If the fudge seems to have lighter streaks on the surface or seems different about the edges, it may well change to fudge without your doing anything.

If it doesn't, pass it off as soft caramel. Simply wrap half-teaspoonfuls in wax paper, twist the ends, and tell the world to try this delicious caramel you just made.

Cure 2: Dehydrate it in a frost-free refrigerator.

Simply place the pan uncovered near the refrigerator fan and allow it to stay that way overnight or longer. The fan will withdraw water and turn the fudge hard.

Cure 3: Recook it as in cure 4 for coarse and grainy fudge (page 227) unless it contains fruit or marshmallow. See page 230 for instructions on handling these.

Cure 4: Add enough confectioners' sugar to thicken it. The result will probably be sickeningly sweet. *Not recommended.*

Cure 5: Make something else out of it. (See recipes beginning on page 231.)

IF FUDGE IS FIRM BUT AWFULLY SUGARY

Cause: The grain wasn't controlled, there was not enough corn syrup in the recipe, or it was beaten at too warm a temperature or for too long.

Cure: Cheer up.

Some people have gone through life eating sugary fudge. Sugary fudge is real fudge, they'll tell you; that other stuff lacks character and texture. (Which explains the popularity of many brownies.)

To prevent sugaring, use a recipe with a crystal preventor (professionals call them "crystal doctors"), such as corn syrup, honey, molasses, lemon juice, or anything acidic. Wash down the crystals from the side of the pan before cooking to a ball and/or pouring—using a pastry brush dipped in the thermometer bath, or cover pan with wax paper and tight-fitting lid and steam 1 to 2 minutes. Be sure to allow the pan to cool to lukewarm before stirring. Don't overbeat. Pour as soon as fudge loses its gloss.

IF FUDGE DEVELOPS SPOTS AFTER COOLING

Cause: Spots are usually air bubbles caused by several things: too vigorous beating that incorporates too much air, or too small a pan, which traps bubbles inside too thick a layer. Or you failed to bang the pan sharply. Or you beat at too high a temperature. Spots could even be caused by impurities in the sugar. Those recipes using water as the dissolver usually require you to skim the sugar syrup of any impurities. When a milk-based product is used as a dissolver, the impurities do not come to the surface at the beginning of the boil, only after the fudge has cooled. A third possible cause is "fat bloom," or molecules of fat coming to the surface. That's the bad news. The good news is this is only a cosmetic problem. The spots won't affect the taste and certainly won't hurt you.

Cure 1: Ignore.

Cure 2: Cut fudge into very small pieces to disguise the spots.

Cure 3: Hide the spots by covering the fudge with melted semisweet chocolate (melt in microwave, but don't apply while hot or the fudge may melt).

Cure 4: Make something else out of it.

MARSHMALLOW-BASED FAILED FUDGES

This is one of those d----d if you do, and d----d if you don't situations. Marshmallows help prevent fudge failures. They are the basis of 99.9 percent of all "no-fail" recipes—which do not have a 100 percent success rate, otherwise you wouldn't be reading this.

When marshmallow-based fudges fail, the marshmallow makes rescuing it almost impossible. That is because, like oil and water, fat and gelatin don't mix.

You will have less of a problem if you have used marshmallows and not marshmallow creme. When you melt the fudge, simply remove the marshmallows before proceeding with the recipe and reincorporate them just before pouring, as you do with soft nuts in cure 3 on page 228.

If you have used marshmallow creme, you may be in trouble. Although the mixture will cook back up to the soft ball—it takes a while—when you go to stir it, you have to be a fine judge of when to stop. Stir just until it thickens slightly and pour immediately; it will grain in the pan. Go beyond that and you may see a miracle of fudge chemistry before your eyes. Suddenly the fudge will get watery. (The first time it happened to me, I thought my pot had sprung a leak.) It is actually throwing off the excess cocoa butter or fat. Fear not, you can simply drain it, refrigerate, and your fudge will be fine. It may not look as great as some, but it will taste fine.

Another solution is to make a wonderful caramel out of the marshmallow failure. Add ½ of the original amount of liquid, 1 tablespoon corn syrup per original cup of sugar, and recook to the firm-ball stage— it must hold its shape when taken out of water and be chewy to the bite. Pour immediately into a prepared pan. You can even add more mini-marshmallows if you'd like. Either wrap in wax paper or refrigerate, for this makes a very sticky caramel.

Other solutions:

1. Fight fire with fire. Remelt, adding water—one-half the amount of the original liquid—bring back to ball (it should hold its shape when removed from water), and pour over more marshmallow creme. If you wish, you can even flavor that creme and simply streak the fudge through it. I've had great success adding both ½ teaspoon peppermint and several drops of red food coloring to the creme (the food coloring doesn't blend in all that well but no matter), then streaking it with remelted chocolate fudge. Chill until cold. It makes a very tender fudge.

2. Remelt, adding water as in the first step, recook to ball, then pour over one can of ready-made canned frosting in a complementary flavor. Add nuts if you like and refrigerate. This approaches the soft consistency of the best store-bought fudge.

3. Remelt as in the first step, bring to a ball, let cool for about 10 minutes or to about 200°F (93.5°C), then pour over fondant in a mixing bowl (this will cause fudge to cool down immediately). Mix well and pour—what you have here is identical to professional fudges.

FANTASTIC FLOPPEROOS

Okay, you've tried your best and the fudge failed, probably due to circumstances beyond your control. What you need is a no-fail success. And that's what these recipes are. They'll turn failures into triumphs, rescue all that hard work you've done, and earn you compliments without your ever having to confess you flopped.

Drizzle Bars

How good are these bars? All I can say is that there are people hoping that my fudge will fail so that I'll make these, they're that good! I offer you a choice of crusts, one more buttery than the other. For those trying to limit their butterfat intake, the first will appeal. Between you and me, taste-testers favor Crust 2.

CRUST 1	CRUST 2
¼ cup (½ stick) butter	½ cup (1 stick) butter
¼ cup confectioners' sugar	¼ cup confectioners' sugar
1 cup all-purpose flour	1 cup all-purpose flour

3½ to 7 ounces shredded sweetened coconut

1 to 2 cups (6 to 12 ounces) chips in complementary flavor

1 recipe failed fudge (too hard, too soft, too runny, too sugary, too chewy)

1 cup chopped walnuts

One 14-ounce can sweetened condensed milk

Preheat oven to 375°F. Melt butter (in microwave or saucepan) and blend with sugar and flour until cohesive. Then press into ungreased pan (8 × 8-inch or 9 × 9-inch). Bake Crust 1 for 15 to 20 minutes, until firm and barely browned; bake Crust 2 for 20 to 30 minutes. While crust is still hot, spread coconut over it. Top with chips (butterscotch or peanut butter chips with chocolate fudge, semisweet chocolate with almost anything else). Pour too-thin fudge haphazardly over chips; dice too-hard or grainy or chewy fudge and scatter over chips. Scatter walnuts over that. Drizzle sweetened condensed milk over everything. Bake for 20 minutes, then use a spatula to press down and compact the bars. Finish baking for 15 to 20 minutes. Cool on a rack and cut.

YIELD: APPROXIMATELY 2½ DOZEN 2 × 2-INCH BARS. Can freeze and can double, using two pans.

You don't have failed fudge? Despair not, substitute 2 cups (12 ounces) chips in the flavor of your choice. You don't have coconut? Omit. You have two recipes of failed fudge? If they're complementary (and most are), use both. You have a nut fudge that won't go with walnuts? Omit walnuts or substitute peanuts. Or try doubling the chocolate chips. If you're really short of ingredients, go with Crust 2 (which is a delicious shortbread and has more character than Crust 1) and use what little you have.

There is only one constant and without it you'll have another failure: You must use sweetened condensed milk. Everything else? Use what you've got. These are, after all, no-fail bars.

Taffy-Apple Bars

Crust 2 from Drizzle Bars (see page 232)

½ of 14-ounce can apple pie filling, or one 12-ounce jar grape jelly, strawberry preserves, or other fruit-flavored jelly

1 recipe failed fudge

One 14-ounce can sweetened condensed milk

Follow directions for Drizzle Bars, using filling in place of coconut and chips. Cook 40 to 45 minutes until center is done. Let cool before cutting.

Failed-Fudge Brownies

Your fudge has failed . . . you don't have chips or other ingredients to make Drizzle Bars. What to do now? If you have milk, an egg, and all-purpose flour, you can make a deliciously chewy brownie out of the failed fudge.

Proportions are as follows: For every 2 cups (roughly 1 pound yield) of any failed fudge that is not runny, you'll need 1 egg, ½ cup scooped all-purpose flour, and ½ cup milk. (For fudge soup, halve the milk. If fudge is as thin as bouillon, eliminate the milk.) Mix egg, milk, and flour together until mixture is smooth, then stir into fudge mixture. Bake in buttered 8 × 8-inch pan in preheated 325°F oven for 40 to 45 minutes. A cake tester inserted around the edge should come out clean; center will obviously still be soft. Place on rack to cool.

Failed-Fudge Cereal Treats

1 recipe failed fudge, remelted
2½ cups crisp rice cereal
Optional: ½ cup chopped nuts

If you are planning to use nuts, add them to the hot fudge first, then the cereal. Mound in 5 × 10-inch buttered pan. Refrigerate. Frequently you'll end up with a caramel or fudge on the bottom and a crunchy layer on top. It's very good either way.

Fudgamon Buns

1 recipe failed fudge
One 8-pack triangular refrigerator rolls
One 4-pack triangular refrigerator rolls
Optional: ¼ cup granulated white sugar
½ cup seedless raisins

Preheat oven to 350°F. Spread fudge if too thin or chop and scatter fudge if too thick over the bottom of 6 × 10-inch baking pan. Unroll rolls and press perforations together. Sprinkle with sugar, if desired, and press raisins firmly into dough. Cut each four-triangle portion into four long ribbons. Roll each ribbon up pinwheel fashion and place, pinwheel side down, on top of fudge. Space rolls about ½ inch apart. Put pan inside larger pan; add water to larger pan so that it comes up about ½ inch on smaller pan (to prevent fudge from burning). Bake 35 to 40 minutes, or until rolls are brown.

YIELD: 12 BUNS.

No-Good Nougat

Next to fudge, nougat is the most temperamental candy. Although it should set at room temperature, if it is still too soft after 12 hours or so, try putting it in the refrigerator. Still too soft? Forget freezing, it won't. Instead, gell.

2 envelopes (2 tablespoons or ½ ounce) unflavored gelatin
¼ cup cold water
Optional: *flavorings*
1 recipe failed nougat

Soften gelatin in water for 10 minutes, or until it swells up. Heat in microwave or atop range until gelatin dissolves. Flavor gelatin, if desired, depending on flavor of nougat. For chocolate nougat, use ½ teaspoon instant coffee; for vanilla nougat, use ½ teaspoon flavoring of your choice, including more vanilla. Blend gelatin and nougat and chill in refrigerator for several hours. Texture will be soft. Serve as a dessert or cube (1-inch pieces) and roll in ground nuts.

One Failed Fudge =
One Magnificent Mousse

If your fudge has at least partially thickened, so its consistency is more like a custard than a beverage, you have the makings of two quick and easy desserts (which seems only fair, considering all the time you put in on the failed fudge): a not-so-ordinary mousse and a frozen soufflé. (This is particularly good with failed Apple Fudge à la Barbara Bush.)

Chill 1 pound fudge soup (soft and/or chewy) for at least 1 hour (who knows, it might decide to go thick in the refrigerator). At the same time, chill a small mixer bowl, the electric mixer beaters, and 1 cup heavy (whipping) cream. Beat cream to stiff peaks—watch that it doesn't turn to butter. Fold failed fudge into cream thoroughly. Mound into individual dishes, and keep chilled until ready to serve. Or pile into lightly greased mold and freeze.

To make this exquisite dessert deliberately, simply follow the instructions for making a sauce: When fudge thickens and bubbles become noisy, remove from heat, and in the case of Apple Fudge à la Barbara Bush, add spices and 1 cup diced apple. Stir well (to cook apples). The mixture will thicken slightly but never grain. Chill several hours, then fold into whipped cream. This is Apple Fudge à la Mode with a delicious twist.

Failed-Fudge Bavarian Cream

If the fudge is very, very runny, turn it into a Bavarian Cream.

1 recipe failed fudge, soupy
2 envelopes (2 tablespoons or ½ ounce) unflavored gelatin
2 large egg whites
Pinch (⅛ teaspoon) of cream of tartar
1 cup heavy (whipping) cream

Take ½ cup runny fudge and sprinkle gelatin over it. Allow to sit until gelatin softens and swells. Dissolve gelatin completely by microwaving on MEDIUM (50%) for 15 to 30 seconds, or by placing over hot water. Mix warmed fudge back into the rest of fudge and let cool to room temperature. Beat egg whites, adding cream of tartar when they become frothy. Continue beating to stiff peaks, and fold into fudge mixture. Beat cream in chilled bowl using chilled beaters until stiffened but not thick—it should hold soft peaks—and fold into fudge mixture. Pour into 6-cup mold and chill until ready to serve.

Failed-Fudge Frosting

1 recipe failed fudge
Up to 2 tablespoons cold milk

Make a fondantlike, glossy frosting by warming fudge in top of double boiler to 110°F to 120°F (43.5°C to 49°C), stirring constantly. Stirring will release any air that may be present. If fudge separates on warming, add a little cold milk to bind it back together. Let cool, then pour or spread over cakes or cupcakes. Frosting should set with a fine gloss.

Mock Pecan Pie
a.k.a. Failed-Fudge Pie

Let me ask you, would your family members turn up their noses at a luscious pecan pie? No? Then don't tell them your chocolate or caramel fudge failed, just add pecans to it and follow these directions, telling them you were trying out a new recipe for chocolate or caramel pecan pie. Results are good with almost any fudge recipe, but are best with sour cream– or buttermilk-based fudges. The result is a very dense, very chewy pie—exactly like a pecan pie.

1 pie crust, or Crust 2 from Drizzle Bars (see page 232)
3 ounces cream cheese, softened
1 recipe failed fudge (1 pound), soupy, at room temperature
2 large eggs, separated
Pinch (⅛ teaspoon) of cream of tartar
Pecans or walnuts

Preheat oven to 350°F. Line 8-inch round pan with pie crust or Crust 2 and prebake as directed. Allow to cool while you make filling. Blend cream cheese and fudge with electric mixer or in food processor. Add egg yolks and beat well. In separate bowl, with clean beaters, beat egg whites till frothy. Add cream of tartar, and continue beating until whites form stiff peaks. Fold whites lightly into fudge mixture. Mound mixture in center of nut-filled prebaked crust or put nuts on top. (Mixture will spread during baking.) Bake for 45 minutes, or until center has fallen. Let cool. Serve with whipped cream or ice cream.

TWELVE

Mishmash

VERSION III
MELTING MORSELS, CHIPS, OR BITS
CHOCOLATE "RIBBON" WRAPPING

Every book has one of these, a potpourri, a miscellany, a catch-all chapter in which to insert recipes that are misfits but essential.

Basic Recipe for Fudge Sauce

Make any fudge recipe in this book (if you've done it before and noted a temperature at which it balled, your life is simplified), and cook just until sauce thickens, or 6°F (3.5°C) lower than the temperature at which it balled. Add flavorings and let cool without shocking or stirring.

Making Sauce from Frozen Fudge

Let's suppose you made a double batch of fudge and froze half. That frozen fudge can be converted into a sauce. Microwave at DEFROST (30%) for 3 minutes, uncovered; stir, repeat for 2 minutes. If too thick, add heavy cream, 1 teaspoon at a time. Or melt fudge in double boiler, adding heavy cream 1 teaspoon at a time until desired thickness is reached. Do not let it get so hot that it begins recooking.

Neat Trick for Hot Fudge Sauce

Use a slow cooker, on lowest heat, to melt and hold fudge or to hold melted sauce.

Taffy

After spending page after page extolling the virtues of old-fashioned candy-making sessions, how could I leave out the most fun candy of them all: taffy. It is truly helpful to have a group session when pulling this, although, thanks to the microwave, one person really can handle it. But that's no fun. By the way, in the old days, before fudge shops put marble slabs in their windows, the big attraction for passersby at a candy store was watching taffy being pulled singlehandedly. An enormous hook hanging from the ceiling or placed high up on a wall would not only take the place of a partner, but it used gravity to do the stretching.

Plain Molasses Taffy

An old-fashioned taffy made simply from molasses and baking soda, this makes enough for two people to pull. But for groups, it is easily doubled or tripled, providing you have a pot big enough (I'm talking soup kettle) to hold the mixture. Molasses treated with baking soda follows the Benning Law of Junk Expanding to Fill a Boy's Room: It just swells and swells. The molasses itself will expand fourfold during boiling. Then when you add the baking soda, it will inflate again— alarmingly so.

> *2 cups good molasses*
> *⅛ teaspoon stirred, lump-free baking soda*

STEP 1: PREPARE: Prewarm thermometer; fill glass with ice cubes and water; butter jelly-roll pan or surface to pour taffy on (it will spread to about 8 by 12 inches). Cut 3 × 5-inch pieces of wax paper while waiting for molasses to cook. Use at least a 3-quart heavy saucepan because molasses tends to boil up.

STEP 2: WET cup before measuring molasses. Pour into saucepan, scraping cup out well. Set over low heat until it thins out.

STEP 3: BOIL, over medium heat, for about 20 to 30 minutes, stirring occasionally and watching to prevent its boiling too high. When froth subsides a bit, rinse down any accumulated sugar crystals on sides of pan with pastry brush dipped in water from thermometer bath, using as little water as necessary. Introduce prewarmed thermometer.

STEP 4: TEST in ice-cold water when mixture thickens and becomes foamy, for soft crack. Syrup separates into individual, somewhat brittle strands in ice-cold water, but when removed, it softens from warmth of your fingers and becomes stretchy. Taste it; if it's chewy and taffylike, it's ready. Approximately 270°F to 290°F (132°C to 143°C).

STEP 5: ADD baking soda, stir down, and continue cooking to brittle stage. Retest with clean ice-cold water. Syrup, when it hits ice-cold water, forms strands that can be broken on removal from water. Approximately 300°F to 310°F (149°C to 154°C); try to stay on low side.

STEP 6: POUR, but do not scrape, taffy onto buttered jelly-roll pan or any cold, buttered, nonporous surface.

STEP 7: COOL until safe to handle. (Hold hand over taffy: When taffy stops giving off heat, test with a tentative buttered finger. If cool, not cold, go to it.)

STEP 8: WORK taffy, but first butter your hands. (You may want to use a scraper or spatula at first when it's fairly thin and sticky.) Fold taffy in upon itself a couple of times until you have a long thin rectangle. Then pick it up, s-t-r-e-t-c-h it as far as you can reach, then fold it in half like a jump rope, twist together into one rope, pull, bring ends together, twist, and so on. At first you'll be able to work the whole batch at one time. But when it becomes completely streaked with pale brown, it will begin hardening up. So, divide in half and let someone else work one while you do the other. (Or set it aside and microwave as below.) Repeat until taffy is all one color—a light *dull* tan. Then pull out again to about a yard, fold in half, and twist while working taffy so that it is all of one width (about the size of your ring finger).

It will look exactly like a spiral-wound telephone cord. Cut with a scissors into 1-inch lengths. The cutting will compress it and turn each piece into a candy cushion. Wrap in wax paper, twisting ends if you are not planning to use within an hour or so (if you are planning to use soon, place pieces on a heavily buttered platter but don't let them touch).

About that other half. Put it on a micro-proof dish and zap it on DEFROST (30%) for 20 to 30 seconds. Take it out. Handling it gingerly with buttered hands—there may be hot spots—begin working it just like the first batch.

If at any time candy hardens while you are working, microwave it on DEFROST (30%) in small segments (about the size of a frankfurter) for 5 to 10 seconds; depending on microwave, it may take a few seconds longer to make candy pliable.

YIELD: 72 PIECES. Recipe can be doubled (or tripled) and frozen.

Peanut Taffy

A richer candy than plain Molasses Taffy, this one also requires just a few ingredients, but you have a lot of leeway in terms of how many peanuts you wish to include. My family votes for as many as you can possibly work in.

⅔ cup unsulfured molasses

1¼ cups firmly packed light brown sugar

6 tablespoons (¾ stick) butter, cut into thin slices

Approximately 1 cup roasted peanuts

STEP 1: PREPARE: Prewarm thermometer; fill glass with ice cubes and water; butter a shiny or nonporous surface to pour taffy on (it will spread to about 9 × 12 inches), scatter handful of peanuts in center of pan, over an area 6 by 9 inches, approximately.

STEP 2: DISSOLVE sugar in molasses, stirring constantly with wooden spoon over low heat until gritty sounds cease, spoon glides smoothly over bottom of pan. Increase heat to medium and bring to a boil. Cut

3 × 5-inch pieces of wax paper while waiting for molasses to cook. Use at least a 3-quart heavy saucepan because molasses has a tendency to boil up.

STEP 3: BOIL after washing down any crystals that may have formed with pastry brush dipped in hot water from thermometer bath, using as little water as possible. Introduce prewarmed thermometer. Reduce heat while retaining boil. Stir occasionally, mostly to scrape along edges.

STEP 4: ADD butter, scattering pieces about on top of pan, when mixture thickens and makes smacking noises. Approximately 240°F (115.5°C). Continue cooking.

STEP 5: TEST in ice-cold water when mixture thickens and foam gets darker, approximately 265°F (129.5°C). Continue testing until it comes to the soft crack. Syrup separates into individual, somewhat brittle strands in ice-cold water, but when removed, it softens from warmth of your fingers and becomes stretchy. Taste it; if it's chewy and taffylike, it's ready. Approximately 270°F to 290°F (132°C to 145°C).

STEP 6: POUR, but do not scrape pan, over peanuts on greased surface. Scatter more peanuts on top.

STEP 7: COOL until safe to handle. (Hold hand over taffy: When taffy stops giving off heat, test with a tentative buttered finger. If cool, not cold, go to it.)

STEP 8: WORK taffy, but first butter your hands. (You may want to use a scraper or spatula at first when it's fairly thin and sticky.) Incorporate peanuts as you go. The fewer peanuts you add and the less working you do, the shinier the candy and the harder it will be to the initial bite.

YIELD: 72 PIECES, MORE OR LESS, depending on how small you cut the pieces and how many peanuts you incorporate. Can double and freeze.

For other peanutty candies, check out the First Lady candies in chapter 13.

Simple Sugar Syrup

This syrup is used to remelt fondant in the classic manner. You can also use it when making iced tea or mixed drinks that call for a simple syrup. Also, if you brush this on warm baked goods before sprinkling with vanilla sugar or sifting on confectioners' sugar, the sugar will stick!

> 1 cup granulated white sugar
>
> ⅓ cup water

Dissolve sugar in water, stirring constantly until gritty sound ceases. Introduce thermometer. Turn up heat, and bring syrup to a boil without stirring (may need to skim scum). Boil to 225°F (107°C). Remove from heat and let cool until lukewarm. Pour, without scraping pan, into a clean jar. Store in refrigerator until needed. If it should crystallize at some point, simply remelt.

WORKING WITH CHOCOLATE

Homemade Chocolate Cups

Version I

This is the classic method; version III is the fastest. Personally I prefer the simpler, but admittedly less elegant version II.

> 2 squares (2 ounces) semisweet or unsweetened chocolate
>
> 2 teaspoons margarine or vegetable shortening
>
> 48 paper candy cups

Melt chocolate with margarine or vegetable shortening in top of double boiler over hot, not boiling, water. Use doubled paper candy cups, one inside another, to help support chocolate filling. Pour ½ teaspoon chocolate into each cup and spread up sides with an artist's brush. Chill in freezer for a few minutes, then recoat.

YIELD: 24 DOUBLE-COATED CUPS. Store for up to 1 week in refrigerator.

Version II

½ cup (3 ounces) semisweet chocolate chips

48 paper candy cups

Heat chocolate chips in microwave on HIGH (100%) for 60 seconds, stir, then heat for 30 seconds, stir. Use double paper candy cups, one inside another, to help support chocolate filling. Put ½ teaspoon chocolate in each cup and smear up the sides. To be fancy, you could use a brush for these as in recipe I, but work fast. Although these have a tendency to get a "bloom," or discolor (which is not harmful and does not affect the taste), after days of standing, they do not soften easily, even at warm room temperatures.

YIELD: 24 DOUBLE-COATED CUPS. Can be doubled and frozen.

Version III

2 packets premelted unsweetened chocolate

48 paper candy cups

Knead packets or place, unopened, in hot water to liquefy (dry packets thoroughly before opening to prevent any drops of water getting into chocolate). Cut corner of packet, squeeze ½ teaspoon or so in each cup and use a brush to coat sides of cup. Refrigerate between coatings and afterward.

This is the easiest way to make chocolate cups with a brush, but they must be refrigerated or else they soften. You may wish to do a third or fourth coating (double the chocolate) if you plan to serve them without the paper candy cup.

YIELD: 24 DOUBLE-COATED CUPS.

Melting Morsels, Chips, or Bits

OPTION 1: Melt chocolate by placing in heat-proof bowl over the hot water in your thermometer bath.

OPTION 2: Place in micro-proof measuring cup. Heat in microwave on HIGH (100%) for 60 seconds, then stir. Heat another 30 seconds, stir again thoroughly. Many chips will finish melting during the second stirring. Others will require another 30 seconds.

Chocolate "Ribbon" Wrapping

For the perfect hostess gift, here is an edible way to jazz up an assortment of homemade fudges. Cut fudge into same size pieces and place in a deep gift box. Then "wrap" box with a ribbon of chocolate.

6 squares (6 ounces) semisweet chocolate

¼ cup light corn syrup

Melt chocolate with corn syrup in top of a double boiler over simmering water. Stir until smooth. Pour into small bowl (I use 12-ounce heat-proof) and cover with plastic wrap to prevent evaporation, pressing wrap down onto surface to prevent condensation. Let stand in cool spot until mixture loses its gloss and is pliable (about 4 hours).

Remove from bowl with your hands, working into flattened oblong. Place on waxy side of freezer paper (at least 12 inches long) and top with wax paper. Roll out into a rectangle no more than ⅛-inch thick. (Or put through pasta machine to get as thin as possible. If chocolate begins to get too soft, let rest before working again.) Let rest and cool down about 1 hour before attempting to remove wax paper.

Cut the long way into ¾-inch-wide ribbons. Drape one ribbon lengthwise, another crosswise, over box or fudge, tucking ends under. Form balance of ribbons into a multilooped bow (if not pliable enough, stand ribbon on its side—heat from hands will help soften it, too) and flip over onto fudge. Allow two ends, trimmed ribbon–style, to dangle. If at any time heat from hands makes chocolate go soft, stop and let ribbons rest a bit. Garnish bow with berries or candied fruit or small candy cane at Christmastime.

THIRTEEN

A

Chronology of

Historic Fudges

1849 GINGER CANDY
1879 COCOANUT CARAMELS
1887 VASSAR FUDGE
1890 VANILLA CANDY
1900 FUDGE
     NO. 1 CHOCOLATE
     NO. 2 CHOCOLATE-NUT
     NO. 3 MAPLE SUGAR
1902 CHOCOLATE CARAMELS
1904 FUDGES
     PONOUCHI
     COMANCHE
1909 SMITH COLLEGE FUDGE
     WELLESLEY COLLEGE FUDGE
1920s TREACLE TOFFEE

FIRST LADY CANDIES AND CONFECTIONS

1887 FRENCH CREAM CANDY

1940s WHITE HOUSE FUDGE

      LADY BIRD JOHNSON'S QUICK PEANUT CANDY

      ROSALYNN CARTER'S PEANUT BRITTLE

      NANCY REAGAN'S VIENNA CHOCOLATE BARS

      BARBARA BUSH'S APPLE CRISP WITH ORANGE JUICE

        APPLE FUDGE À LA BARBARA BUSH

REQUESTED RECIPES

      NEVER-FAIL FUDGE

      HERSHEY'S COCOA CAN FUDGE

      KNOX DAINTIES

FUDGE PALACE FUDGE

      BASIC SINGLE 2½-POUND BATCH

      BASIC QUANTITY 6¼-POUND BATCH

See for yourself how much sweet-making has changed in America since the days of the 1849 gold rush. The following recipes are from the cookbook bibles of the past, running the gamut from simple to difficult. There are fondants, caramels, fudges, as well as others. Each is presented as originally written. Imagine as you read that you were there, doing the cooking. Note the nonstandard measurements and the vague instructions, and remember that you would also have had to cope with the treacherous fire beneath the pot, building it up or stoking it down in a constant attempt to keep it stable.

For our mothers and grandmothers and great-grandmothers, making confections was a chore and a challenge. Yet those same women, knowing the difficulties but desiring to please their families, mastered a diverse repertoire of confection recipes . . . and then, in the late 1800s, faced the most apparently simple yet devilishly complex confection of them all, fudge!

The recipes that follow work as is; modern measurements or equivalents are given in brackets. If you follow them as written, as I did, you will discover what the sweets of the last 140 years were like. Many of them are really tasty, others produce sugary, grainy candies. Therefore, after each recipe are suggestions to make them more like today's candies.

A CHRONOLOGY OF RECIPES

1849: *Cook and Confectioner*, by J. M. Sanderson, one of the oldest and most complete manuals for professionals

Ginger Candy

Although J. M. Sanderson could not supply us with a fudge, his ginger candy is a delicious fondant, the predecessor of fudge. Traditionally, ginger has been combined with sugar to make a most effective, palatable medication. Herbalists use it to soothe indigestion and to take the wind out of our rearward sails and the oops out of motion sickness. And many people love ginger ale, which, although caffeine free, still delivers some *oomph* since ginger is a mild stimulant.

> *Take clarified sugar and boil it to the ball; flavor it either with the essence of ginger or the root in powder; then with a spoon or spatula rub some [as much as you can] of it against the side of the pan until you perceive it turn white; pour it into small square tins with edges or paper cases, which have been oiled or buttered and put it in a warm place, or on a hot stone, that it may become dappled [some parts clear, the rest like rock candy; will take a day unless you place the pan on a heating pad set on low heat]. The syrup should be coloured yellow, while boiling, with a little saffron.*

MODERN METHOD:

(See chapter 8): Dissolve 2 cups granulated sugar, 1 cup water, several strands of saffron (can substitute food coloring and add later). Add pinch (⅛ teaspoon) of cream of tartar. Cook in 1½-quart saucepan. When it comes to the boil, cover with square of wax paper and lid, and steam to remove crystals—1 to 2 minutes. Continue cooking without stirring to soft-ball stage (approximately 236°F to 240°F

[113.5°C to 115.5°C]). Remove from heat, add 1 teaspoon powdered ginger and a few drops yellow food coloring, if desired. Proceed as for a basic fondant made in the food processor. The result is a creamy, mildly gingery candy.

To use fresh ginger: Place 3-inch-long, 3-ounce piece fresh ginger in bowl of hot water for a few minutes to make it easy to peel. Peel, then slice into ⅛-inch-thick pieces and cook along with syrup. When candy reaches soft-ball stage, pour syrup into food processor bowl through a sieve to catch the slices—these are now candied and can be used for another purpose if kept refrigerated. However, for a cream with crunch, a candy with a bite, process slices in food processor along with the syrup.

For an orange or lemon version: Follow same procedure to candy citrus peel, then either remove it or leave it in. Add orange or lemon extract (1 teaspoon, or to taste).

YIELD: 1 POUND. Can freeze; do not double.

1879: *Housekeeping in Old Virginia,* by Marion Cabell Tyree (Louisville, Ky: John P. Morton and Company)

Cocoanut Caramels

This was most likely the inspiration for the Smith College Fudge of thirty years later. I was amazed at how truly delicious this is. You can turn it into a fudge or a caramel, depending on how you interpret the instructions. This is not extremely chocolatey or coconutty or even molassessy, but a great blending of all three. If you use the original instructions, please note that if you halve the recipe, the times, inaccurate to begin with, will be totally askew. If you eliminate the coconut, it is a delicious penuche.

I am grateful to Mrs. Tyree who, later in her book, taught me how to "pound chocolate." Simply place unsweetened chocolate in a plastic bag and whack it with a mallet or hammer.

One-quarter pound Baker's chocolate (half cake) [4 ounces], one-quarter pound butter, two pounds [4½ firmly packed cups] nice [dark] brown sugar, one teacup [½ cup] rich milk, [light cream]. Stew half an hour or till thick. Add a grated cocoanut [see below]. Stir till mixture begins to boil again. Take from the fire, stir in a tablespoonful vanilla, and pour into buttered dishes. When cool enough to handle, make into balls the size of a walnut and place on buttered dishes—Mrs. S.T. [Mrs. Samuel Tyree of Lynchburg, Virginia, who contributed a third of all the confectionery recipes in the book].

MODERN METHOD TO MAKE A CARAMEL:

Melt chocolate, butter, sugar, and cream in a 4- or 5-quart saucepan. When completely dissolved, boil for approximately 20 minutes, or until very thick and to firm-ball stage (ball will hold its shape except under pressure and be chewy to the bite, approximately 242°F to 244°F [116.5°C to 118°C]). Pour boiling water over 3¾ to 4 cups dried or flaked coconut, drain in a sieve, and add to the mixture, which will drop the temperature immediately. Bring back to boil and cook an additional 10 to 15 minutes, or until very thick and returned to the firm-ball stage (should come in at slightly lower temperature than before). Remove from heat, stir in vanilla, pour into 8 × 12-inch buttered pan. When cool enough to handle, take teaspoonfuls and mold into balls—heat from your hands will do it—and place in paper candy cups. These will harden and become crusty outside. Inside, they will be fudgy and yet, because of coconut, remain chewy. If you don't want to bother making balls, simply let sit until cool and cut into squares. The result will be chewy with a sugary texture—a very unusual candy.

YIELD: MAKES 1½ POUNDS. Can store in airtight containers at room temperature for days at a time. Will freeze but do not double.

MODERN METHOD TO MAKE INTO A FUDGE:

Follow directions for making a caramel, but after you add coconut, continue cooking only to the soft-ball stage—approximately 236°F to

238°F (113.5°C to 114.5°C)—or until ball taken from cold water holds its shape until the heat from your fingers begins to soften it. Remove candy from heat, add vanilla, place pan in sink filled with ½ inch water. Let sit until lukewarm. Stir thoroughly by hand, pausing frequently. Because of coconut, it will be difficult to tell when it loses its sheen, but it should "snap" and become very thick. Pour into 8 × 12-inch buttered pan. Score while lukewarm, store in airtight container at room temperature or in refrigerator.

YIELD: 1½ POUNDS.

1887: Fudge introduced at Vassar; the recipe, supplied to me by Elizabeth Daniels, Vassar Historian, appeared in a newspaper for the first time in the *Wichita Kansas Beacon*, February 4, 1916.

Vassar Fudge

2 cups granulated white sugar

1 tablespoon butter

1 cup of cream

¼ of a cake of Baker's Premium No. 1 [unsweetened] Chocolate [see Note]

Put in the sugar and cream, and when this becomes hot, put in the chocolate, broken up into fine pieces. Stir vigorously and constantly. Put in butter when it begins to boil. Stir until it creams when beaten on a saucer. Then remove and beat until quite cool and pour into buttered tins. When cold, cut in diamond-shaped pieces.

NOTE: Many cookbook authors have taken "cake" to mean ¼ pound chocolate, or 4 ounces. Not so. Baker marketed its Premium No. 1 in 8-ounce cakes, so only 2 ounces of chocolate would have been used. And having tried it both ways, this is one case where less chocolate is better.

MODERN METHOD OF MAKING VASSAR FUDGE:

See Bread & Butter Fudge, page 64.

1890: *American Domestic Cyclopedia, A Volume of Universal Ready Reference for American Women in American Homes* (New York: F. M. Lupton)

In this work, the authors chose to use the technical term "candy" instead of fudge. But it's fudge through and through, from the emphasis on "unskimmed" milk to the seeding with vanilla to the cooling before beating. Easy to make, easy to get to candy, it requires and rewards gentle treatment: It will be light and delicate and very creamy. You'll like it. I do.

Vanilla Candy

Three teacups [1½ cups] of white or coffee sugar, one and a half teacups [¾ cup] unskimmed sweet milk [half-and-half] to dissolve it; boil till done [soft-ball stage], and flavor with [1 teaspoon] vanilla; after it cools a little [a lot], stir until hard and eat when you please.

MODERN METHOD:

Take precautions to prevent premature candying. Be sure to butter sides of 1½-quart saucepan to prevent boiling over, wash down crystals with pastry brush dipped in hot-water bath, and turn heat down once a boil is achieved. If heat is low enough, do not stir. Test in ice water when it thickens and bubbles become noisy. Ball, formed in ice water, should hold its shape until heat from your hand begins to flatten it and should be al dente—slightly chewy. Approximately 234°F to 240°F (112°C to 115.5°C). This candy must be treated very gently. Remove from heat and place on heat-proof pad. Under no circumstances shock by placing pot on cold surface or in cold water. Seeding with vanilla is enough to start candying. With these sugar-milk proportions, it is almost impossible to keep this white—it will darken more as it cools— so use regular vanilla extract for flavoring. Let cool to very low temperature, below the usual 110°F (43.5°C). In fact, 100°F (38°C) is better. And finally, *stir*, don't beat, and don't stir vigorously either, gently does it. It will begin to "snap" within the first few strokes. Doubling the vanilla or adding a handful of chopped pecans just before it candies will give it more jazz; as is, it has a delicate flavor.

1900: *New Century Home Book* by Frank A. DePuy (New York: Eaton & Main's)

You will note in these recipes just how much more sophisticated candy-making, fudge-making in particular, has become in less than two decades. Also note that "fudge" is used here for multiples, while in other books of the same period, the term for one recipe is "fudges." Mr. DePuy gave six recipes, but the last three were simply variations on the first three, adding nuts, coconut, fruit (chopped figs, dates, raisins, and citron).

Fudge

No. 1. Mix three quarters of a cupful [6 squares or ounces] of un-sweetened chocolate, grated or cut into small pieces, one cupful of milk [8 ounces], and two cupfuls [16 ounces] of white granulated sugar. Boil, stirring constantly. When fairly boiling, add a small piece [1 tablespoon] of butter. After twenty [15] minutes, it will begin to thicken. Watch carefully, and when the spoon leaves a trace on the bottom of the kettle, take it off, add one teaspoonful of vanilla quickly, and beat until the mixture is thick. Pour into buttered pans [one 8 × 8-inch pan] in layers about three quarters of an inch thick and cut into squares.

The success of fudge depends upon its being removed from the fire at the right moment. [AMEN!]

MODERN METHOD:

This is a very, very chocolatey fudge—just the thing for dedicated chocoholics. For the rest of us, cut that chocolate back at the very least to 4 squares (ounces); 2 squares (ounces) are more my style. As written with all that chocolate, the fudge candies quickly and looks very grainy when poured out.

In 3-quart saucepan, mix chocolate smashed with half-and-half and sugar. Stir constantly until sugar is dissolved and chocolate melted, then bring to a boil, add butter, and introduce prewarmed thermometer. After 15 to 20 minutes it will thicken and spoon will leave a trace on the bottom of kettle. When bubbles become noisy, use ice-cold water to test for soft ball. Ball, formed in ice water, should hold its shape until heat from your hand begins to flatten it and should be al dente—slightly chewy. Approximately 234°F to 240°F (112°C to 115.5°C). Remove from heat but do not shock. Add vanilla quickly but without stirring. Let cool until lukewarm and "skin" forms on top (110°F [43.5°C]). Return thermometer to its hot-water bath to soak clean. Stir fudge thoroughly but not vigorously. Pause frequently to allow fudge to thicken, lose its sheen, become lighter in color or streaked with lighter shades, give off some heat, suddenly stiffen. Pour into buttered 8 × 8-inch pan and cut into squares. As the author says, "The success of fudge depends upon its being removed from the fire at the right moment." If it candies on you, butter your fingers and spread it into place; butter will leave a most attractive gloss on top. Candy will still be grainy underneath.

YIELD: 1½ POUNDS. Can freeze; can double.

No. 2. Prepare as in No. 1, and add [1 cup] chopped nuts when the vanilla is put in. Walnuts, hickory nuts, peanuts, or any preferred nuts may be used. Almonds are too hard to be desirable [being fond of almonds in fudge, I disagree; I've used blanched and/or slivered, as well as hazelnuts].

No. 3. Substitute maple sugar for the chocolate, and prepare as in No. 1.

SUGGESTION: If you are unable to get maple sugar, substitute ½ cup plus 1 tablespoon maple syrup and reduce half-and-half to 1 cup less 3 tablespoons. It should ball about 15 minutes after adding the butter. Even after letting it sit until cool before mixing, the result is grainy. In fact, it looks and tastes exactly like maple sugar. Good thing to know if your family is fond of maple sugar.

1902: *Woman's Favorite Cookbook*, by Annie R. Gregory "assisted by 1000 Homekeepers" [Homekeepers, what a nice way of putting it!] (Chicago: Monarch Book Co.)

This book contains, in the section "How to Tell When Candy Is Sufficiently Cooked," the first reference I could document on using a thermometer in sugar boiling. However, only a succinct recipe for caramel actually specifies a temperature.

Chocolate Caramels

Two cupfuls of [firmly packed] brown sugar, one-quarter pound [4 ounces/4 squares unsweetened] of chocolate, one half cupful [4 ounces] of molasses, one half cupful of milk, one half cupful of butter. Cook to 254°, stir in one teaspoonful of vanilla and pour in buttered pan.

MODERN METHOD:

A caution or two: Remember to dissolve sugar before bringing to the boil, to test in ice water (syrup will be difficult to scrape up and must be forced into a hard ball), and to take steps to prevent candying. Use an 8 × 8-inch pan. Also, this makes for a somewhat harder caramel as it is cooked to a higher temperature than caramels usually are. The intensity of its flavor is matched only by the brevity of its instructions.

1904: *Consolidated Library of Modern Cooking & Household Recipes* by Christine Terhune Herrick (editor-in-chief) and Marion Harland, *et al.*, volume 2 (New York: R. J. Bodner Company)

This is one of the early recipes that attempted to cut back on the molasses taste of brown sugar of the time by using half brown and half white. You won't find many shorter recipes either.

Fudges

2 cupfuls [firmly packed light] brown sugar, 2 cupfuls white sugar (or use all white sugar), 1 cupful milk, a piece of butter size of a walnut [1½ tablespoons], 2 squares [2 ounces unsweetened] chocolate. Stir all the time it is boiling. Flavor with vanilla [1 teaspoon]. After you take it off the stove, stir until it is almost hard, then pour into buttered pans.

MODERN METHOD:

Butter sides of 3-quart saucepan, prewarm thermometer. Use same ingredients as in original recipe but substitute 1 cup half-and-half for the milk. Dump in pan. Stir constantly until sugar is dissolved and it comes to a boil. Reduce heat while retaining boil and continue cooking, stirring infrequently if at all. When it reaches soft ball, around 234°F to 240°F (112°C to 115.5°C), remove from heat and flavor with 1 teaspoon vanilla. Do not shock immediately. However, when fudge cools on top (hold hand over the candy to check) place pan in cool water to equalize heat between bottom and top of pan. Stir gently, it will candy almost immediately; pour into buttered 8 × 8-inch pan.

Ponouchi

2 cupfuls [dark or light firmly packed] brown sugar, 2 cupfuls white sugar, 1 cupful milk, a piece of butter size of a walnut [1½ tablespoons]. Use either walnuts or hickory nuts, chopped very fine. [End of recipe.]

MODERN METHOD:

Follow directions for Fudges (page 262), eliminating the chocolate.

Comanche

(One has to think that the following recipe was either fudged or written by "*et al.*"!)

> *Make both the above recipes [simultaneously? one after the other?]. Pour the brown [both are brown] fudge into a buttered pan, and pour the white [is no white fudge, ponouchi is brown] fudge over it.*

MODERN METHOD OF MAKING TWO-TONED FUDGE:

1. Make a double batch of Fudges using all white sugar and a 5-quart or larger saucepan with buttered sides. Melt 2 squares (2 ounces unsweetened) chocolate separately, *or* use 2 packets premelted chocolate (warm in thermometer bath to liquefy). When fudge has reached soft-ball stage, pour some hot water from thermometer bath into a large heat-proof bowl. Swish it around to preheat it and pour it back into thermometer bath. Pour half the batch into the preheated bowl and flavor with melted chocolate. Add 1 teaspoon vanilla to fudge remaining in pan. Let both cool until lukewarm. The one in the bowl will be ready to stir first, and when about to candy—the moment it loses its gloss—spread in a 6 × 10-inch or larger pan. Place in refrigerator to chill while you stir the second batch. Then pour that over first batch to get your "Comanche."

2. For two shades of brown, follow Ponouchi recipe using half dark brown sugar and half white sugar, adding melted chocolate to one-half as described above.

1909: *Chocolate and Cocoa Recipes by Miss Parloa, and Home Made Candy Recipes* by Mrs. Janet McKenzie Hill (Dorchester, Mass.: Walter Baker & Company, Ltd. [now part of General Foods])

This pamphlet was the first to provide recipes for Smith, Wellesley, and Vassar fudges all in one place. It is most often cited—inaccurately, we know now—as the first source to ever mention fudge. The Vassar recipe is a variation of the one cited earlier (page 257). Copies of the recipes were supplied to me by Maida Goodwin, archives specialist at Smith College.

Smith College Fudge

Melt one-quarter cup of butter. Mix together in a separate dish one cup of white sugar, one cup of brown sugar, one-quarter cup of molasses and one-half cup of cream. Add this to the butter, and after it has been brought to a boil continue boiling for two and one-half minutes, stirring rapidly. Then add two squares of Baker's Premium No. 1 Chocolate, scraped fine. Boil this five minutes, stirring it first rapidly and then more slowly towards the end. After it has been taken from the fire, add one and one-half teaspoonfuls of vanilla. Then stir constantly until the mass thickens. Pour into buttered pan and set in a cool place.

MODERN METHOD:

Add molasses sparingly; many fudge testers found ¼ cup too strong. The times cited are unreliable. For step-by-step method of making this fudge, see Brown Sugar Fudge, page 74.

Wellesley College Fudge

Heat two cups of granulated sugar and one cup of rich milk [heavy cream is better]. Add two squares [2 ounces] of Baker's Chocolate and boil until it hardens in cold water. Just before it is done, add a small piece of butter, then begin to stir in marshmallows, crushing and beating them with a spoon. Continue to stir in marshmallows, after the fudge has been taken from the fire, until half a pound has been stirred into the fudge. Cool in sheets three-quarters of an inch thick, and cut in cubes.

MODERN METHOD:

Marshmallow Creme Fudge (page 79) is an easier, less labor-intensive way of making this fudge.

1920s: *The Science of Home-Making* by Kate Kennedy (London: T. H. Nelson & Sons, Ltd.)

This is one of the earliest home economics textbooks to discuss testing. The author, a Scottish teacher, spends a great deal of time differentiating between the handling of toffee and "tablet," her name for fudge. For example, she explains that to test for toffee, "drop a teaspoonful of toffee into a cup of cold water. It should harden and crack if ready . . . for 'tablet' put a teaspoonful of tablet into a saucer and work it with a teaspoon. It should form into a ball if ready." Not for a butterfingers like me, it won't. Note in the following recipe that Mrs. Kennedy has adopted the "new" method of specifying ingredients and then giving directions.

Treacle Toffee

Treacle, in case you didn't know—and I didn't—is the term used in Great Britain for either molasses, as in *Alice in Wonderland*, or golden syrup, which is a very light molasses mixed with corn syrup. To us this particular toffee is a brittle, as it is cooked to the hard crack.

Two pounds moist brown sugar

Quarter pound margarine or butter [use unsalted butter]

Two tablespoons treacle [if using dark brown sugar, use golden syrup or light corn syrup; if using light brown sugar, use very light molasses]

One gill water [½ cup]

The toffee must not be stirred. Put the sugar and water into a [3-quart] pan and leave at the side of the fire [cook on lowest heat] until most of the sugar is dissolved. Put the pan over a gentle [medium-low] heat, and add the treacle and butter. Boil steadily for thirty to forty minutes [or even longer]. Test a few drops in a cup of cold water, to see if the toffee hardens and cracks. If it does so [around 270°F to 280°F (135°C to 138°C)], pour at once into a buttered tin [large jelly-roll pan], and mark [score] when nearly cold.

MODERN METHOD:

Again, with a little translation, the recipe works very well. But do stir until the sugar has dissolved. And you might want to use a pre-warmed thermometer, introduced when the mixture comes to the boil. If you do, be sure to take the thermometer out now and again to shake it free of accumulated toffee, otherwise it will just mislead you. This makes 2 pounds, a very large quantity of toffee. You might want to halve it or convert half into a toffee-krunch.

To make a toffee-krunch: Either make only half of the above recipe or divide hot toffee into two batches, by pouring half into a buttered 8 × 8-inch pan. To balance remaining in saucepan, stir in ½ teaspoon baking soda and watch it foam up (the action of the baking soda on the candy causes it to separate into dozens of thin, brittle, crunchy layers), then pour into a second buttered 8 × 8-inch pan. After allowing toffee to cool for 5 to 10 minutes, top with scattered chocolate chips or miniature candy bars; spread when melted. You can go even further and sprinkle chopped nuts on top of those.

FIRST LADY CANDIES AND CONFECTIONS

1887: *The Original White House Cookbook*, by Hugo Ziemann (steward of the White House) and Mrs. F. L. Gillette, Facsimile Edition (Old Greenwich, Conn.: The Devon Adair Company, 1983)

Although this book contains no recipes for fudge, it devotes much space to "creams." The following recipe in particular is of interest. This French Cream is a delicious improvement on earlier recipes for so-called Martha Washington Creams and/or Dolley Madison Creams. The candy is fondantlike, and the recipe itself is very detailed. Note the attempts made to help the cook determine whether the candy is ready, first to ball, then to beat. And it even contains suggestions for dealing with a failure—a first!

French Cream Candy

Put four cupfuls of white sugar and one cupful of water into a bright tin pan on the range and let it boil without stirring for ten minutes. If it looks somewhat thick, test it by letting some drop from the spoon, and if it threads, remove the pan to the table. Take out a small spoonful, and rub it against the side of a cake bowl; if it becomes creamy, and will roll into a ball between the fingers, pour the whole into the bowl. When cool enough to bear your finger in it, take it in your lap [this could be dangerous], stir or beat it with a large spoon, or pudding-stick. It will soon begin to look like cream, and then grow stiffer until you find it necessary to take your hands and work it like bread dough. If it is not boiled enough to cream, set it back upon the range and let it remain one or two minutes, or as long as is necessary, taking care not to cook it too much. Add the flavoring as soon as it begins to cool. This is the foundation of all French creams. It can be made into rolls, and sliced off, or packed in plates and cut into small cubes, or made into any shape imitating French candies. A pretty form is made by coloring some of the cream pink, taking a piece about as large as a hazel nut, and crowding an almond meat halfway into one side, till it looks like a bursting kernel. In working, should the cream get too cold, warm it.

To be successful in making this cream, several points are to be remembered; when the boiled sugar is cool enough to beat, if it looks rough and has turned to sugar, it is because it has been boiled too much, or has been stirred. If, after it is beaten, it does not look like lard or thick cream, and is sandy or sugary instead, it is because you did not let it get cool enough before beating. It is not boiled enough if it does not harden so as to work like dough, and should not stick to the hands; in this case put it back into the pan with an ounce of hot water, and cook over just enough, by testing in water as above. After it is turned into the bowl to cool, it should look clear as jelly. Practice and patience will make perfect.

MODERN METHOD:

Not only practice and patience make perfect, but a food processor practically guarantees it. Follow instructions for Homemade Butter Creams on page 171.

White House Fudge

Dating back to the 1940s, this recipe is also known as Mamie's Fudge, Mrs. Eisenhower's Fudge, Million Dollar Fudge, Mamie's Million Dollar Fudge . . . and it is a variation of Wellesley Marshmallow Fudge. It has spawned as many variations as it has names, but this is the original. If made properly, its taste and texture are more that of a candy bar than a piece of fudge. I think the fudge is just as good, maybe better, without the nuts.

4½ cups sugar
2 tablespoons butter
Pinch of salt
1 tall can (12 ounces) evaporated milk

12 ounces semi-sweet chocolate bits

12 ounces German sweet chocolate

1 pint marshmallow creme

2 cups nut meats

Boil sugar, butter, salt, and milk for 6 minutes. In a bowl, put: chocolate bits, German chocolate, marshmallow creme, and nuts. Pour the boiling syrup over the ingredients. Beat until chocolate is melted. Pour into pan. Let stand a few hours before cutting. "Remember it's better the second day. Store in a tin box."

MODERN METHOD:

Melt chocolates together in microwave—1 minute on HIGH (100%)—stir—another 30 seconds on HIGH—and fold into marshmallow and add nuts. Mix sugar, butter, salt, and milk in 4-quart saucepan. Dissolve sugar, then bring to a boil, and continue boiling—stirring no more than necessary—for 6 to 7 minutes, or until syrup comes to a soft ball (approximately 234°F to 240°F [112°C to 115.5°C]). Pour hot syrup over chocolates, marshmallows, and nuts. Working fast, fold until syrup is incorporated. Pour into buttered 9×9-inch pan. Fudge will set up almost immediately. For dense fudge, pat down into pan. For lighter fudge, bang pan against counter to remove air pockets. When cool (bottom of pan should not feel warm to your hand), cut into squares. And while it is awfully good the first day, it is indeed better the second.

YIELD: 1½ POUNDS, OR 36 OR MORE SQUARES. Should not be doubled.

Tracking down the original version of Mamie Eisenhower's fudge took some doing. However, getting a recipe from a current First Lady is another story. Easy as pie. Simply write a letter requesting the recipe and address it to the White House, Washington, D.C. 20500. In return, you'll receive up to four family recipes. You sort of take pot luck in the sense that you don't know in advance what they'll be for, but they do come on heavy, white card stock, beautifully printed, with a picture of the White House and the signature of the current First Lady.

Lady Bird Johnson's Quick Peanut Candy

Mrs. Lyndon Baines Johnson's family cook, Zephyr Wright, prepared this quick chocolatey peanut-laden confection for the Johnsons in the White House.

1 stick margarine

3 tablespoons cocoa

1¾ cups quick oats

1 cup chopped peanuts (can use roasted, lightly salted peanuts)

2 cups granulated white sugar

½ cup milk

½ cup peanut butter

In a large skillet, combine margarine, sugar, cocoa, and milk. Bring to a boil and boil for 2 minutes, stirring constantly. Remove from heat and add oats, peanut butter, and peanuts. Stir to blend well. Let cool and drop by teaspoons on wax paper.

Rosalynn Carter's Peanut Brittle

I know people who bought a peanut cookbook just for this recipe, which is labeled Jimmy's Carter's favorite peanut brittle. I think you'll agree they got their money's worth.

3 cups granulated white sugar

1½ cups water

1 cup white (light) corn syrup

3 cups raw peanuts

2 tablespoons baking soda

4 tablespoons (½ stick) butter

1 teaspoon vanilla

Boil sugar, water, and syrup until spins thread; add peanuts. After adding peanuts, stir continually until syrup turns golden brown. Remove from heat; add remaining ingredients; stir until butter melts. Pour quickly on 2 cookie sheets with sides. As mixture begins to harden around edges, pull until thin.

NOTE: For those of you using a candy thermometer, you can spin a thread from a spoon, around 230°F (110°C). Be sure mixture has cooled sufficiently before handling. Also I think you'll be more successful if you lightly oil the cookie sheets and butter your hands before pulling. Lift the edge of the candy with a spatula if necessary, grasp gently and pull. Continue going round and round until candy threatens to break. Let sit until hard, then break by rapping sharply with a mallet or tack hammer, or lift candy and use a spoon.

Nancy Reagan's Vienna Chocolate Bars

An elegant lady, an elegant dessert.

2 sticks butter

1½ cups sugar

2 egg yolks

¼ teaspoon salt

2½ cups flour

1 cup [6 ounces] chocolate bits

1 10-ounce jar jelly [Mrs. Reagan doesn't specify a particular jelly; I'm fond of raspberry.]

4 egg whites

2 cups finely chopped nuts

Cream the butter and ½ cup sugar. Add egg yolks and salt. Add the flour and knead with fingers. Pat batter out onto a greased cookie sheet. Bake for 15 to 20 minutes at 350°F until lightly browned. Remove from oven, spread with jelly and top with chocolate bits. Beat egg whites until stiff. Fold in remaining sugar and nuts. Gently spread on top of jelly and chocolate. Bake for about 25 minutes at 350°F. Cut into squares or bars.

NOTE: If you're not sure of your patting ability, you might want to use a low-sided greased 8×10-inch pan instead of the cookie sheet. Be sure your oven is preheated. You can vary this recipe by beating the sugar into the egg whites to make a meringue, then folding in the nuts. The top layer of the resulting bar has a texture like divinity.

Barbara Bush's Apple Crisp with Orange Juice

This recipe and three other equally delicious ones were sent in response to my request for a fudge recipe. I was so taken with this that I converted it to fudge (see following recipe), which was the universal favorite of all the traditionalist taste-testers, even partisan Democrats.

4 cups sliced pared tart apples

¼ cup orange juice

1 cup sugar

¾ cup flour, sifted

½ teaspoon ground cinnamon

¼ teaspoon ground nutmeg

Dash of salt

⅓ cup butter

Mound apples in buttered pie plate and pour orange juice over them. In separate bowl, combine sugar, flour, spices, and salt; cut in butter until mixture is crumbly. Sprinkle over apples.

Bake at 375 degrees for 45 minutes or until apples are tender and topping is crisp. Serve warm with cream.

Apple Fudge à la Barbara Bush

Converting this recipe was easy. However, it would be remiss of me not to remind you that fresh fruit and fudge don't really mix so this should be stored in the refrigerator once it has cooled. The apple juices working on the fudge will create a very thin, very delicious sauce beneath the fudge. (You can lessen this by sautéing the apple slices first in a little extra butter and then draining them.) Because this is an up-to-date fudge recipe, it is done by the ten-step method.

¼ cup orange juice

2 cups granulated white sugar

½ cup or one 5-ounce can evaporated whole milk

4 tablespoons (½ stick) butter, divided

Pinch (⅛ teaspoon) of salt

½ teaspoon ground cinnamon

¼ teaspoon (preferably freshly grated) nutmeg

Optional: ½ teaspoon vanilla extract

1 cup pared and diced apples (prepare in step 6)

STEP 1: PREPARE: Prewarm thermometer; use 2-quart saucepan; measure all ingredients except apples, spices, and optional vanilla and 1 tablespoon butter, and dump into saucepan; butter upper sides of saucepan. Grease and, if necessary, line a 5 × 10-inch pan. Freeze 1 tablespoon butter. Fill glass with ice cubes and water and sink ½-inch full of water.

STEP 2: DISSOLVE sugar, stirring constantly with wooden spoon over low heat until butter melts, gritty sounds cease, spoon glides smoothly over bottom of pan. Increase heat to medium and bring to a boil.

STEP 3: BOIL after washing down any crystals that may have formed with pastry brush dipped in hot water from thermometer bath, using as little water as possible. Introduce prewarmed thermometer. Reduce heat while retaining boil. Stir no more than necessary.

STEP 4: TEST in ice-cold water when mixture thickens and bubbles become noisy. Ball, formed in ice water, should hold its shape until heat from your hand begins to flatten it and should be al dente—slightly chewy. Approximately 236°F to 242°F (113.5°C to 116.5°C).

STEP 5: SHOCK by placing saucepan in sink.

STEP 6: SEED by adding, without stirring, spices and ice-cold butter (and optional vanilla for an apple pie à la mode flavor). Then allow to cool while you pare apples, slice ¼ inch thick, then dice into ½-inch pieces. Drain between paper towels until ready to use. Better still, sauté quickly in extra butter before draining on paper towels.

STEP 7: STIR when lukewarm, and "skin" forms on top (110°F [43.5°C]). Return thermometer to its hot-water bath to soak clean. Stir fudge thoroughly but not vigorously by hand, with electric mixer, or with food processor. Pause frequently to allow fudge to react.

STEP 8: WATCH for fudge to thicken, lose its sheen, become lighter in color or streaked with lighter shades, give off some heat, suddenly stiffen. If mixing by hand, fudge will "snap" with each stroke; by mixer, mixer waves will become very distinct; by food processor, fudge will flow sluggishly back to center when processor is stopped.

STEP 9: PUT apples, after patting dry, in bottom of pan.

STEP 10: POUR, SCORE, AND STORE, when cool, in airtight plastic bag in refrigerator.

YIELD: 1 POUND. Recipe is not easily doubled but can be frozen.

REQUESTED RECIPES

No group of historical recipes would be complete without those that Americans themselves have voted their favorites by requesting them frequently from manufacturers.

Never-Fail Fudge

According to Don Durkee of Durkee-Mower, Inc., this is a variation of the Mamie Eisenhower recipe and has appeared on containers of Marshmallow Fluff since after World War II. The product itself goes back to 1917. Three years later, H. Allen Durkee and Fred L. Mower purchased the formula for $500. Durkee and Mower spent each evening making the fluff and the following day selling it door to door. From those humble beginnings, their factory has expanded and expanded.

5 cups sugar

1 large (12-ounce) can evaporated milk

¼ pound butter or margarine

12 ounces (¾ of 16-ounce jar) Marshmallow Fluff

1 teaspoon salt

1 teaspoon vanilla

1 cup walnut meats

2 large (12-ounce) packages semi-sweet chocolate pieces

Combine first five ingredients in 4-quart saucepan. Stir over low heat until blended.

Bring to a boil over moderate heat, being careful not to mistake escaping air bubbles for boiling. *Then boil slowly, stirring constantly, for 5 minutes.* To soft-ball stage.

Remove from heat. Stir in chocolate and vanilla (and nuts if used) until chocolate is melted. Pour into 2 buttered 9 × 9-inch pans and cool.

YIELD: APPROXIMATELY 5 POUNDS.

Hershey's Cocoa Can Fudge

⅔ *cup cocoa*

3 cups granulated sugar

⅛ *teaspoon salt*

1½ cups milk

¼ *cup (½ of a stick) butter*

1 teaspoon vanilla

Combine cocoa, sugar and salt in a large saucepan [3-quart with buttered sides]. Add milk gradually, mix thoroughly; bring to a "bubbly" boil on high heat, stirring continuously. Reduce heat to medium and continue to boil the mixture, without stirring, until it reaches a temperature of 232°F (111°C) [higher, higher!] or until a small amount of mixture forms a soft ball when dropped into cold water. Be sure that thermometer bulb is not resting on bottom of saucepan. Remove saucepan from heat; add butter and vanilla to mixture. DO NOT STIR. Allow fudge to cool at room temperature until it reaches 110°F (43.5°C). [Note: Lovers of sugary fudge, ignore the DO NOT STIR directive and begin stirring immediately.] Beat by hand or with portable electric mixer until the fudge thickens and loses some of its gloss. Quickly pour and spread fudge in lightly buttered 8 × 8 × 2-inch pan. Cool. Cut into squares.

YIELD: ABOUT 3 DOZEN SQUARES.

Knox Dainties

Year after year, the letters come in to Knox Gelatin asking for a copy of this recipe. Although it was recently updated (the amount of gelatin used was increased to five envelopes), for all of you who believe that old is best, here is the original.

4 envelopes Knox unflavored gelatin

1 cup cold water

1½ cups boiling water

4 cups sugar

¼ teaspoonful salt

red and green food coloring (optional)

1 teaspoonful cinnamon extract, not powder [see Note]

½ teaspoonful peppermint extract [see Note]

Heat sugar, salt, and boiling water to boiling point. Soften gelatin in cold water. Add to hot syrup and stir until dissolved. Boil slowly for 15 minutes. Remove from fire and divide into two equal parts. Color one part a delicate red and flavor with cinnamon extract; color the other part a delicate green and flavor with peppermint extract. Rinse two pans (size about 8 × 4 inches) in cold water, and pour in candy mixture to the depth of about three-fourths inch and put in a cool place (not a refrigerator), allowing candy to thicken for at least twelve hours. With a wet sharp knife loosen around edges of pan, pull out on board lightly covered with powdered sugar. Cut in cubes and roll in powdered or fine granulated sugar.

[NOTE: You can also use 10 drops oil of cinnamon. Or substitute lemon: add 3 tablespoons lemon juice and 2 teaspoons lemon extract to one part of the candy and leave it uncolored or tint pale yellow. You also can substitute ½ teaspoon strawberry extract for either the cinnamon or the peppermint. Other flavor suggestions include using 2 teaspoons coconut extract.]

Fudge Palace Fudge

As mentioned previously, it is almost impossible to duplicate any of the slab-made fudges from shops like Jim "Seamus" Garrahy's. And for several good reasons:

1. The fudge palaces are set up to make fudge, and usually only fudge. For example, their thermometers are suspended in the center of the fudge pot; furthermore, the closest we can come to duplicating their fudge pot is a wok (which works well but is difficult to shock).
2. They make essentially the same recipe over and over again and so will detect signs of candying you or I would miss.
3. They have specialized equipment and ingredients—the marble slab itself with its cooling-shocking properties, the ingredients such as extracts (which can cost up to $2,000 per gallon) as well as the special corn syrup available only in giant drums.

In spite of this, this recipe comes close, very close, to slab fudge.

Basic Single 2½-Pound Batch

4 cups superfine white sugar

½ cup corn syrup, less 2 teaspoons

⅓ teaspoon salt

1¼ cups heavy (whipping) cream

Optional (*see Note for vanilla fudge*):

1½ teaspoons vanilla extract

⅓ cup cocoa, for chocolate fudge

¾ cup peanut butter, for peanut butter fudge

Optional: *1 cup (about) chopped or whole nuts—pecans, walnuts, etc.*

Basic Quantity 6¼-Pound Batch

10 cups superfine sugar

1 cup plus 2 tablespoons light corn syrup

¾ teaspoon salt

3 cups heavy (whipping) cream

Optional (*see Note for vanilla fudge*):

4 teaspoons vanilla extract
¾ cup plus 2 tablespoons cocoa, for chocolate fudge
2 cups peanut butter, for peanut butter fudge

Optional: 2½ cups chopped or whole nuts—pecans, walnuts, etc.

STEP 1: PREPARE: Prewarm thermometer; use 3-quart saucepan for small batch, 8-quart stockpot for large batch; measure all ingredients including optional cocoa and/or peanut butter (but not other flavorings or optional nuts), and dump into saucepan; butter upper sides of saucepan. Grease and, if necessary, line an 8 × 8-inch pan for single batch, jelly-roll pan for larger batch. Fill glass with ice cubes and water and sink ½ inch full of water.

STEP 2: DISSOLVE sugar, stirring constantly with wooden spoon over low heat until butter melts, gritty sounds cease, spoon glides smoothly over bottom of pan. Increase heat to medium and bring to a boil.

STEP 3: BOIL after washing down any crystals that may have formed with pastry brush dipped in hot water from thermometer bath, using as little water as possible. Introduce prewarmed thermometer. Reduce heat while retaining boil. Stir no more than necessary.

STEP 4: TEST in ice-cold water when mixture thickens and bubbles become noisy. Ball, formed in ice water, should hold its shape until heat from your hand begins to flatten it and should be al dente— slightly chewy. Approximately 236°F to 240°F (113.5°C to 115.5°C). Seamus Garrahy says, on the average, their fudge comes in at 238°F (114.5°C).

STEP 5: SHOCK by placing saucepan in sink.

STEP 6: SEED by adding, without stirring, extract. Then allow to cool.

STEP 7: STIR when lukewarm and "skin" forms on top, 110°F (43.5°C). Return thermometer to its hot-water bath to soak clean. Stir fudge thoroughly but not vigorously by hand, with electric mixer, or with food processor. Pause frequently to allow fudge to react.

STEP 8: WATCH for fudge to thicken, lose its sheen, become lighter in color or streaked with lighter shades, give off some heat, suddenly stiffen. If mixing by hand, fudge will "snap" with each stroke; by mixer, mixer waves will become very distinct; by food processor, fudge will flow sluggishly back to center with processor stopped.

STEP 9: ADD any optional nuts before fudge totally candies.

STEP 10: POUR, SCORE, AND STORE when cool in airtight container in refrigerator or at room temperature. Recipe can be frozen.

NOTE: To make different flavors, use concentrated pure extracts— maple, cherry, strawberry, etc.—available in .125-fluid-ounce bottles. 1 bottle per 2½-pound batch, 2½ to 3 bottles for 6¼-pound batch.

WHERE TO GO OR SEND
FOR FUDGE

We Americans take our candy seriously, so seriously that we've made two towns in Pennsylvania big tourist attractions. Hershey bills itself as the "Chocolate Capital of the U.S.A." and is famous for its unusual streetlamps in the form of Kisses. It's grown so large, it's added a theme park to its list of attractions. The other, a teeny, tiny town compared to Hershey, is Lititz. And smack-dab in its center is the Candy Americana Museum, founded in October 1972. Begun to take advantage of the large number of tourists visiting the land of the Amish near Lancaster, Pennsylvania, it is now a major tourist attraction in itself. The day I visited, when there was no tour bus in sight, people were standing three deep before the window where chocolates were being hand-dipped. Admission, which is free, enables you to see in operation an actual antique candy-maker's kitchen, circa 1900. In addition, you'll find an interesting assortment of old tins, candy molds, as well as 150 porcelain pots for drinking chocolate from the most famous china makers in the world.

The museum is an annex of the Wilbur Candy Outlet and Chocolate Factory, home of Wilbur Buds and hundreds of other candies, including a rich, creamy pan fudge. Available in a modest assortment of flavors, it's inexpensive compared to most and worth seeking out. But even more noteworthy than that is the fact that it's been around for more than a hundred years. Longevity and fudge-making do not seem to go hand in hand. Fudge shops are, literally, here today and gone tomorrow. So the following list of sources, although accurate at press time, may not be so the day you read this. Call ahead to check before seeking one out. Call, also, for mail order, to determine the policy on shipping fudge during the summer months. Most won't, not between May 31 and October 1.

CALIFORNIA
Meyenberg Goat Milk
Jackson-Mitchell Pharmaceuticals, Inc.
P.O. Box 5425
Santa Barbara, CA 93150
(805) 565-1538

If you want to try something truly different, send for the goat's milk Blue Ribbon Microwave Fudge in a can. In less than three minutes, it's done! This fudge was discovered by word of mouth. But once word got out, it rated columns in newsprint. Take my word, you'll love it.

Nut Tree Candy and Foods
Nut Tree, CA 95696
(707) 448-6411

One visitor called it "fudge beyond compare," which may be why Nut Tree has its own post office and zip code, just to handle mail orders. They offer chocolate, milk chocolate bark, vanilla bark, and penuche among other flavors.

Preston's Candies
1170 Broadway
Burlingame, CA 94010
(415) 344-3254

The fudge is creamy, the caramel dreamy. They offer chocolate slab fudge with or without nuts made in their own kitchens.

See's Candy Shops, Inc.
3431 South La Cienega Boulevard
Los Angeles, CA 90016
(213) 870-3761

This is one of over a hundred See's shops along the West Coast offering chocolate and vanilla pan fudge.

KENTUCKY
Rebecca-Ruth Candy, Inc.
112 East Second Street
Frankfort, KY 40602-0064
(800) 444-3766

The wonderful, wonderful fudge from this company comes in marsh-mallow, peanut butter, rocky road made with pecans, and vanilla, and vanilla with pecans. Actually, Rebecca-Ruth is more famous for Kentucky bourbon chocolate-covered creams, including Irish and cognac, coffee, and scotch. In business since 1919, they'll be delighted to send you a free catalog so you can pick and choose among all their candy delights. They have five shops of their own, and you'll find Rebecca-Ruth candies at twenty-seven other locations.

LOUISIANA
Creole Delicacies Company
533 St. Ann Street
New Orleans, LA 70116
(504) 525-9508

There's no fudge here, but their rich, creamy pralines, made fresh daily, deserve a try. In original (brown sugary) flavor, chewy, chocolate, or rum.

MASSACHUSETTS
Putnam Pantry
Route One
Danvers, MA 01923
(508) 774-2383

These four shops are not strictly fudge shops. They also make fudge toppings for their smorgasbord of sauces, including butterscotch, cherry-caramel, chocolate, hot chocolate fudge, hot penuche, marsh-mallow, and so on.

Trappistine Quality Candy
Mount Saint Mary's Abbey
Wrentham, MA 02093
(508) 384-6465

Both chocolate fudge and penuche are offered here and they're so good, they sell out early in the day.

MICHIGAN
Marshall's Mackinac Trail Fudge
308 E. Central Avenue
Mackinaw City, MI 49701

52 N. State Street
St. Ignace, MI 49781
1-800-34-FUDGE

If you call that number during the off-season, the gentle voice that answers will probably belong to Jeannie, the Marshalls' daughter-in-law. In season (July, August, and Christmas) you can sample from as many as twenty-five different flavors of slab fudge, including butter pecan, cherry, chocolate caramel, chocolate cashew, chocolate chip, chocolate mint, chocolate peanut butter, piña colada, strawberry, triple chip . . . and even a chocolate orange. They make a magnificent nougat-centered pecan roll, as well as caramels and brittles and chocolate barks and old-fashioned divinity—a rarity! They'll time their shipping of your order so your candy won't have to sit, unrefrigerated, over a weekend.

Sydney Bogg Chocolates
18932 Woodward Avenue
Detroit, MI 48203
(313) 368-2470

This shop has a great assortment of chocolate bark, brittles, and fudges, especially at the peak of the season when they dream up a wondrous variety, including amaretto, chocolate coconut, and chocolate with raspberry.

MISSOURI
The Candy Factory
1016 E. Broadway
Columbia, MO 65201
(314) 443-8222

Once upon a time they specialized in old-fashioned goat's milk fudge; alas, no longer. But they do have the standards plus a variety of nut-enhanced ones, including chocolate-almond.

NEW JERSEY
The Fudge Boat
21 Spinnaker North
35th & Boardwalk
Sea Isle City, NJ 08243

This shop offers typical seashore fudge: creamy and not too intensely flavored. Open only for the summer season.

A. L. Roth
On the Boardwalk
Atlantic City, NJ 08401
(609) 344-1145

Try their sample packs before buying. In addition to fudge, they offer a great many other chocolate candies plus a large assortment of carob candies.

Steel Candies
On the Boardwalk
Atlantic City, NJ 08401
(609) 345-4051

They offer the same nine flavors of seashore fudge, including pistachio, all year round at both of their locations. Some people use Steel's fudge as the yardstick against which to judge all other fudges.

NEW YORK
Speach Candy Company
1012 Burnet Avenue
Syracuse, NY 13203
(315) 472-2271

Although Sue Speach is justifiably proud of her chocolate-covered crunch, I was equally impressed by her pure white vanilla fudge. She gets her ingredients where you and I do, at the supermarket. But oh, what she does with them!

OHIO
Candy Shop
South Shore Shopping Center
Vermilion, Ohio 44089
(216) 967-6318 or 967-6363

There are two shops featuring pan fudge in chocolate, maple and maple walnut, peanut butter swirl, rocky road, and vanilla. They'll be happy to handle mail orders.

Harry London's Candies, Inc.
1281 South Main Street
North Canton, Ohio 44720
(216) 494-2757

This shop offers mail-order pan fudge in basic, time-tested flavors. They are especially well known for their caramels, including amaretto and chocolate meltaways.

Malley's Chocolates
14822 Madison Avenue
Lakewood, Ohio 44107
(216) 226-8300

To place an order, call collect. They make fascinating fudges: chocolate mint; chocolate peanut butter swirl; chocolate–pecan praline; dark chocolate, plain or with nuts; maple walnut; milk chocolate, plain and with walnuts; peanut butter; pineapple; strawberry pecan— and would you believe, bubblegum-flavored fudge? That's not all: in the fall, they offer pumpkin fudge.

OREGON
Briggittine Monks
23300 Walker Lane
Amity, OR 97101
(503) 835-8080

This fudge has earned a Medallion of Excellence award from *Chocolate News Magazine*. Flavors offered include butterscotch, with and without nuts; chocolate, with and without nuts; chocolate–peanut butter; golden peanut butter; and divinity, with and without nuts. At last report, chocolate-amaretto, chocolate mint, and pecan-praline are also available.

PENNSYLVANIA
Bolan's Candies
6018 Penn Avenue, Penn Mall
Pittsburgh, PA 15206
(412) 441-1220

Students write home about Bolan's coconut bars, but you'll like their fudge, as well. Flavors include chocolate, penuci, praline, and vanilla.

Wilbur Chocolate Company
48 North Broad Street
Lititz, PA 17543
(717) 626-1131

Their fudge is great, especially at the price. But if they happen to have any opera creams in the refrigerator, you're really in luck. Be sure to take home some of their candy coatings, as well as their many-colored miniature Wilbur Buds to add to your fudge for some variety.

RHODE ISLAND
Country Kettle Fudge
Newport Fudgery
359 Thames Street
Newport, RI 02849
(401) 849-2228

They offer hand-whipped fudge in a dozen flavors, including chocolate chip mint and triple chocolate (plain or with almonds). It's a little on the pricey side, but then their motto is "We send your love in a box of fudge."

TENNESSEE
Dinstuhl's
5280 Pleasant View Road
Memphis, TN 38124
(901) 377-2639

They make a fudge roll that's hard to beat: chocolate fudge totally plastered with pecans.

TEXAS
Acme Candy Company
4839 Don Drive
Dallas, TX 75247
(214) 634-2825

Pralines in four delicious flavors including chocolate, maple, pecan, and rum are the specialty here.

Lamme's Candies
P.O. Box 1885
Austin, TX 78767
(512) 835-6794 for mail orders

They offer soft, buttery-rich confections including pralines with a real cream caramel base, surrounding sweet pecans.

UTAH
Cummings Candies
Highland Avenue
Salt Lake City, Utah 84105
(801) 487-1031

Here you can find smooth fudge with that deep, dark, rich taste true chocolate lovers crave.

Maxfields' Candy Company
1050 South 200 West
Salt Lake City, Utah 84110
(801) 355-5321

Fudge logs are a specialty here. Once you try one, you'll know why they rate raves.

WISCONSIN
Kilwin's of Lake Geneva
772 West Main Street
Lake Geneva, WI 53147
(414) 248-4400

Thousands of customers attest to the excellence of fourteen different slab fudge flavors including butter pecan, maple walnut, and German chocolate. They are also known for 100 flavors of homemade chocolates and forty flavors of their own ice cream.

Tremblay's Sweet Shop
P.O. Box 228
Hayward, WI 54843
(715) 634-2785

Tremblay's offers slab fudge in your basic flavors: chocolate (the best seller), maple, peanut butter, and vanilla are smooth and loaded with nuts. They are solid, not soft, but without a hint of graininess.

CANADA
Laura Secord Candy Shops
Laura Secord Walk
P.O. Box 1812, Station "D"
Scarborough, Ontario
(416) 751-0500

This chain, with 225 stores in Canada, offers both creams and fudge.

SLAB FUDGE FROM JIM GARRAHY

And last, but not least, Jim Garrahy's Fudge Kitchens are all over the place:

California: Solvang and Universal Studios/Los Angeles
Florida: Cypress Gardens, Marineland, St. Augustine, Shell Factory
    in Fort Myers, and Universal Studios
Georgia: Helen, Rock City, and Savannah
Illinois: Long Grove
Maryland: Annapolis
Ohio: Sea World
Pennsylvania: Gettysburg, Intercourse, and Lancaster
Rhode Island: Rocky Point
Tennessee: Dixie's Stampede in Pigeon Forge and Gatlinburg
Virginia: Luray Caverns
Wyoming: Jackson Hole

Plus his shops in Great Britain: in Bath, Canterbury, American Adventure in Derbyshire, Camelot in Preston, and Windsor Park Safari in Windsor, plus York.

If there isn't a shop near you, Garrahy's is delighted to ship mail order: write Jim Garrahy's Fudge Kitchen, Inc., Kitchen Kettle Village, P.O. Box 258, Intercourse, PA 17534, or call (717) 768-3740. His slab fudge comes in 1-pound boxes, containing four slices of your choice of flavors.

TESTING AND TEMPERATURES

There are as many ways to test as there are cooks. For example, back in 1849, confection manual author J. M. Sanderson directed you to test candy syrup: "Provide a jug of clean cold water and a piece of round stick. First dip in the water, then in the sugar, and again in the water." (To which he added the footnote, "This should be performed as speedily as possible." To which I add amen and good luck.) To continue: "Take off the sugar which has adhered to it, and endeavor to roll it into a ball between the finger and thumb in the water: when this can be done, it has attained the desired degree. If it forms large hard ball which will bite hard and adhere to the teeth when eaten, it is then termed the large ball."

In 1896, Oscar Tschirky ("Oscar of the Waldorf") advised would-be candy-makers to dip a clay pipe-stem into the sugar syrup when it is boiling, pull it out, and draw the hot syrup between finger and thumb to test for thread. To test for the ball, dip the pipe into the syrup, "plunge it into some cold water and when you take it out, the sugar should work up like putty."

A 1920s domestic science teacher recommended putting a teaspoon of syrup in a saucer and rolling it into a ball.

Julia Child recommends the continental method of testing: Dip a finger first in cold water, then in the boiling sugar, and immediately in cold water once more, rolling the syrup into a ball.

She has my admiration; my fingers burn at the thought of it. I once touched hot taffy, and the resulting blisters on my fingers were half an inch thick and an inch long. Nor am I adept enough to make the saucer method work. As for clay pipe-stems, I just hope they were unused.

The method I use is very simple, very basic:

1. Use *fresh*, ice-cold water (so that your water will be the same temperature as mine). Pour it into a custard cup just before testing so you know it's ice cold (but don't let ice get into the test cup itself, as that skews the test results).

2. Slowly pour ½ teaspoon syrup into the cup. You can tell a lot about the state of your fudge by what happens initially to the syrup:

- If it immediately dissipates, it is not up to thread.
- If it immediately oozes into a round flat mass, it is at the beginning of the soft-ball stage.
- If the end of the pour remains elevated, it is at the soft-ball stage.
- If the whole looks like a stalagmite, sticking up in the air, it is at the firm-ball stage.
- If the first drips solidify immediately, it is at the hard-ball stage.

3. When the action of the syrup looks promising, gather the syrup into a ball in the water. The easiest way, especially on your fingers, is to let the syrup cool a second or two, then pour out the water as you gather up the ball.

- If, when you take it out, it is runny and gooey, like a thick gelatin—and when tasted it dissolves instantly in your mouth—it is not ready yet.
- If, when taken out of the water, it can be formed into a cohesive ball that will soften only under pressure or after several seconds of resting on your hand, it is probably done. Next, taste it. Is it al dente—offering some resistance to your teeth? Then your fudge is ready.
- If, when taken out of the water, it easily forms a ball and is really chewy to the taste—that's for caramel.
- If the syrup forms threads the moment it hits the water and resists your bite momentarily, it is at the hard-ball stage.
- If the syrup contracts when it hits the water, but when removed can be pulled and made stretchy, it is at the soft-crack stage and will stick to your teeth.
- If the syrup contracts when it hits the water and, when removed, breaks easily, resisting being made into a ball—it is at the hard-crack stage.

INDEX